Origins of a Civilization

By the same authors:

RAYMOND ALLCHIN

Piklihal Excavations (1960).
Neolithic Cattle-keepers of South India (1963).
Kavitavali (1964) and Vinayapatrika, The Petition to Ram (1966).
The Archaeology of Afghanistan (1978) ed. with Norman Hammond.
Shahr-i-Zohak and the History of the Bamiyan Valley with P.B. Baker.
The Archaeology of Early Historic South Asia (1995) with B. Allchin,
D.K. Chakraborti, R. Coningham and G. Erdosy.

BRIDGET ALLCHIN

The Stone Tipped Arrow (1966).
The Prehistory and Palaeogeography of the Great Indian Desert (1978).
South Asian Archaeology 1981, 1984 (ed.).
Living Traditions, Studies in the Ethnoarchaeology of South Asia (1994).

RAYMOND AND BRIDGET ALLCHIN

The Birth of Indian Civilization (1968; reprinted 1993).
The Rise of Civilization in India and Pakistan (1982; reprinted 1986,
1988).
Conservation of the Indian Heritage (1986) with B.K. Thapar (ed).

ORIGINS OF A CIVILIZATION

The
Prehistory and Early Archaeology
of South Asia

BRIDGET AND RAYMOND
ALLCHIN

VIKING

VIKING

Penguin Books India (P) Ltd., 210, Chiranjiv Tower, 43, Nehru Place, New Delhi 110 019, India
Penguin Books Ltd., 27 Wrights Lane, London W8 5TZ, UK
Penguin Books USA Inc., 375 Hudson Street, New York, NY 10014, USA
Penguin Books Australia Ltd., Ringwood, Victoria, Australia
Penguin Books Canada Ltd., 10 Alcorn Avenue, Suite 300, Toronto, Ontario M4V 3B2, Canada
Penguin Books (NZ) Ltd., 182-190 Wairau Road, Auckland 10, New Zealand

First published in Viking by Penguin Books India (P) Ltd. 1997

Copyright © Bridget and Raymond Allchin 1997

All rights reserved

10 9 8 7 6 5 4 3 2 1

Typeset in New Baskerville by FOLIO, G-68, Connaught Circus, New Delhi-1
Printed in India at Rekha Printers Pvt. Ltd., New Delhi-20

The image of the Mohenjo-daro terracotta seated figure of a woman, reproduced on the front cover, is from the National Museum, New Delhi.

This book is sold subject to the condition that it shall not, by way of trade or otherwise, be lent, resold, hired out, or otherwise circulated without the publisher's prior written consent in any form of binding or cover other than that in which it is published and without a similar condition including this condition being imposed on the subsequent purchaser and without limiting the rights under copyright reserved above, no part of this publication may be reproduced, stored in or introduced into a retrieval system, or transmitted in any form or by any means (electronic, mechanical, photocopying, recording or otherwise), without the prior written permission of both the copyright owner and the above-mentioned publisher of this book.

CONTENTS

Preface	vii
List of Plates	ix
List of Figures	xvii
List of Maps	xxi
1 The Rediscovery of the Past	1
2 The South Asian Setting	12
3 Roots: Ancestors of Mankind and the Beginning of Culture	33
4 The Long Climb: The Middle and Upper Palaeolithic	55
5 Pathways to Settled Life: The Mesolithic and Early Neolithic	88
6 The Indus World: The Context of the First South Asian Towns and Cities	113
7 Farmers and Village Communities of the Indus System	125
8 The Indus Empire: Sites and Structure	153
9 The Indus Empire: People and Culture	183
10 Changing Scenes: Indus to Ganges	206
11 The Second Urbanization	223
Bibliography	263
Index	277

PREFACE

We would like to acknowledge our gratitude and appreciation to all our friends and colleagues in the field of South Asian archaeology and early history, in the countries of South Asia, Europe and the New World, too numerous to mention individually, whose books and papers we have read and with whom we have had many exciting and valuable discussions over the years. Some of these to whom we are indebted had already retired or passed away when we embarked upon the study of South Asia's past nearly fifty years ago. Others who were then in senior positions helped us in many ways and taught us a great deal. Many of them too sadly have now passed away.

Fortunately many more scholars have entered the field and new generations of archaeologists and historians, with all kinds of new and valuable expertise, continue to do so. The necessity for interdisciplinary collaboration is now well established, and scientists and others are being drawn into research projects alongside archaeologists to help unravel the problems of the past to an extent scarcely conceivable fifty years ago. Indeed, this is one of the most important developments that has taken place. After fifty years of independence pressures of population and economic advance, together with growing public awareness, have increased the need for research and conservation to protect, study and make known the cultural heritage. Happily it seems that the younger generation are qualified and prepared to tackle these problems. We wish them every success.

New Delhi
19 February 1997

LIST OF PLATES

Plate 1. Riwat artefact. (Photo: SAS, 1988)

Plate 2. The deposit at Dina in which one of the hand-axes illustrated (Fig. 3) was found in 1983 by members of the British Archaeological Mission to Pakistan. The way in which the artefacts became incorporated in a conglomerate of this kind and are later exposed is shown in the diagram (Fig. 2). (Photo: Derrill)

Plate 3. Milestone 101, a Stone Age factory site where many hand-axes were made, overlooking the Indus plains in Lower Sindh. (Photo: Allchin)

Plate 4. The Belan river, 1973, with a party from Allahabad University. The coarse conglomerate below the path includes Lower Palaeolithic artefacts, the gravels halfway up the section Middle Paleolithic and those near the top Upper Paleolithic. Mesolithic material is located below the topsoil. (Photo: Allchin)

Plate 5. Budha Pushkar Lake, Rajasthan, with the permanent lake in the foreground & the lake basin which fills occasionally after rain ringed by trees behind it. (Photo: Allchin)

Plate 6. The Potwar Plateau, northern Punjab, Pakistan, near the village of Aurangzeb, showing a spread of cobbles and pebbles, most of which are artefacts or debris from tool-making, in this case recently exposed by the erosion of overlying loess, in a rapidly eroding landscape. (Photo: Allchin)

Plate 7. The Rohri hills, Upper Sindh (1975), showing the old red soil with flint nodules capping the flat tops, and a man leading a x *Origins of a Civilization*

camel loaded with firewood in the foreground. (Photo: Allchin)

Plate 8. The Rohri hills, Upper Sindh (1975), view along the tops of the hills, with flint worked at many periods. The hills in the middle distance were being quarried to obtain limestone for cement-making. (Photo: Allchin)

Plate 9. An Upper Palaeolithic workplace in the Rohri hills with cores, blades and debris. (Photo: Allchin)

Plate 10. A bead-maker in Cambay (1968), blocking out agate beads by the traditional method using a hammer with a buffalo-horn head and flexible, cane handle and an iron spike fixed in the ground. (Photo: Allchin)

Plate 11. Sangao Cave, North West Frontier Province, Pakistan, 1963. (Photo: Allchin)

Plate 12. Excavated trench Sangao Cave, as it was in 1963. The man on the right was over six feet tall. (Photo: Allchin)

Plate 13. Kitugala, a mountain cave in south-west Sri Lanka formerly occupied by the makers of stone artefacts of the kind shown in Fig. 8. (Photo: Allchin)

Plate 14. A Vedda family in a rock shelter in south-western Sri Lanka, photographed by the Seligmans at the beginning of this century. (After Allchin 1966)

Plate 15. An excavation in progress (1983) at Alu Lena cave, currently part of a Buddhist residential complex. (Photo: Allchin)

Plate 16. Fishermen with traditional sea-going catamarans on the south-east coast of India, south of Madras. (Photo: Allchin)

Plate 17. Baghe Kor, a Central Indian rock shelter formed in Vindhyan sandstone. (Photo: Allchin)

Plates 18. Outline drawing of a female Sambar deer. (Photo: Allchin)

Plate 19. Outline drawing of a rhinoceros in red ochre in Lekhahiya rock shelter in the Vindhyas. (Photo: Allchin)

List of Plates

Plate 20. Bhimbetka, a hunting scene showing two hunters killing a buffalo bull superimposed on & surrounded by pictures of other animals. (Photo: Allchin)

Plate 21. Nawishta, Baluchistan, an ibex with two goats. (Photo: Courtesy, Brigardier Usman Hassan)

Plate 22. Microlithic artefacts from Barkaccha, a factory site on the edge of the Vindhyas from which tools were exported to sites in the Ganges plains, made of grey agate.
Line 1, cores; lines 2, 5 & 6, flakes; lines 3 & 4, sections of microlithic blades & 'geometric' microliths. (Photo: Allchin)

Plate 23 a & b. Hunter-gatherers. (Photo: M.L.K. Murty)

Plate 24. Neolithic living & field terraces, Tekkalakota, Karnataka, South India. (Photo: Allchin)

Plate 25. Modern houses on a terraced hillside at Tekkalakota, Karnataka, built in a similar way to those of Neolithic times. (Photo: Allchin)

Plate 26. A rock bruising of a bull from the Neolithic site of Maski, Raichure District, South India. (Photo: Allchin)

Plate 27. A hoof impression in vitrified cowdung from Utnur, an 'ash mound' or Neolithic cattle pen. (Photo: Allchin)

Plate 28. A large saddle quern from Tarakai Qila, a settlement of the early Harappan period, NWFP Pakistan; similar to those in use from Neolithic times forward, those from Mesolithic contexts being smaller. (Photo: Allchin)

Plate 29. Microliths made of fine grained quartzite, chert and crystal from a site on the surface of the final sand sheet at Pushkar.
Row 1, a carinated scraper & three broken blade cores;
Row 2, five blade cores & a carefully trimmed crystal;
Row 3, five triangular microliths, probably arrow barbs, & three small points, probably drill heads;
Row 4, sections of small parallel side-blades each trimmed and blunted along one edge, perhaps parts for composite knife blades. (Photo: Allchin)

xii   *Origins of a Civilization*

Plate 30. View of Lewan factory site, Bannu Basin, NWPF, Pakistan. (Photo: Allchin)

Plate 31. A hut similar in plan, floor and other features to that from Lewan excavation (Fig. 13), being constructed near Attock, Pakistan, in 1980 by Afghan refugees from Jalalabad. The frame was afterwards thatched with straw. (Photo: Allchin)

Plate 32. The Indus in the Karakoram. (Photo: Courtesy, H. Rendell)

Plate 33. The Indus in flood near Bilot, at the north-western edge of the plain on the NWFP-Punjab border. (Photo: Allchin)

Plate 34. The Indus near Mohenjo-daro (winter 1992), showing the wide shallow bed and low bank. Flood water may overspill the bank at any point, tending to do so upstream from Mohenjo-daro, and inundates different parts of the plain. (Photo: Allchin)

Plate 35. The Lower Indus plains from the north-west side of the valley opposite Hyderabad. (Photo: Allchin)

Plate 36. The Indus in Lower Sindh from the north-west side of the valley, showing some of the remaining gallery forest on the river's edge. (Photo: Allchin)

Plate 37. Mehrgarh, view of site, with entrance to the Bolan Pass in the distance. (Photo: Allchin)

Plate 38. Rahman Dheri, aerial photograph of mound. The outline of the massive brick defences is clearly visible on the east and west sides. (After Durrani, 1988)

Plate 39. Kalibangan, ploughed field surface, junction of Early and Mature Harappan, c. 2600 BC. (Courtesy: Archaeological Survey of India)

Plate 40. Tarakai Qila, group of miniature pots of Early Harappan period. (Photo: Allchin)

Plate 41. Tarakai Qila. Terracotta model of an ox. (Photo: Allchin)

Plate 42. Tarakai Qila. Terracotta models of oxen of Early Harappan period. (Photo: Allchin)

List of Plates xiii

Plate 43. Tarakai Qila, terracotta model cart-wheels, some with painted designs. (Photo: Allchin)

Plate 44. Modern wooden plough photographed in fields near Mohenjo-daro. (Photo: Allchin)

Plate 45. Harappan stone-working floor exposed on hilltop near Sakkhar. At the time of the photograph (1976), and since, the area has been in imminent danger of destruction by modern industrial quarrying. (Photo: Allchin)

Plate 46. Chanhu-daro, terracotta model of a bullock-cart.

Plate 47. Indus river transport, photographed near Sakkhar. (Photo: Arbuthnot)

Plate 48. Carved stone representation of a river boat from Mohenjo-daro. (After Parpola, 1991)

Plate 49. Rahman Dheri, potsherds with pre-firing graffiti on exterior face. Such shards belong to the Early Harappan period or its regional equivalent. (After Parpola, 1991)

Plate 50. Mohenjo-daro: 1. stone seal with inscription, but without other symbols (M-314); 2. oblong seal with inscription only (M-1262). (After Parpola, 1987, 1991)

Plate 51. Mohenjo-daro: 1. inscribed seal impression on neck of jar (M-1372); 2, inscribed stoneware bangle (M-1629). (After Parpola, 1991)

Plate 52. Mohenjo-daro: terracotta seated figure of woman, perhaps making dough. (Photograph: Allchin. Courtesy: National Museum, New Delhi).

Plate 53. Standing female terracotta figure with heavy ornaments. (Courtesy: National Museum, Pakistan)

Plate 54. Mohenjo-daro, terracotta figurine of a bison (bos guarus). (Courtesy: Archaeological Survey of India)

Plate 55. Mohenjo-daro: terracotta monkey with pierced hole for inserting climbing string, height c.3.5 cm. (Photograph: Allchin. Courtesy: National Museum, New Delhi)

xiv
Origins of a Civilization

Plate 56. Mohenjo-daro: stone ram of uncertain provenance, maximum length 49 cms and height 27 cms. This is probably the largest and best preserved item in the whole repertoire of Harappan sculptures. (Courtesy: H. Mahboubian)

Plate 57. Mohenjo-daro: tiny figure of a seated squirrel in faience, height c. 2.3 cm. (Photograph: Allchin. Courtesy: National Museum, New Delhi)

Plate 58. Mohenjo-daro, steatite seal of unicorn standing in front of characteristic ritual stand (M-8). (After Parpola 1987)

Plate 59. Mohenjo-daro, steatite seal of Indian rhinoceros (M-1134). (After Parpola 1991)

Plate 60. Mohenjo-daro, steatite seal depicting composite beast (M-300). (After Parpola 1987)

Plate 61. Mohenjo-daro, steatite seal of seated figure with horned headdress, surrounded by wild beasts (M-304). (After Parpola, 1987)

Plate 62. Mohenjo-daro, steatite seal with complex mythological content (M-1186). (After Parpola 1991)

Plate 63. View of the modern town of Sehwan from the top of the high mound (of archaeologically undetermined age), with the Indus in far left distance. The tall flagpole to the left in the middle distance marks the site of the shrine containing the grave of the celebrated saint Lal Shahbaz Kalandar. (Photograph: Allchin)

Plate 64. View of the dried-up flood plain of the river Sarasvati (Ghaggar), from the site of the Harappan town at Kalibangan. The former flood plain is clearly recognizable in the areas under crops. The far edge of the plain may be recognized in the line of trees in the far distance towards the right of the picture. (Photograph: Allchin)

Plate 65. Kausambi, brick facing of rampart. (After G.R. Sharma)

Plate 66. Mahasthangarh, view of moat from ramparts. Although the moat is now almost filled with alluvial deposits, it is still clearly visible on the ground. (Photograph: Allchin)

List of Plates xv

Plate 67. Aerial photograph of Sisupalgarh. (Courtesy: Archaeological Survey of India)

Plate 68. Diagrammatic section through a moat and rampart.

Plate 69. Part of stone city walls of Rajagriha. (Photograph: Allchin)

Plate 70. Shards of Rouletted ware from Arikamedu. (After Wheeler)

Plate 71. Anuradhapura, inscribed shards from periods J and I. 1. and 2. from period J5 (calibrated dates c. 340-370 BC); 3. from period I2 (calibrated date c.300 BC); and 4 from period G5 (calibrated date c. 1st century AD). (Photograph: Coningham)

Plate 72. Sarnath; Lion capital of the time of Ashoka. (Courtesy: ASI)

List of Figures

Fig. 1. Diagram illustrating the incorporation of artefacts into the Siwalik deposits. (Courtesy: H. Rendell)

Fig. 2. Lower Palaeolithic stone tools from early collections made in the northern Punjab (Nos 1 to 4) and Madras (Nos 5 to 8). Nos 1, 2 & 6, chopping tools; Nos 3 & 7, hand-axes; Nos 4 & 8, cleavers. (Drawing: Allchin. After Allchin, 1963)

Fig. 3. Hand-axes from dated contexts (c. 500,000 BP) from Jalalpur and Dina, Jhelum valley, northern Punjab, Pakistan.

Fig. 4a & 4b Middle Palaeolithic artefacts from the surface of the red fossil soil at Hokra, near Budha Pushkar. a. Nos 1, unidirectional core; 2 & 5, flakes struck from prepared cores; 3, burin; 4, carinated scraper; 6, scraper made on a flake; 7, discoidal core.
b. No 1, utilized flake or adze blade; 2, broken palette stone; 3. tip of a broken hand-axe; 4, core; 5, hammer stone.
(After Allchin & Goudie 1978. Drawing: Allchin)

Fig. 5. Hafted stone artefacts from Australia in their original mounts of wood and resin or other mastic. (From the British Museum collection, now in the Museum of Mankind.)
Nos 1, fighting pick; 2, ground stone axe; 3, finely worked point used as a spearhead; 4, knife with a composite blade made from ten sharp-edged fragments of stone; 5, a man's knife; 6 & 6a, a woman's knife and sheath; 7 & 8, knives; 9 & 10, various types of mounted adze blades; a double adze with a blade at each end of the handle; 2, a spear thrower with an adze blade at one end. (After Allchin 1966. Drawing: Allchin. Courtesy, Trustees of the British Museum)

xviii *Origins of a Civilization*

Fig. 6. A schematic interpretation of the Late Pleistocene to Early Holocene stratigraphic and cultural sequence at Pushkar. (After Allchin & Goudie, 1974)

Fig. 7. Upper Palaeolithic artefacts from the site in the Rohri hills, shown in Plate 9.
Nos 1, blade core; 2 & 3, blades; 4, blade core trimming flake—a characteristic by-product of core preparation. (Drawing: Allchin)

Fig. 8a & b. Sri Lankan quartz artefacts from the factory site of Bandarawela, south-west Highlands.
a. Nos 1 & 2, scrapers; 3 & 4, small discoidal cores; 5 to 8 & 21 to 30, a range of 'microliths' characteristic of the later quartz industry of Sri Lankan; 31 & 33, awls or borers; 34, a quartz crystal.
b. Nos 1 & 6, concave scrapers; 2, 3, 4 & 8, convex scrapers or adze blades; 5 & 7, carinated scrapers; 9, 4 & 18, bifacial points; 10 to 13 microliths; 15, burin; 17, tanged point. (Drawing: Allchin)

Fig. 9. Artefacts from Barasimla, an Upper Paleolithic/Microlithic factory site in Central India recorded in the 1930s. Nos 1 & 19, awls or borers; Nos 3, 4, 5 & 8, scrapers; Nos 6 & 4, triangles; Nos 6, 7 & 12 – 17, 'geometric' microliths all made from sections of small parallel-sided blades struck from cores resembling Nos 18 & 20; No 10, blade struck from a large Upper Palaeolithic type core; No 18, very small microlithic blade core; No 20, top part of a somewhat large microlithic blade core. (Collection of Col. D.H. Gordon, now in the Institute of Archaeology, London; Drawing: Allchin)

Fig. 10. Eastern style Neolithic ground stone axes oradzes from Mahagara. (Drawing: after G.R. Sharma)

Fig. 11. Southern Neolithic stone axes. (Drawing: Allchin)

Fig. 12a & b. Heavy stone artefacts from Lewan factory site.
a. No 1, hammer; 2, broken blade of an axe; 3, axe, hammer dressed with ground blade; part of a broken palette stone; small hammer/sling ball; pointed stone dressing hammer.
b. No 1, natural cylindrical pebble used at both ends as a hammer; 2 – 4, natural pebbles used as stone dressing hammers, all showing wear &/or shattering of the ends characteristic of this group of tools;

List of Figures xix

broken ring stones probably made with stone dressing hammers similar to those illustrated here. (Drawing: Allchin)

Fig. 13. Lewan excavations; outline-plans of huts or houses of c. 3,000 BC. (Drawing: Allchin)

Fig. 14. Mehrgarh, section through river bank, showing original mound and subsequent flood deposits. (After Lechevallier and Quivron, *South Asian Archaeology 1983*. Fig. 4)

Fig. 15. Mehrgarh, sickles with stone blades set in bitumen. (After Jarrige and Jarrige, 1995. *Mehrgarh, Field Reports 1974-1985*)

Fig. 16. Mehrgarh, period I. Burial with stone blades, cores and a ground stone axe as grave goods. (After Lechevallier and Quivron, *South Asian Archaeology, 1979*. Fig. 12)

Fig. 17. Mehrgarh, mud brick compartmented building, period IIA. (After Jarrige, *South Asian Archaeology 1981*, Fig. 4.4.)

Fig. 18. Mehrgarh, comparative frequencies of animal remains, periods I-III. (After Meadows, 1993)

Fig. 19. Kalibangan, plan of Early Harappan town. (After Thapar, 1985, Fig. 23)

Fig. 20. Kot Diji, Early Harappan 'horned deity' painted on pot. (Courtesy: R. Mughal)

Fig. 21. Lewan Early Harappan 'horned deities' painted on pot. (Drawing: Allchin)

Fig. 22. Plan of Harappan Kalibangan. (After Thapar)

Fig. 23. Plan of Harappan Surkotada. (After J.P. Joshi)

Fig. 24. Plan of Harappan Dholavira. (Courtesy: Archaeological Survey of India. After Bisht)

Fig. 25. Plan of Harappan trading station at Lothal. (After S.R. Rao)

Origins of a Civilization

Fig. 26. Banawali, drawing of terracotta model of a wooden plough, Harappan period. (After Bisht)

Fig. 27. Reconstruction of the several elements employed in the manufacture of stoneware bangles. (After Vidale, 1989)

Fig. 28. Plan of Sankissa (Sankasya). (After Cunningham)

Fig. 29. Plan of Ahicchatra. (After Cunningham)

Fig. 30. Ujjain, plan and section of ramparts. (Courtesy: ASI)

Fig. 31. Ujjain detail of culture sequence for periods II and III. (Courtesy: ASI)

Fig. 32. Map showing the fortified city of Sisupalgarh in relation to neighbouring monuments. (Courtesy: ASI)

LIST OF MAPS

Map 1. South Asia and surrounding regions.

Map 2. South Asian rainfall. (After the Imperial Gazetteer, 1910)

Map 3. Principal archaeological sites and localities referred to in Chapters 3, 4 and 5.

Map 4. The Indus system in the Early Harappan and earlier periods showing sites referred to in Chapter 7.

Map 5. The Indus Civilization, showing main regions and sites discussed in Chapters 8 and 9:— I. Sindh Province; II. Punjab and the Northwest; III. Eastern Province; IV. Central and Southern Rajasthan; V. Southern Province.

Map 6. Northern India-Pakistan in the late second and early first millennia BC, showing sites mentioned in Chapters 10 and 11.

Map 7. The distribution and relative size of principal cities of South Asia in the third century BC. (After Allchin et al., 1995, Map 0.5 and 206-208)

Map 8. The approximate areas occupied by the Sixteen Great States (Mahajanapadas) and other major tribal Janapadas, 5th-6th centuries BC together with their probable capital cities. (After Allchin et al., 1995, Map 7.4)

Origins of a Civilization

Map 1. *(Facing page) South Asia and Surrounding Regions.*
Courtesy: Worlsat International and J. Knighton/Science Photo Library

Chapter 1

THE REDISCOVERY OF THE PAST

This book has been written to celebrate the fiftieth anniversary of the independence of India and Pakistan. Virtually ever since that time the authors have been in touch with the Indian subcontinent, and in particular with the development of archaeological studies there. The book is intended for the general reader with an interest in the culture of South Asia, and how it came to be as it is. It may also perhaps be useful to the student embarking on the study of South Asian archaeology or ancient history, or looking for a preliminary overview to give perspective to more detailed scholarly study of particular periods or aspects of the subject. It is emphatically not a compilation or compendium of available information; nor does it claim to be comprehensive at the level of theory or ideas within the fields it touches. What we have tried to do is to tell as coherent a story as is possible at the present time, of the development of human life and culture within the subcontinent, indicating the main trends, principal motivating factors and important turning-points, as we see them, on the long road from the earliest tool-makers, over two million years ago, to Early Historic times in the early centuries BC. We have also tried to indicate the relationship of South Asian culture to that of adjacent regions of the world, which played what seem to us significant roles at various points in the story.

Throughout we have tried to use plain standard English, avoiding special terms or jargon. Likewise, we have tried to avoid as far as possible specialized theoretical concepts and approaches. These can be helpful to specialists in advancing ideas but tend, in our view, to make the subject over-complicated for others.

In earlier books, *The Birth of Indian Civilization* (1968), *The Prehistory and Palaeogeography of the Great Indian Desert* (1978), *The Rise of Civilization in India and Pakistan* (1982), *The Archaeology of Early Historic South Asia* (1995), we have covered as much of the same

Origins of a Civilization

ground as was then possible in each case, on the basis of the material available, and as was appropriate to the point of view from which each book was written. These books all included more specific detail and discussion of alternative interpretations, etc., as they were intended primarily for students and scholars rather than for more general reading. Obviously, therefore, in the present book there is a certain amount of repetition. Although, we have tried to use new illustrative material as far as possible, in some cases we have used the same illustrations simply because they appear to be the best or only suitable examples available.

This book does however contain new material on all phases of prehistory, and on climatic and environmental change, and new ranges of physical dates, all of which has come to light during the last ten to fifteen years. It also includes new information on the emergence of the first South Asian urbanization, the Indus civilization; and on the transitional processes that linked this to the second urbanization in the Ganges valley, and its subsequent spread. Indeed, these subjects may seem to occupy more than their share of the book; if so it is because of the central position they occupy in important formative phases of the history of South Asian culture. We have tried to make it clear throughout the book that parallel, if less carefully documented, and apparently less dramatic, developments were taking place in many regions of the subcontinent, and to indicate what they were and how they related to the mainstream, if interrupted, process of urban and state development. Much of the new material has been synthesized and summarized directly from primary sources and research reports: it has not had time to pass through the process of digestion by critical assessment that earlier material has been subject to. Therefore, what we have said on some topics may be considered by some to be controversial and in need of further confirmation. This we freely admit: we are sticking our necks out, but we feel it is worth the risk in order to include much interesting and relatively up-to-date material, and much of our own recent thinking.

Why should we try to rediscover the past? Before looking for the origins of a civilization, or any civilization, in the remote depths of time before the beginning of history, one must ask oneself, 'Why?'

First of all, perhaps, the answer many people would give is because it is intriguing and exciting to try to find out about the things that remain from the past. It is like being a detective. An interest in archaeology is a response to a challenge. Undoubtedly, this is what motivated many of the first archaeologists of the eighteenth and early nineteenth century in India, as it did in other parts of the world. They wanted to find out more about ancient abandoned cities; to examine works of art and objects of everyday life that were different from those of their own time; to try to understand the meaning of rock paintings and what stone artefacts were used for, and to know how old they all were. All these things are still part of the immediate challenge to which the archaeologist responds, although the questions are now more informed and carefully considered; and both more comprehensive and more detailed. Today, we know from experience that the search is and will continue to be laborious. It involves painstaking investigations, surveys and excavations; the minute examination of objects and evidence of all kinds; testing the evidence in a number of ways, and dating by elaborate scientific processes. The rewards for all the hard work and thinking and planning are great, though seldom precisely what we expect they will be. What we find frequently raises more questions than it answers, and so we are led on to further investigations.

Individual finds are sometimes very exciting—the piece of gold, the beautiful stone sculpture, the burial accompanied by stone artefacts or pots from remote prehistory, are thrilling. One can never forget making such a discovery. But it is the relationship of these and many other less dramatic things to one another and to their context that gives them meaning. The piece of gold becomes much more interesting if it is found hidden beneath the mud floor of an ancient house; the sculpture has a much deeper meaning if it comes from a niche in the wall of a building about which other facts are known or can be discovered; the burial takes on quite a new significance if it can be shown to be related to a particular phase in the development of a nearby settlement or an occupied cave or rock shelter. That is to say, once any of these finds is given a cultural context of this sort they acquire new dimensions of meaning. They are no longer merely objects of interest, but an important part of an emerging picture of the human past of the region from which they come. By going one or two steps further and relating the immediate contexts in which finds like these are made to localities or settlements, and also discovering the relationship of those settlements to others of the same period, and of earlier and later periods, we achieve a wider cultural perspective and start to be able to place our finds in a time-frame. The patterns that archaeological finds then form, and the stories they tell, begin to show us something of what the past was like, and how, as a result of natural change combined with human activity, conditions changed.

By piecing things together we begin to see how people lived and

4 *Origins of a Civilization*

traded and fought; a picture begins to emerge of what was actually going on in a particular locality at a particular time in the past. Archaeological investigations always aim to discover a sequence of such pictures. This is something to which the excavation of settlement sites, where people have lived for a long time, lends itself because every time a new floor or road surface is laid down a new, recognizable layer is formed which can be seen in the section cut through the occupation deposit by the excavation trench. As a result one tends to get the impression that the archaeological past consists of a series of tableaux or 'stills' representing a series of designated cultural phases which replace one another like transparencies on a screen. In fact, of course what we are seeing, represented by the sequence of old floor levels or surfaces, is a continuous process of development and change such as we witness in the course of our own lives. When elderly people say regretfully 'things aren't what they were', the archaeologist is tempted to reply, 'of course not, just look at the past, things have always been changing!' The development of human cultures is an ongoing dynamic process involving continuous change: and, fortunately for the archaeologist, leaving behind the detritus resulting from all the human activities that went on, which reflects the process of change, and which is the stuff of archaeology.

Differing Cultural Traditions. There is another way of looking at the past which is equally important in understanding it. If one stands back and considers the physical remains of past cultures generally, taking a broad overview, one sees that in spite of a number of differences all must have been created by people whose minds by and large worked very much as our own do. At the same time, there are quite profound differences between the cultures of different regions which manifest themselves clearly in the archaeological record much as they do today. These include things affecting all aspects of life, ranging from architecture and house and settlement patterns to tools and cooking utensils, pottery styles, and all kinds of decorative crafts and arts. Anyone who has even a slight familiarity with the pottery of indigenous Central American cultures, or with sculpture of the Gandhara or the classical Indian tradition, for example, would be unlikely to mistake any one of them for artefacts from any other culture than their own.

If we now go on to look more closely at prehistoric cultures of different regions, we can nearly always see features which relate to those of historical and modern cultures of the same region—features that are not shared with the past or present cultures of other regions.

The Rediscovery of the Past 5

In the following chapters we shall see a number of examples of prehistoric house and settlement patterns from various regions of India which have counterparts in present-day traditional buildings. A striking example is the huts built by nomadic people in the North West Frontier province of Pakistan which have close parallels at sites of the fourth to third millennium BC in the same region (*Plate 31*). Another example is the ploughed field, associated with the major Harappan urban settlement at Kalibangan in Rajasthan, where the distinctive pattern of ploughing is identical with that used for cultivating certain combinations of crops in the same region today (*Plate 39*).

At first sight the kind of strong local or regional continuity indicated by the foregoing examples may seem surprising, but looked at in a broader perspective such continuity is not difficult to understand. It is a truism that we are all to a large extent what our past has made us, as individuals, as communities and as nations, and also as part of the human race. It is generally accepted that to understand a person one needs to know something of their family background and position in society. When considering a local community or a nation, no thinking person can seriously doubt that both are what their circumstances, that is to say their geographical environment, traditions and history, have made them. Indeed, the purpose behind the study of geography and history is clear: accurately and critically approached they enable one to understand one's own country, one's own cultural traditions, and how we came to be as we are. By extension they can help one to understand something of other countries and other cultures and how they came to be as they are. How far the human race as a whole has been moulded by its past is perhaps not so obvious, but that too will perhaps become clearer when we look at the earlier phases of prehistory.

Environment. By environment we mean the totality of our surroundings. Today, many people live in urban environments which seem far removed from the natural world. In the Indian subcontinent the majority of the population still live in rural or semi-rural environments in villages and small towns. Most of these are surrounded by agricultural land where only occasional vestiges of the natural environment survive. In the Lower Ganges valley, for example, artificially levelled and irrigated paddy fields extend as far as the eye can see, constituting a man-made landscape. Where there are mountains and hills, nature asserts itself rather more. But even there, hillsides are sometimes artificially terraced to a height of several

6 *Origins of a Civilization*

thousand feet, as in the valley of Nepal, and everywhere tree-cutting has changed the landscape and profoundly affected the countryside in a variety of ways. However much humans may try to control and modify the environment, they are still to a large extent controlled by it and dependent upon it.

Climate and weather form a significant part of the environment, and the first basic ingredient of our environment is the underlying land formations—more locally the rocks and soil upon which we live; the second is the climate, the weather, which is constantly interacting with and modifying the land, and is equally important. The character of continents and regions is formed from these basic ingredients; on them depends the kind of crops that can be grown, the animals that can be reared, the building materials that are available. They are, in fact, the basis of life and the formative factors in the life-style of a population. Some understanding of the environment of the Indian subcontinent therefore is essential to a meaningful study of the development of its cultural past in both prehistoric and historic times. For this reason, one chapter of this book attempts to give an overview of the environmental mosaic of South Asia in so far as it is essential to understanding its cultural development.

History and Prehistory. History depends primarily upon written records such as edicts of kings and important people, inscriptions, state documents, letters and other written material and, of course, coins. These tell us about dynasties and individual kings and queens, their policies, their military campaigns, and the laws they made. All these things are liable to be inaccurate for a variety of reasons, and perhaps on occasions deliberately falsified. Furthermore, they do not tell us much about the lives led by ordinary people. In these respects archaeological evidence is likely to come nearer to the truth, and taken together the two categories of evidence can obviously give a fuller and more accurate picture than either can alone.

When we turn to prehistory, or what happened before written records were available, we have only archaeological evidence from which to reconstruct the past. Therefore, we must treat all potential sources of information with great care and respect. If we in our enthusiasm inadvertently destroy the evidence we hope to use, we are indeed killing the goose that lays the golden egg. The further back in time we go, the more scarce and ephemeral become the surviving material remains and traces of human activity.

Geographical and environmental considerations remain equally important, but instead of inscriptions, the edicts of emperors and

The Rediscovery of the Past

kings and historical documents of all kinds, the prehistorian looks at the outlines of ancient settlements, the remains of huts and houses abandoned long ago, and the things found associated with them, such as fragments of pottery and objects of stone, bone and metal which survive the ravages of time. If they are not disturbed and are carefully recorded, the relationship of objects to one another within a living space such as a hut or the room of a house can tell us about what took place there. Occasionally, spectacular finds are made, such as burials with rich grave goods or settlements overwhelmed and preserved by lava or volcanic ash. But these are exceptional. Prehistory normally relies on observations carefully recorded in the course of surveys, and examination and excavation of ancient sites and monuments. From this database, ways of life, economic and political developments and other major factors affecting human societies of the past can be to some extent reconstructed. The dating of events and cultural phases of the prehistoric past require particular care and skillful use of both deductive reasoning and of the scientific techniques available today.

It must be clear from what has been said that no archaeologist today can work in isolation. No archaeological research in the field can be complete without the collaboration of experts in other fields of knowledge. Depending upon the problems being investigated these can range from geology and palaeontology, in the case of early prehistoric investigations, through soil science, the study of ancient plant and animal remains, the study of ancient human bones from many points of view including the evidence for disease, nutrition and other factors, to a knowledge of ancient languages and literature which are necessary in order to assess early historical documents. Most investigations also need to use one or more methods of physical dating, for which the collaboration of laboratories specializing in this work is essential. Thus, most worthwhile archaeological projects today depend upon broad-based interdisciplinary collaboration. The days of the great loner are long gone, and the successful archaeologist today must be an expert in management, fund-raising and human relations as well as archaeology, and know enough about related disciplines to know when to call upon their collaboration.

Approaches. The urge to investigate the past seems always to have been associated with a wish to collect, classify and preserve objects of interest from the past. In its early stages the acquisition of objects of beauty and interest from ancient cultures was seen as the primary objective of archaeology. It is from these beginnings, from the

8 *Origins of a Civilization*

collections of kings and wealthy people interested in antiquities in the seventeenth and eighteenth centuries, that today's museums have grown.

The surveying and recording of monuments, buildings and settlements, sometimes accompanied by clearing of buildings and a certain amount of excavation, was probably the next aspect of archaeology and prehistory as we see them today to be addressed. In pre-Partition India, this was one of the first tasks of the Archaeological Survey, set up in 1861 under the direction of General Cunningham. Measured drawings and descriptions of many major monuments such as the Mahabodhi temple at Bodh Gaya, Fatehpur Sikri and the Taj Mahal were made and put on record. Excavation at this stage frequently meant digging out the centre of a megalithic monument in search of grave goods, or breaking open a stupa in the hope of finding relics in rich reliquary caskets.

Systematic excavation to investigate ancient sites of all kinds, with the object of finding out about their character and chronology and the part they played in cultural development, came to the fore at the end of the nineteenth century. It was practiced with notable success by Sir John Marshall at such places as Bhita, Taxila and Mohenjo-daro, and by his colleagues, M.S. Vats at Harappa, and Dayā Ram Sahni and N.G. Majumdar at other sites. The work of this distinguished band of archaeologists was chiefly concerned with carrying out large-scale excavations at major city-sites of the third millennium BC and later times, and interpreting what they found as fully as possible.

The concept upon which the new, more comprehensive and scholarly approach was based was that archaeology should aim to gain the fullest possible information about the past. It saw individual town and city-sites as part of local and regional groupings with shared or interrelated patterns of life, or cultures, which changed through time, and passed through a series of phases as part of an ongoing dynamic process involving cultural change, expansion, amalgamation, and sometimes periods of decline. It assumed that these processes could be inferred from archaeological findings just as historical processes could be inferred from written sources of various kinds. Obviously, the kind of information that can be obtained from archaeological as opposed to historical sources is somewhat different, but carefully and thoughtfully used, each can tell a significant part of a story. In theory, the ideal situation is to have both sets of evidence available so that they can be used to complement and check one another. This can sometimes be achieved when excavating sites of historical importance such as Taxila or Fatehpur Sikri, where it

The Rediscovery of the Past

proves very rewarding. In interpreting what has been found in excavations all possible sources of information were used. Marshall in his Mohenjo-daro report frequently refers to local practice in Sindh to interpret what an object was used for, as for example wooden bullock-carts, clay sling-balls, and articles of women's adornment.

Part of the more comprehensive culturally-oriented approach is to investigate the extent of established cultures, how they change in differing geographical situations, whether there are distinct frontiers with other cultures, and if so, where they occur. These, too, were questions that began to be investigated in India at the turn of the century, notably by R.D. Banerji and N.G. Majumdar of the Archeological Survey of India (ASI), the latter tragically killed by bandits on the Sindh-Baluchistan border when making a survey of Indus and pre-Indus sites.

Inevitably, as part of the new attitude to investigating the past, different approaches began to be developed for different kinds of archaeological sites. Sites whose history was reasonably well-known would obviously be excavated with different objects in view, and therefore in a different manner, to prehistoric sites with little or no history beyond that provided by local traditions. Caves and rock shelters containing stone artefacts and other occupation material would again call for a special kind of approach. This book is concerned primarily with prehistoric cultures, ranging from those represented only by stone artefacts in geologically stratified contexts, and dating back over a million years, to sophisticated cultures centred upon cities of considerable size which were on the threshold of history. Therefore, throughout, we are dealing largely with situations where archaeological methods prevail, and only in the later chapters with the beginnings of historical archaeology. Examples of approaches used by archaeologists to different kinds of sites over the last hundred or more years will be referred to from time to time. The many different approaches and investigative techniques used have profoundly affected the outcome of investigations, and therefore one needs to know about them. But, at the same time, what is most significant in all archaeological investigations is clear thinking. An archaeologist must be able to define the problems being tackled and work out the most practical and economical ways of solving them so as to extend understanding of the situation concerned.

When archaeology is viewed in this way, the relationship of individual sites and cultural groups to their geographical setting becomes increasingly significant. This is another aspect of the study of archaeology which developed during the earlier decades of the

Origins of a Civilization

present century. From considering exclusively cultural questions, and objects and buildings of cultural, artistic and architectural interest, the focus shifted to include the relationship of cultures, and the political entities of which they formed a part, and to their surroundings. Agriculture and the exploitation of natural resources, commerce, long-distance trade and communications, and their development through time—all began to be considered as being within the scope of archaeology. Gordon Childe was the chief initiator of this approach. His books, written in the second quarter of the twentieth century, were widely read and have played an important part in forming the ideas of subsequent generations of archaeologists.

Following Partition, in both India and Pakistan, Mortimer Wheeler gave a fresh impetus to the Archaeological Survey which during the War years had been going through a low period. A successful brigadier, his forte was organization, and he applied this to excavations and to training staff with considerable success. But in doing so he imposed a rigid pattern of excavating which, while simple to learn, was restricting in practice, and not conducive to the kind of thinking needed to address new and complex problems. His legacy, while extremely valuable in some respects, has tended to inhibit the adoption of new ideas and methods current in the rest of the western world.

Archaeology and Conservation of the Cultural Heritage. The part played by archaeology in the conservation of historical monuments does not need much explanation. The more fully the original purpose of a building is understood, and the more information is available regarding the way it was planned and built, how it was used, and the ways in which it has been altered and added to, the better can its character be maintained and made clear for posterity. A clear understanding of the part it has played in the history of the surrounding region is also essential in order to assess the relative priority of spending thought, effort and money on the preservation and conservation of different historical monuments. It is not difficult to see that both historians and archaeologists have an essential role in this. When we come to prehistoric monuments and ancient city-sites such as Mohenjo-daro, Kalibangan, Sisupalgarh, Taxila and many more, clearly the same applies, although as we go back in time the expertise must come increasingly from the archaeologist. Sites which consist chiefly of stone or brick structures present relatively clearer problems, and the more difficult questions often arise in connection with their immediate surroundings which also need knowledge of the past combined with strong control if the character

The Rediscovery of the Past

of the monument is to be maintained. A Mughal monument, a temple or a group of old town houses can be totally dominated and eclipsed by a factory or a tower block in too close proximity.

As we go back in time the more ephemeral remains of earlier settlements, prehistoric workplaces, rock art, and the remnants of ancient landscapes all present different problems. To protect such places and at the same time make them available to the public is no easy task, and demands the united expertise of prehistorians, conservationists, local authorities and governments—and of course public interest and pressure. It is something very hard to achieve in the face of the rapid rate of development of present times, genuine economic pressures, and the powerful vested interests that are always part of development. Many major monuments throughout the subcontinent have been successfully conserved: the Taj Mahal and many of the Mughal and earlier buildings at Agra, Delhi and Lahore; Mahabalipuram and the many great early South Indian temples; cave temples of Ajanta and Ellora; Mathura, Taxila, Kausambi; Mohenjo-daro, Harappa, Kalibangan and other major sites of the Indus culture—and many others spring to mind. But many more are in a perilous state, and many monuments of great interest have already been lost. Neolithic rock art on the granite hills of Karnataka has been broken up for road metal, as has much of the rock art of prehistoric and later periods along the Karakoram Highway. Prehistoric stone alignments, ancient temples and mosques and settlements of all periods regularly disappear beneath factory and housing developments throughout the subcontinent. In many cases this is due to lack of funds or, more tragically, to misappropriation or misdirection of funds. An outstanding example of the last is the destruction of many unique prehistoric sites in the Rohri hills of Upper Sindh by quarrying away the limestone on which they are located in order to ship it downstream for use to build flood barriers to protect Mohenjo-daro—a process which has now been going on in recent years with the aid of UNESCO funds.

The conservation of the cultural heritage is a world problem, both because great monuments, like great works of art, are the cultural heritage of the human race, and because all countries have things that deserve and demand conservation. South Asia is particularly rich in such things, of all kinds, but it is also at present going through a period of rapid economic development together with an ongoing population explosion. This combination presents a situation of unique intensity and urgency, and a peculiar challenge to nations and governments, and to conservationists and all their allies among archaeologists, art historians, architects and scientists.

Chapter 2

THE SOUTH ASIAN SETTING

In order to begin to understand the cultural history of the Indian subcontinent, we need to consider it from two points of view. First of all, we should think of South Asian culture as an entity in itself, because it is one of the major cultures of the world, and has very ancient roots within the subcontinent. At the same time we should try to look at it in relation to the rest of the world, especially to cultures of adjacent regions, and lands to which there is and has been in past times, ready access by land or sea.

In physical terms the subcontinent is quite clearly defined, being a peninsula bounded by seas and divided from the rest of Asia by high mountain ranges. In this respect it is not unlike Europe, except that South Asia's land frontiers are more clearly demarcated by major mountain ranges than those of Europe. Like Europe and other major cultural entities of the world such as China or Central America, the Indian subcontinent has an unmistakable character of its own. This may be hard to define in a few words and hard to analyze but, once experienced, it is instantly recognizable. One of the underlying reasons for such a clear cultural identity in all these major regions, including South Asia, is that each has had a long history of internal cultural development which has formed deeply rooted patterns of thought, religious and philosophical attitudes, social behaviour, artistic expression, and a range of different but interrelated life-styles.

In common with other major cultures South Asia has been constantly influenced by external forces, as a result of invasion, military conquest, trade and the spread of ideas and technology. In any or all of these ways, at different times, the cultural structure and development of the subcontinent has been interrupted, stimulated, enhanced or otherwise influenced. In world terms this can be seen as part of an ongoing process of cultural cross-fertilization whereby major cultural entities continually influence one another.

The tension and balance between internal cultural development and external influence is complex and subtle, and it is something an archaeologist needs to keep constantly under review in trying to understand the past. The two processes, internal development and external influence, are also apparent on a smaller scale between regional cultures within a major subcontinental culture, as will become clear when we look more closely at the internal character and cultural history of South Asia. But before we begin to consider the regional differences that exist within the subcontinent, a closer look at it is necessary, in the world context both, as a part of Asia and of the Old World generally.

SOUTH ASIA IN RELATION TO ASIA AND THE WORLD

In a physical map of Asia, or on a globe of the world, the Indian subcontinent is seen as a triangular peninsula extending southward between two other major peninsulas, Arabia and South-east Asia, with the great ranges of the Hindu Kush, the Karakoram and the Himalayas enclosing it on the north (Map 1, xxi). Access by land would always have been difficult, but not impossible for those who knew the routes through the mountains and deserts. Access by sea would have been relatively easy once seagoing boats were available, and more readily and quickly achievable when the seasonal patterns of prevailing winds in the Arabian Sea and the Indian Ocean were understood by navigators. These factors would need to be borne in mind when considering every phase of the cultural development of South Asia, from the time of its earliest human or ancestrally human inhabitants to the Early Historic period—and indeed beyond, extending into the realms of later history which are outside the scope of this book.

There are further factors that are also important throughout, for understanding South Asia's cultural development. The first of these is the physical structure of the subcontinent which has already been touched upon; that is to say, the interrelationship of the major mountain ranges, plains and plateaux constituting it. Another is climate, both as it is today, and in terms of the extent to which it has changed during the periods being considered. Together, structure and climate form the natural environment upon which all human societies ultimately depend, and it follows that the environment of a major region in turn plays an important part in creating its cultural character.

Structure. Viewing the Indian subcontinent as part of the continent of Asia (Map 1), it is not difficult to understand one of the underlying formative processes of physical geography that has important bearing upon its past and present character. This is the part played by the process known as Plate Tectonics in giving the subcontinent its shape. Briefly, Plate Tectonics concerns the movement of blocks or plates of the earth's crust which form the major land areas or continents of the world. Over many millions of years, due to complex processes within the earth's core, these plates have been divided and been driven apart, and subsequently the parts have become attached to one another in different ways, forming new patterns and new major blocks or continents. Many millions of years ago, peninsular India was part of an older landmass, or plate, known as Gondwanaland which included, among other major blocks, what are now the continent of Australia and the island of Mauritius. When this block broke up the Indian plate became a separate entity, or large island, which drifted northward. Some twenty million years ago it made contact with the main Asian plate, and with time the convergence became more forceful, the Indian plate pushing against and going under the Asian one and forcing up the Himalayas and Tibetan plateau in the course of a series of massive upheavals interspersed by quieter phases. The periods of uplift are considered to have had widespread effects upon surrounding regions as far away as Japan and the Philippines. The latest is thought to have occurred c. 2.4 million years ago and is still continuing. Recent research has shown that the Tibetan plateau, the northern Himalayas, Nanga Parbat in Kashmir and Mount Gongga in Sichuan are all rising at an average rate of between five and ten millimetres per year.

The ongoing process of convergence accounts for much of the physical structure of northern parts of the subcontinent and of surrounding regions to the north. The height of the Tibetan Plateau and intermontane basins of Baluchistan, eastern Iran and south-western Afghanistan; and the height, youthful steepness and jagged outlines of the mountain ranges are its direct outcome. The great depths of alluvial silts and gravels that constitute the riverine plains of Pakistan and North India, filling the Indus and Ganges valleys, have accumulated in the trough or foredeep that has been formed in front of the main mountain ranges. Like the foothills and piedmont zone between the mountains and plains, the silts, gravels and boulders of which they are built have been derived in large part from the mountains. This kind of material continues to be washed down as the result of the rapid rate of uplift.

The South Asian Setting 15

These processes, the upthrust of the mountains, the accelerated rate of erosion, and the massive deposition of eroded material in the plains, have been going on very actively during the periods covered by this book, and continue till today. The collision or convergence process further manifests itself in a very immediate sense by the occurrence of earthquakes and related events. Such events include changes in the courses of major rivers like those recorded in the Punjab in historic times; and changes of level such as the twenty foot drop of a large block of land near the Rann of Kacch at the time of the Kacch earthquake in 1819 (Allchin et al, 1978).

Secondary effects of the collision are witnessed in the extensive erosion of soil over wide areas by seasonal torrents, and the rapid down-cutting and lateral movement of streams seen in the foothill valleys of the piedmont zone between the major mountain ranges and the plains, as for instance in and around the Bannu Basin in the southern NWFP. Other examples are the much-dissected silts and rapidly changing 'bad land' topography through which the main Islamabad-Peshawar road and railway pass south-east of Attock in the northern Punjab; and again in the Pabbi Hills near Jhelum. Similar conditions prevail in hilly regions like the Las Bela district north of Karachi. They are also found to some extent in parts of the Indian Siwaliks, and Himalayan valleys, although moving eastward the effects of erosion tend to be mitigated by more humid conditions. The notorious Chambal ravines which occur where the Chambal river emerges from the Central Indian hills into the Jamuna plain, south of Agra, are a similar phenomenon associated with local uplift.

The large-scale erosion in regions effected by the intercontinental collision is essentially a natural process, but clearly it is being accelerated by over-grazing, woodcutting, road-building and other human activities. The richness and productivity of the soils of the plains of Pakistan and North India, which are constantly refreshed by silts carried out of the mountains by rivers and streams, is a further result of the collision process, and it has had immeasurable effects, directly and indirectly, upon cultural development in the regions concerned and on the subcontinent as a whole.

In the longer term, but still well within the period of this book, the increasing height of the Himalayan and Karakoram mountain ranges has been shown to have had far-reaching effects upon the climate, and on the environment generally. Most important of these are the conditions thus created to bring rainfall to the subcontinent in the form of the south-west and north-east monsoons. It is evident that the world we live in is constantly being altered by a series of

16   *Origins of a Civilization*

dynamic processes on a scale quite beyond human control. Today, in addition to all the natural changes taking place, environmental change is being increasingly brought about by the activities of mankind.

Climate. The greater part of the Indian peninsula lies south of the Tropic of Cancer, and receives virtually all its rainfall in the summer with the south-west monsoon. Exceptions to this are Sri Lanka and the extreme north of the subcontinent—that is to say Chitral, Kohistan, Swat and most of the North West Frontier Province of Pakistan, together with Kashmir and some of the other Himalayan valleys of India—lie in the winter rainfall zone of the northern hemisphere. They receive a large part of their water from winter storms in the form of rain and melting snow.

Looking at the world map we see that, by and large, in the continents of the northern hemisphere the more northerly winter rainfall zone and southerly summer rainfall zone are divided by deserts; and that within the desert zone the degree of aridity varies somewhat. The most regular, extensive and intensely arid sections are the Sahara and the Arabian Desert, while in both North America and West and Central Asia the pattern is thrown out by mountains and high plateaux which have a modifying effect on the climate in various ways.

In South Asia the modifying effect of the physical structure is very marked. In climatic terms much of the north-western third of the subcontinent forms an extension of the Arabia/Persian desert. The climate is marginally less arid in parts of the region, but everywhere approaches desert conditions. But moving eastward conditions change significantly. The south-easterly curving arc of the Himalayas sweeps down into latitudes that would otherwise be desert. It deflects winter rains southward to overlap with the monsoon zone, and increasingly on moving eastward, contributes to the precipitation of summer monsoon rains in North India. The escarpment of the Western Ghats increases monsoon precipitation along the western coastal strip and much of the plateau of peninsular India, but also causes a rain shadow, or zone of lower rainfall, a certain distance inland (Map 2). The subcontinent has its own climatic patterns which, while clearly part of the pattern of similar latitudes throughout the world, are at the same time considerably modified by its structure and by the effects of its ongoing collision with Asia.

Climatic Change. Like the conformation of the landscape, the climatic patterns of the past varied considerably from those existing today and during historic and later prehistoric times; and there have been

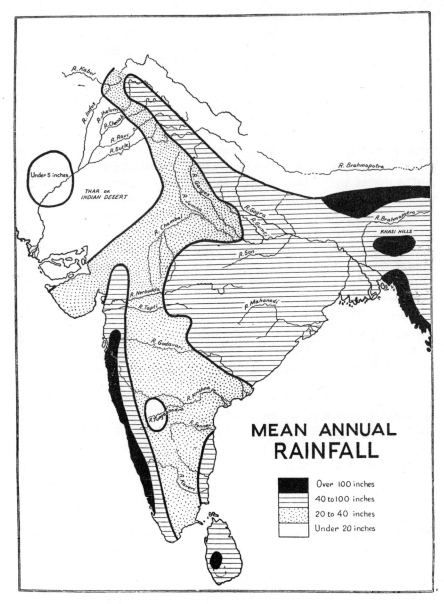

Map 2. South Asian rainfall (after the Imperial Gazetteer, 1910)

much greater variations during the longer periods of time covered by earlier prehistory. These changes have been part of world patterns, but like other such patterns they differ somewhat from continent to continent and from region to region. In the course of the last two million years the world has passed through a number of alternating colder and warmer phases, commonly referred to as glacials and inter-glacials. Formerly, there were thought to have been four glacial phases during the Pleistocene, but as a result of the study of deep sea cores taken from the sediments of the ocean floors there is now a continuous record which shows that there were many more changes of varying intensity.

Major glacial phases had a radical effect on the climate of temperate regions as both northern and southern polar ice-caps greatly increased in size. As a result much of northern Europe, Asia and America were continuously covered by ice and snow for long periods, and a great deal of the earth's water was locked in the extended polar ice-caps, causing the sea level to fall by c.150 metres. In equatorial regions the difference does not appear to have been so strongly marked, but in tropical and semi-tropical regions both rainfall and evaporation were reduced and winds were stronger. Consequently, there was more sand-dune formation in deserts and increased amounts of windborne dust or loess were carried for long distances over land and sea. Rivers became highly seasonal, many drying up entirely for much of the year, but carrying large quantities of coarse gravel and boulders when in flood. The force of rivers when in flood was further increased by down-cutting due to falling sea levels.

These conditions prevailed during the last glacial maximum, c. 16,000 to 18,000 years ago. After this the ice began to melt and the sea level rose rapidly, but conditions did not get much warmer for some time, because the temperature of the sea remained cold due to melting ice. This was a time of maximum aridity in tropical and semi-tropical regions, including North India, when many lakes and rivers dried up. By about 12,000 BP (before present) the rate of sea-level rise began to slow down, the sea became warmer and rainfall and humidity increased. Forests and grasslands spread into previously arid regions, deserts contracted, and rivers flowed more regularly, carrying silt in suspension rather than coarse material when in spate. It is clear that earlier glacial phases had followed somewhat similar courses, but the end of the last glaciation is of particular significance because it marks the beginning of the Holocene (from c. 10,000 years to the present), with conditions generally like those we know today. This was a considerable landmark in terms of human development in South Asia. The improvement and diversity of the environment provided humanity the opportunity for cultural and technological experimentation.

The South Asian Setting   19

The minor climatic fluctuations of the Holocene clearly had considerable effects upon human life and culture. Changes in sea level, even on a small scale, combined with changing temperatures and rainfall regimes, can have far-reaching effects upon the environment as a whole. A slight rise in sea level can flood fertile valleys and submerge coastal plains or turn them into salt marshes or saline lagoons. Relative changes in land and sea level can be caused by tectonic movements of the land, causing areas or blocks of land to rise or sink.

A change of a few degrees in average annual temperature over a period of two or three decades can cause glaciers to advance or retreat measurably within their valleys. An increase of a few centimetres in average annual rainfall over a period of years, particularly if it is accompanied by a slight fall in average temperature and/or an increase in humidity, will turn a desert into grassland suitable for grazing animals. A corresponding decrease in average precipitation and humidity, or a rise in temperature can reverse the change even more rapidly. Such changes, as we know well today, can be crucial to the livelihood and survival of human communities. The same has been the case in the past.

One of the ways in which climatic change can come about is through a slight alteration in the seasonal patterns of rain-bearing winds, the monsoons of the tropics and the cyclones and anti-cyclones of temperate regions. The causes of such widespread changes are complex and somewhat controversial, and are in any case beyond the scope of this book. However, they have undoubtedly taken place in the past, and if we look once again at the climatic map it is clear, for example, that a very slight southward shift of the northern winter rainfall belt would greatly increase the fertility of the Lower Indus valley which at present has an annual rainfall of between zero and five inches. We shall not go any further into general questions of climatic and environmental change here, as it is sufficient for the present to be aware that such changes take place, and have been of crucial importance to human development in South Asia as in the rest of the world. But we shall come back from time to time to questions of environment and environmental change at many points in the story, because they have had profound effects upon human life and culture.

It would now be in order to look at the various regions of the subcontinent, and assess the widely differing environments that its structure and climate have provided for human communities.

Origins of a Civilization

INTERNAL DIVERSITY WITHIN OVERALL UNITY: DIFFERENT ENVIRONMENTS, DIFFERENT CULTURES

Hitherto, we have been looking at the Indian subcontinent as part of the continent of Asia, and of the world. We have noted its distinctive cultural character and overall unity. We have seen how it is placed in relation to the pattern of climatic zones of the northern hemisphere; and the way in which its physical conformation, that is to say its mountain ranges, plains, hills, plateaux and escarpments, modify the overall pattern of climatic zones in certain respects. As a result South Asia has a number of climatic and environmental features, resulting from its physical structure and tectonic history, that are peculiar to itself and have helped to form its individual character.

Looking more closely at the character of the subcontinent, and the variations within it, we see that it includes a great many different kinds of natural environments, ranging from deserts to tropical rain forests, and from some of the highest mountains in the world to immense, low-lying, flat alluvial plains with rich, highly productive soils. Of the total range of tropical and semi-tropical environments found in the world, almost all are represented in the Indian subcontinent. Almost every possible combination of environmental factors can be found. Each different type of environment means a variation in the life-style of the human communities who live and support themselves within it.

This does not mean, however, that the environment of a region completely controls the cultural development of human communities who live there, for within any situation there are always a number of choices regarding what to do and how to do it. What the environment does in every region is to put a number of negative controls on the range of activities possible there. For example, in much of the north-western third of South Asia, agriculture has never been possible because of lack of water either in the form of rain or supplied by rivers. This has meant that pastoralism and hunting are the only available means of obtaining a livelihood. The situation has changed in certain regions from time to time due to advances in technology, such as understanding how to store surplus rainwater in tanks or bunds (*bandhs*), to dig deep wells, or to construct irrigation schemes and bring in water from outside the region. The applications of technological discoveries of this kind can transform a landscape and increase the productivity and range of possible activities out of all recognition.

In many instances, by exploiting the potential of their regional environment, human communities have brought about radical changes. Forests have been cleared, hillsides terraced, and deserts irrigated by means of canal systems. This has been done in order to increase the productivity of cereals and other food crops, cotton or other cash crops, and to increase the total range of crops cultivated. When successful, such works make possible enormous increases in population, as is the case with rice cultivation in the Lower Ganges valley, for instance. When misjudged or imperfectly maintained, such human interventions have frequently led to disaster and the loss of much good land, due to erosion, salination and other causes. The character of the different regions of South Asia, as we see them today, has been formed by a combination of its natural potential and the way the communities who live there have used it.

South Asian Environments

We shall now look in more detail at the range of environments found in South Asia today. Then we shall go on to consider the extent to which climatic and environmental conditions during prehistoric and early historic times differed from the present.

The Arid North-west. In the north-western third of the subcontinent there is a large area of desert or near-desert conditions which, in world terms, forms an extension of the Persian desert. This includes the semi-desert mountainous regions of Baluchistan and parts of the North West Frontier Province of Pakistan, consisting of arid hills and almost equally arid mountain ranges divided by deep valleys, with streams that provide narrow belts of secluded fertile, and often irrigated, agricultural land. Whatever rainfall there is comes mainly in the form of winter storms. Much of this region appears to have had many more trees and more natural vegetation in the past. This is confirmed by historical sources. The degree of aridity seen today appears to be due in part at any rate to cutting of trees for commercial purposes and excessive grazing by sheep and goats.

The Thar desert occupies the province of Rajasthan and parts of surrounding provinces of western India and the south-eastern borderlands of Pakistan, and conditions are consistently more arid than in the north-western mountains. Thar, means a dry place or wilderness, perhaps even a place of death, and, although it is not quite so profoundly arid as the Sahara or the Arabian desert, it has and does form a formidable obstacle for men and animals. The underlying structure of almost the entire Thar is a low rocky plateau which is part of the Indian plate. From it, rise widely spaced groups of dry rocky hills. Between them, in places, there are dune fields consisting of rows of sand-dunes sometimes a hundred feet or more in height, running approximately at right angles to the prevailing south-westerly wind. Formed by the wind, before which they are very slowly advancing in a north-easterly direction, they look like giant waves on the sea. Elsewhere there are great undulating stretches of bare rock interrupted here and there by small rocky hillocks and by shallow valleys in which streams flowed in the past at times when the climate was somewhat less arid than today. The valleys form part of ancient drainage systems, some of which debouched into the Rann of Kacch or the Gulf of Cambay and others forming part of the Indus system. Today they carry water only for a few days following the rare rainstorms that occur in the desert, and many of them are blocked by sand so that the water spreads out to form shallow lakes or *dhandhs* which rapidly evaporate and become saline before they disappear.

The 'dead' drainage systems of the Thar are of great interest to archaeologists, as they give a clear indication that it was not always so arid as it is today. This and other evidence, both archaeological and geomorphological, shows that at times, in the past the Thar has been a more hospitable region both for grazing animals and for people. The Thar lies on the northern fringes of the south-westerly monsoon zone, which is the source of the sparse and unreliable rainfall it receives today. None of the hills are high enough to modify the climate. In terms of structure and climate the Thar is part of peninsular India.

The Indus System. The valley of the Lower Indus, which divides the rocky plateau of the Thar from the north-western mountain region of Pakistan, coincides with the province of Sindh and part of the Punjab in Pakistan. It lies between the northern winter rainfall zone and that of the summer monsoon, receiving little or no rain from either. Thus the Lower Indus valley is one of the few parts of the world where a major perennial river flows through a desert with virtually no rainfall. Two other regions which provide parallels for the Indus valley are the valleys of the Tigris-Euphrates and the Nile. Each of the three has been the home of one of the earth's earliest civilizations. Such a situation provides exceptionally propitious conditions for early agriculture, combined with a highway for inland water transport. It is easy today to forget that until the advent of

The South Asian Setting

mechanized road and rail transport, waterways were of great practical and commercial importance both for travel and for the transport of heavy materials such as stone, timber, grain or cloth in substantial quantities. This is why throughout South Asia, as in other parts of the world, there is a tendency for important regional cultures to grow up around major river systems, as has happened in the case of the Indus, the Ganges, the Cauvery (Kaveri) and a number of other rivers at various periods.

The Lower Indus valley as we see it today is an extremely arid region totally dependent upon the Indus to sustain human life. As in the Thar, there are indications that it may not always have been quite so arid, and that areas along the north-western margin of the plain in particular may have been able to support grazing animals and sustain dry cultivation in a way that is not possible today. In chapter 5 we shall consider the environment of the Lower Indus valley, and the Indus system generally. But at this point a little needs to be said about the Indus and its tributaries, because it is such a major river, and together they are so important to understanding the mosaic of South Asian environment complex.

The Indus rises in south-western Tibet, and flows between two ranges of the inner Himalayas, in a north-westerly direction, until it meets the Gilgit river flowing in the opposite direction down from the Pamirs. There the Indus turns south-westward, and makes its way through the mountains in a series of gorges to the plains of the northern Punjab, to start on its final eight-hundred-mile journey to the Arabian Sea.

In the first half of its course through the Himalayan and Karakoram ranges the Indus is fed by melting snow in spring and monsoon rain in summer. Near the point where it enters the plains it is joined by the Kabul River, flowing out of the Afghan mountains to the north, fed by winter rains and melting snow. In the Punjab, it receives the water of four major tributaries, the Jhelum, Chenab, Ravi and Sutlej, all of which rise in the outer Himalayas and are both snow and rain fed like the upper Indus. It also continues to receive water from a series of minor rivers, such as the Kuram, flowing from the north-western mountains, and fed primarily by winter rains. Similar rivers continue to emerge from the mountains on the final part of its course through Sindh. Today, they tend, like the Bolan river for example, to lose themselves in the silts of the plain before reaching the Indus. But there is evidence that five thousand years ago the Bolan, and probably other streams, carried sufficient water to flow directly into the Indus. The Indus has always been an unstable

24 *Origins of a Civilization*

river, flowing in its lower course through the southern Punjab and Sindh in a very shallow bed and frequently changing its course. These are characteristics that can be attributed in part to the arid conditions and the flatness of the plain, and in part perhaps directly to the collision factor discussed above.

The upper courses of the Indus and its four major tributaries have been much affected by the uplift of the Himalayan and Karakoram mountains. Together they have a complex history of changing their courses and changing their confluences in the plains, which has continued into recent historical times. The plains of Sindh and the southern Punjab are covered with traces of abandoned river courses, some of which still serve as flood channels in times of spate.

The instability of the Indus system as whole is due to a number of factors. An arid climate and the shallow river beds with low banks tend to result in rivers changing their courses following floods. To this must be added the situation created by the ongoing collision between the Asian and Indian continental plates, briefly outlined in the previous section, which causes continuing intermittent uplift of the mountains where the rivers rise, and disturbance and change of levels in the plains of Punjab and Sindh through which they flow. Such tectonic disturbances, as they are called, (meaning changes in the structure of the earth's crust as, for example, when folded mountains are pushed up, or one block of the crust moves up or down in relation to others) are frequently accompanied by earthquakes, landslides in mountainous regions, and by changes in the courses of shallow-bedded streams and rivers in the plains.

Today the Lower Indus flows near the western margin of its plain. On the eastern margin there is what appears to be the abandoned course of a major river comparable to the present Indus, known as the Hakra. It is usually dry, but during historical times, prior to the building of the Sakhar (Sukkur) barrage and other major dams and irrigation projects, it has been known to carry considerable quantities of water when the Indus was in flood. It is considered that in the past the Hakra may have carried the water of the Sutlej, one of the present major tributaries of the Indus, directly to the sea, debouching into the Rann of Kacch.

Another major change in the system is the disappearance of the Sarasvati, once a major tributary of the Hakra or the Indus. Recorded in the Rig Veda as a major river (between c.1500 and c.1000 BC), it is now a small stream that loses itself in the Punjab plain, its former course marked by abandoned settlement sites of Harappan times. Their distribution indicates that its flow was reduced, causing it to

The South Asian Setting 25

dwindle and retreat back towards the Himalayas in a series of stages. It seems clear that the Sarasvati itself or its tributaries must have been captured by another system, probably that of the Jamuna during later prehistoric or Early Historic times.

Instability of major rivers of the kind we have described can have a catastrophic effect upon human life, destroying houses and whole towns and cities, and ruining agricultural land. In areas of very low rainfall such as Sindh and the south-western Punjab, life depends entirely upon rivers bringing water from regions far away. Settlements, whether villages, towns or cities, are located close to rivers and streams on which they are totally dependent for agricultural purposes and perhaps even for domestic water supplies. Any change in the course of a major river can be devastating, whether it sweeps away a settlement or moves away from its bed, leaving the inhabitants and their fields without water. We shall see when we come to look at the development of the Indus civilization, that it is very much a child of the Indus river system and its environment.

In its long course the Indus and its major tributaries cross the collision zone of the Asian and Indian plates of the earth's crust, the Indus in its early course flowing between ranges of immensely high young folded mountains formed by the collision. Together, they have a very extensive catchment area and receive water from both summer and winter rainfall zones. The Indus system is one of the major river systems of the world, but today, because much of its water is taken off for irrigation, the river is much reduced in its lower reaches. However, it still carries enough water to maintain its character as a major perennial river for several hundred miles through the Sindh desert, where the rate of evaporation is very high and still more water is taken for irrigation, to the sea. But the volume of water carried has been seriously reduced by the demands made on it, so that its flow is no longer sufficiently powerful to carry enough silt to maintain its delta which, in consequence, is being washed away by the sea more quickly than it is being replenished by the river. This has serious effects upon fishing, and also means that land too will be lost if the situation is allowed to continue.

The rivers of the Indus system, which for thousands of years were the principal highways of communication for the whole region, are still used to some extent for transporting goods and people. They began to be superceded by faster mechanized transport towards the end of the last century when the railway was built from Karachi to Rawalpindi and beyond, and improvements in road transport have continued the process. Nevertheless, the importance of the river system in past times should not be forgotten.

26 *Origins of a Civilization*

North and East India. The Ganges-Brahmaputra System. The combined Ganges-Brahmaputra system, like that of the Indus, has a very large catchment area, carrying off the water from a whole range of different regions and different climatic regimes. In these respects it resembles the Indus system, but in others it is very different. The main reason for this is that, with certain exceptions, the entire region is one of moderate to high rainfall, in complete contrast to the deserts and arid mountains of the west. The Brahmaputra drains the mountains of Assam, an area of high rainfall, and the borders of eastern China and northern Burma, from which many relatively short streams fall into the main valley. But the source of one of its major tributaries, the Tsang Po, is in the high cold plateau of southern Tibet, in the same region as the source of the Indus, and flows eastward for several hundred miles before swinging south into eastern Assam.

The Ganges and its companion tributary the Jamuna rise in the outer Himalayas and swing away in great arcs to the east, through what is today a region of moderate rainfall and fairly intensive mixed agriculture, with wheat as the main cereal crop. They meet at Allahabad at the Sangam where the famous Kumbh Mela takes place every twelve years. From there the Ganges flows eastward into a region of increasingly high rainfall and intensive rice cultivation. This climatic situation pertains right across the great Ganges-Brahmaputra delta and along the Brahmaputra valley. The plains of the two great rivers together form an arc of rich low-lying plains at the foot of the Himalayas, the eastern arm of the Indo-Gangetic foredeep filled with alluvium from the Himalayas.

Throughout its course the Ganges is joined by many major and minor tributaries flowing out of the Himalayas to the north and the hill ranges of Central India to the south. Many of these are notoriously unstable and prone to change their courses following floods. The Gangetic plain, like that of the Indus, is studded with abandoned river courses and cut-off meanders, some of which, particularly to the north of the main river, form approximately crescent-shaped lakes or ponds known as ox-bow lakes. Some of the earliest recorded settlements in the region are located close to these. The main river and certain of its major tributaries are deeply incised into the old alluvium of the plain, so that flooding is normally contained and confined to a flood plain on either side of the regular channel of the river, in contrast to the more widespread inundation of the Indus.

Although not such a dramatic boundary as the Himalayas, the Vindhyan escarpment and the hills of Central India form a marked

The South Asian Setting 27

contrast to the wide, flat, extremely productive Ganges plains. Central India is varied, wild and rocky, and historically has always been a contrasting region. Today, the Ganges valley is one of the most densely populated regions of the world. Still largely agricultural, it is thickly studded with villages, intensively cultivated and has few types of trees other than mangoes, besides others which are deliberately planted. Therefore, little or no remnants of the original vegetation remain except along the northern margins of the plains in the Terai where there is still some quite dense natural forest. In view of the climate and the rich soil there can be little doubt that large parts of the Ganges plains were heavily forested before they were cleared and settled by farmers. The process, which had probably been going on for sometime on a limited scale, began in earnest in the first half of the first millennium BC with the establishment of the first Iron Age agricultural settlements. In contrast to the arid north-west, a slight difference in average annual rainfall here would not have greatly effected the environment or the potential for agriculture. What was important was the ability and the technology to clear the forest and to establish and cultivate fields.

The Ganges and its tributaries must have provided the inhabitants of the region from the earliest times with a network of waterways, useful for fishing, travel and communication between groups. In the thickly forested and sometimes marshy plains the waterways would have been a valuable means of communication and transport for the first farmers and early settlements. They must also have been an essential element in establishing the internal trade which made possible the development of the towns and cities of the Iron Age. Later, as the eastern Ganges valley and the delta were developed, they provided an outlet to the Indian Ocean and a gateway for trade with the east coast of peninsular India, Sri Lanka and the world beyond, both to the east and the west. This is something we shall return to in chapter 11 when discussing the Iron Age and the beginning of history.

Central and Peninsular India and Sri Lanka. The boundary between the Ganges valley and peninsular India is effectively the escarpment of the Vindhyas. Although several of the southern tributaries of the Ganges, which rise in the hills of Central India and flow out into the plains as sizable streams, provide a link, the change of landscape upon ascending the escarpment is so marked that there can be no doubt that this is a major regional frontier. Further west, the distinction is not quite so clear as the highlands of Central India

28 *Origins of a Civilization*

merge irregularly into the rocky hills of Rajasthan. The distinction between the arid desert margins and Central India is one of climate rather than topography. Traditionally, however, the Aravalli range running south-west from Delhi has been regarded as an important landmark dividing the Thar Desert from Central India. Where the three main regions of India—the West, the East and the South—meet, we are in a transition zone where the demarcation lines tend to move in response to minor fluctuations of climate, and in accordance with the criteria being used in different situations. This is partly why many geographers have treated the hill region of Central India as a whole as a kind of mutual frontier, or buffer zone, between the three clearly very different regions of the subcontinent. From many points of view this is correct. But even if we treat Central India as a separate entity we are still faced with the problem of defining its frontiers.

Central and peninsular India as a whole have no single unifying feature, such as a great river system with a central region of rich alluvial soil, to provide a focus for cultural development. They consist of a number of different regions, some of them centering upon river systems of considerable size, like the Krishna or Godavari, but of a different character to the Indus or the Ganges. The hills of Central India and the Deccan are all part of a continuous block or hilly plateau, made up largely of rocks of great antiquity, which is part of the Indian plate referred to earlier. Consequently, the underlying rock formations in general are much older than those that from the Himalayas, Karakoram or Hindu Kush and other mountain ranges created by the collision of the Indian and Asian plates. This is an important part of the character of peninsular India. What we see here is on the whole a much more mature and stable landscape, which is not undergoing such rapid change or such large-scale erosion and deposition of waterborne silts and gravels, as regions to the north.

Perhaps, just because the whole character of the region contrasts so decisively with that of the north, the stability of the Central and South Indian landscape has tended to be taken for granted. However, the region has been subject to several severe earthquakes in the present century, and there is no lack of evidence of past tectonic activity. The Vindhyan escarpment mentioned at the beginning of this section results from changing levels of blocks of the earth's crust along a fault line caused by tectonic stress. In this case the floor of the Ganges valley has gone down in relation to the Central Indian plateau in response to the inter-plate collision described earlier. The two major rivers of western Central India, the Narbada and Tapi, flow in rift valleys also formed by the downward movement of blocks of the earth's crust along fault lines.

South of the Tapi there are no major rivers flowing from east to west. The top of the escarpment of the Western Ghats effectively forms the watershed for the rest of the peninsula, and all the major rivers flow from west to east. Much of the northern part of the Deccan plateau is covered by hundreds of metres of Deccan Trapp, a volcanic rock formed of lava from ancient volcanoes, and this gives the landscape a characteristic appearance of horizontal layers overlying one another like irregular steps. This contrasts with the landscape further south, which is predominantly formed by granite and other old igneous rocks. Here groups of hills covered by large rounded boulders rise from the undulating surface of the plateau, today largely cultivated but formerly covered by dry thorn forest and grassland.

The peninsular plateau falls away abruptly on the west in a series of steep escarpments, the Western Ghats, to the narrow, fertile coastal plain studded with small rocky hills. Much of the coast too is rocky with a number of bays and offshore islands which provide well protected harbours. In the extreme south this pattern breaks down somewhat: the plateau begins to fall away, and the Nilgiri and Palni hills rise above it divided by the Palghat gap. Separated from peninsular India by the Mannar Strait, Sri Lanka with its block of mountains and surrounding plains forms the southernmost part of the subcontinent.

Central India and most of peninsular India receive almost all their rain in the late summer with the south-west monsoon. The extreme south of the peninsula and Sri Lanka, in addition, receive rain from the north-east monsoon during the winter. The western coastal plain throughout has a very high rainfall due to high escarpments and mountains immediately inland. The rest of the region has a moderate rainfall, dropping to low in the rainshadow of the Western Ghats. With the exception of the western coast and the deltas of the eastern flowing rivers, of which we shall say more below, the greater part of Central and peninsular India is a region of dry cultivation of cereals, particularly millets, and of cotton. Cultivation has been augmented from prehistoric and early historic times by local irrigation from artificial tanks or dams which conserved rainwater. Recently, large irrigation schemes based on dams built on major rivers have radically changed some areas. In some places there are still considerable areas of dry forest and acacia which provide grazing land for cattle, goats and sheep. On the hillslopes and in the valleys of Central India and in the Eastern and Western Ghats there are denser forests with a whole range of large trees which are the basis of a timber industry.

The major eastward flowing rivers, the Mahanadi, Godavari, Krishna, Penner and Kaveri with their respective deltas have formed the nucleus of successful Iron Age and Early Historic kingdoms: that of Orissa on the Mahanadi; the Andhra kingdom on the combined Krishna-Godavari deltas and extending up both valleys; the Tamil kingdom on the Kaveri system. In each case the deltas and adjoining coastal strips provided an extensive area of rich alluvial soil where tank irrigation could be augmented by local canal irrigation from the numerous distributaries that make up the delta. As a result several crops of rice could be grown in the course of a year, and a large population could be supported. The distributaries also provided a network of waterways throughout the delta, and the main river and its tributaries provided a means of communication with the interior of the country and a means of transport of goods between coastal, delta and inland centres of trade.

Sri Lanka occupies a unique position. It has mountains, hills and plains, and regions of high and relatively low rainfall generally paralleling those of southern India. But the same ingredients form a different mix to that of India, giving it a distinctive pattern and unique character of its own. One basic difference is that while its tropical environment on the whole resembles that of South India, its early historic cities such as Anuradhapura are comparable to those of North India. Being an island at the end of the Indian peninsula, it has been more open to international trade, and has formed a natural link in sea trade between the Mediterranean and western world on the one hand and eastern India, South-east Asia and China on the other. It has remained largely true to its Buddhist roots and Buddhism has remained the state religion, but like India it retains its secular character.

ENVIRONMENT AND CHANGE

When we consider even the recent past, and try to reconstruct the character of any region at a particular period of time, we have to take man-made changes into account. This means working out when certain changes to the natural environment that we see today took place. For example, when considering Mughal times, one would have

The South Asian Setting

31

to think of the countryside without railways, factories, large-scale irrigation schemes; cities and towns as being very much smaller, and areas of natural forest and uncultivated land very much larger and more widespread; the population a fraction of what it is today. Generally speaking, as our research takes us further back in time we can expect the impact of human communities upon the landscape to decrease. Furthermore, the passage of time and the effects of later activities will tend to obliterate or obscure the traces of that impact.

On the positive side, however, some human activities of very early times have left their mark in ways that are recognizable and can increasingly be evaluated with the aid of modern scientific techniques. Almost every human activity has had some effect on the environment. Hunting, fishing and gathering selected plant foods can change the balance of nature and have all kinds of knock-on effects, some of which, such as the extinction of a species, may be irreversible. Cultivating and domesticating certain species of plants and animals, or clearing forests, (even on a small scale) can have even more obvious and far-reaching effects on all kinds of plants and animals, and ultimately upon the climate. Mining for gold, copper and other metals, and for precious stones leaves traces that are recognizable after many centuries or even millennia. Stone embankments or dams (*bandhs*), built to retain water, and stone retaining walls built to reinforce terraces for cultivation on steep hillsides, if not deliberately destroyed in the course of later developments, may last also for centuries or millennia. All sorts of activities of this kind and many others have been having their effect upon the landscape of South Asia for many thousands of years. Although much evidence of this kind has been obliterated by later cultivators and builders of towns, irrigation works, roads, railways and so on, much still remains if we look for it intelligently, and this is the evidence upon which archaeologists base their work.

The regional patterns that we recognize today within South Asia are important as a basis for understanding the past, but further careful research and thought as to how they have been modified are needed in order to understand the surroundings in which past cultures existed, and the complex interrelationship of environmental and cultural change. Generally, the overall outlines of the regional pattern remain, and certain aspects of the environment are modified within it. For example, a slight increase in average rainfall, or in its distribution throughout the year, or a drop in average temperature which reduces the amount of evaporation, may cause the margins of the desert to have a little more vegetation and support more grazing animals, and larger trees may extend into areas of grassland and thorn forest beyond their former limits. If the crucial factors are reversed their effects will be reversed also. Such changes can be crucial to the survival of a community, and they may necessitate a change in ways of life which will be registered in the archaeological record in a variety of ways, such as changes in the tools used or in the nature and distribution of living sites. We shall see numerous examples of this kind of change as we follow the story of South Asian cultural development. In general, minor climatic changes of this kind have more effect in a marginal zone of low rainfall, for example, than in an area of high rainfall where a few inches more or less will not make much difference. In dry regions over-exploitation of the environment can have a similar effect to that of natural decrease in rainfall or humidity.

Changes of climate that have taken place during the Holocene period, that is to say during the last ten thousand years, have been of a relatively minor kind such as we have just described. It is sometimes unclear whether they have been brought about by natural causes or by human activity, or by a combination of both, which seems frequently to have been the situation. Earlier, during the Pleistocene, or the Ice Age as it was formerly called, more profound changes in the climate of the world took place, as we have briefly indicated in an earlier section of this chapter. These and the less massive but still important changes of the last ten thousand years will be further discussed in the following chapters, where they are relevant to the story. The important thing at this point is to understand that nothing in the world as a whole, or for that matter in any regional or local situation, is static. Everything is changing all the time, some things rapidly and dramatically and others so slowly as to be scarcely perceptible. Our aim here is to try to trace the history of cultural development in the Indian subcontinent within a constantly changing environmental context.

Chapter 3

ROOTS: ANCESTORS OF MANKIND AND THE BEGINNING OF CULTURE

ANCESTORS OF MANKIND

The earliest traces of mankind and their immediate ancestors in South Asia are elusive. Like certain later aspects of the story, but for different reasons, they can best be understood when looked at in a wider context. Early human development is an evolutionary process involving the development of body and brain; of manual, social and intellectual skills which decisively distinguish humans from the rest of the animal world. The process of development to a stage that can be generally recognized as human was a long one, extending over several million years. Early ancestors of the human race are referred to as hominids, to distinguish them from later, more fully evolved humans.

The World Picture

For over a century fossil bones and teeth of hominids (the early ancestors of the human race) and early humans have been found from time to time in tropical, semi-tropical and temperate regions of the Old World, in contexts which indicate that they lived during the Pleistocene (c. 1,600,000 to 10,000 years ago), or earlier. Stone artefacts too have been found in such contexts, some with skeletal remains and some without. No such early remains have been found in the New World, although the date of the arrival of human groups both in the Americas and in Australia is still somewhat uncertain, and is being constantly pushed back as new discoveries are made. During the last twenty years, the development of physical dating techniques has enabled early archaeological finds which are beyond the reach of Carbon 14 dating to be independently dated by a

34   *Origins of a Civilization*

number of other scientific methods. The processes involved in most methods of scientific dating are expensive, and often difficult to carry out for scientific or practical reasons, so it has taken time and considerable resources to date new finds and to work through the backlog of important earlier undated finds. As a result we are now steadily getting a clearer idea of the antiquity of mankind and their ancestors in Africa, Europe and Asia.

Africa. Up to the time of the Second World War Asia was regarded as the probable centre of hominid/early human development. But during the fifties, sixties and seventies there were a series of discoveries in East and southern Africa, and particularly in the East African Rift Valley which straddles the equator, that together give us the most complete record of hominid and early human development so far found. The Rift Valley provides peculiarly favourable situations for the discovery of fossils and stone artefacts in geologically stratified contexts suited to various kinds of scientific dating. In both regions the story has now been reconstructed from a whole range of finds including skeletal remains, stone artefacts and living, camping or special activity sites. More recently, important finds have been made in Ethiopia and Chad. Physical dating methods have been used with increasing effectiveness, and there has also been a growing understanding of past environments. Episodes in the story can be therefore independently dated, accurately reconstructed and related to the world pattern of climatic change. As a result the record from Africa can now be seen to extend back for over four million years. There are still many gaps and many unresolved questions, but an outline is emerging which is of great interest in itself, and also helpful in attempting to assess the growing catalogue of finds of hominid and early human remains from Asia.

In brief, it is now reasonably firmly established that in Africa the hominid ancestors of mankind appear to have lived largely in open savannah environments, as opposed to living in tropical forests like the great apes and their ancestors. There is clear skeletal evidence, supported by a remarkable set of fossil footprints at Kanapoi in East Africa, that certain ancestral hominids have walked upright for around four million years. At a fairly early stage they developed opposable fingers and thumbs with which, as their mental powers too developed, they were able to do increasingly precise and delicate tasks. Remains of a number of different early hominids have been found in Africa, of which certain are considered to be directly ancestral to mankind, while others appear to have become extinct.

Roots: Ancestors of Mankind and the Beginning of Culture

Over two million years ago some hominids had begun to make stone tools which became, as time went on, more and more clearly recognizable as artefacts, made deliberately in ways that are virtually impossible in nature. All these discoveries have led many scientists to regard Africa as 'the cradle of mankind', that is to say a centre of evolutionary development from which at times hominids or early humans spread into Asia and Europe, taking with them their ways of life and stone technology. More recent research has cast some doubt upon this view, showing the world picture to be more complex. Schnick and Toth (1993), give a comprehensive view of early hominid/human cultures in Africa and elsewhere.

Asia and Europe. Hominid research in Asia lagged behind Africa for several decades, but during the eighties a number of discoveries began to be made. The earliest hominid skeletal remains together with stone artefacts so far recorded in Asia now appear to come from Longupo Cave in central China, where they are considered to date back to c. two million years on the basis of scientific dating of layers above them in the excavation, and other evidence (Wanpo et al, 1995). The famous 'Peking Man' is somewhat later. Dates of between one and a half and two million years have been obtained for hominid remains with artefacts in Java. Altogether, a considerable number of hominid and early Stone Age sites have now been found in eastern and southeastern Asia, particularly in China, and a fuller dated record can be expected in the not too distant future. Recently, the distribution of early hominid remains in Asia was extended by the discovery of a hominid jaw near Tbilisi in Georgia in a context dated to 1.6my (million years) (Gabunia & Vekua, 1995). Further, early finds have been made in Israel (Bar-Yosef, 1994).

The more northerly parts of Asia and most of Europe remained peripheral to hominid development at this stage. During the glacial periods of the Pleistocene they offered a highly inhospitable environment. There are indications that tool-making hominids ventured north from time to time during inter-glacial periods. During the last glacial, at the end of the Pleistocene, the level of culture and technology attained by that time enabled human communities to continue to live in Europe and western Asia despite cold conditions.

Following the spate of new evidence from Asia the whole question of where the ancestors of modern man evolved, and whether or when they moved to other parts of the Old World has

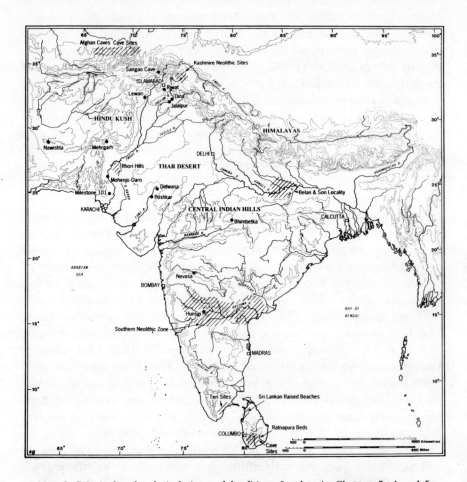

Map 3. Principal archaeological sites and localities referred to in Chapters 3, 4 and 5.

become increasingly more complicated. It continues to be a subject of controversy and energetic debate among scientists; a debate that effects the work of prehistorians everywhere, and especially those concerned with the early prehistory of South Asia.

South Asia. In the Siwaliks, which form the outer foothills of the Himalayas, there are areas rich in fossils which were studied during the last century by the Geological Survey of India and others. Some of the fossil collections from Miocene deposits (23,700,000 to 16,600,000 years ago) included fossil apes. This together with the

Roots: *Ancestors of Mankind and the Beginning of Culture*

discovery during the early 1860s in both Madras and Sindh of stone hand-axes, closely paralleling those found a few years earlier in Pleistocene contexts in Europe, raised hopes of finding a sequence of later hominids and early humans. Though searches have been made from time to time, so far no later hominid or early human fossils have been found. Stone artefacts however have continued to be found throughout the subcontinent in a wide range of situations.

In South Asia one securely dated discovery has so far been made which is comparable to those in China, Java and western Asia. In 1983, at Riwat, near Rawalpindi in the northern Pakistan Punjab, members of the British Archaeological Mission to Pakistan's Potwar Project, working in collaboration with the Department of Archaeology and the Geological Survey of Pakistan found a group of artefacts in a Siwalik deposit, which were subsequently dated by the Paleomagnetic method to 1.9 my. (Rendell, Dennell and Halim, 1989; for a summary of the work of this project, see Allchin, B., 1995). The largest of them was made from a quartzite pebble, with the clear intention of producing a tool with a point and two sharp cutting-edges (*Plate 1*). The butt fitted the hand so that the tool balanced in a suitable way for heavy chopping or hacking. The initial flakes that blocked out the form had been struck off in a controlled manner in at least three directions, and this had been followed by further trimming—a sequence that could not have happened naturally. This tool and the smaller pieces, also clearly man-made, were all in fairly fresh condition. They were shown to have been an integral part of the deposit in which they were found, incorporated into it from the time it was formed.

Riwat is an area close to the collision zone of the Indian and Asian plates described in chapter 2. After the artefacts had been incorporated into the conglomerate the whole deposit had been buried under successive layers of silts and gravels washed out of the rising Himalayan and Karakoram ranges. The layer in which they lay, along with those above and below, had subsequently been folded by further pressure from the Indian plate. The folds or ridges so created were then planed off and dissected by deep gullies and streams (*Fig. 1*). These processes eventually led to the exposure of the artefacts in the conglomerate matrix (by this time a cemented gravel). Inspite of detailed investigation no hominid skeletal remains were found associated with the artefacts, nor in deposits in the same time bracket, in the same locality or elsewhere in the Potwar region.

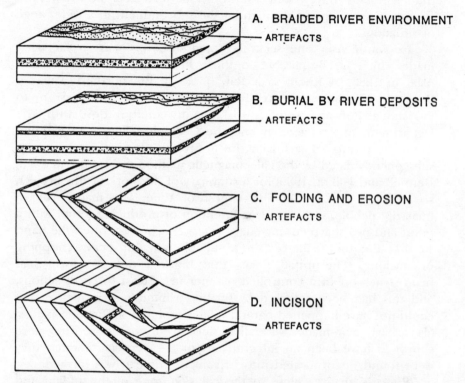

Fig. 1. Diagram illustrating the incorporation of artefacts into the Siwalik deposits.

In the Riwat locality no fossils of any kind were found, as the soil chemistry unfortunately was not conducive to the preservation or fossilization of bone. In another locality in the Potwar plateau members of the project made an exhaustive collection of animal fossils, which have been studied, recorded and labelled and are now in the museum of the Geological Survey of Pakistan in Islamabad. They also made studies of the environment of the last two million years. During this period, which spans the Pleistocene and extends back into the Pliocene (3.5 to 1.6 million years ago), many worldwide climatic changes (glacials and inter-glacials) took place. There were phases of major Himalayan uplift during the Pleistocene, as we have seen in the previous chapter, which must also have affected the environment. Both sets of factors were operative in the region. Throughout, the environment appears to have varied in temperature, rainfall and humidity, while remaining within a general bracket of dry grassland and forest of various kinds. It was inhabited by large herbivorous animals such as the elephant, and rhinoceros, and various types of cattle and antelope, etc. At times lakes formed, marked by fine lacustrine deposits of silt in the sections, and by the fossil bones of crocodiles and turtles. There were many changes in the drainage pattern, due to the proximity of the rising mountains to the north-east which must also have affected the climate. In general terms this picture is consistent with patterns of climatic change in middle latitudes of the world, which appear to have been distinct, involving changes in temperature, rainfall, humidity and vegetation, but less severe than the glacial and inter-glacial phases in more northerly or southerly latitudes.

The significance of the discovery of early artefacts in the Potwar region has also been greatly enhanced by the growing number of comparable early dated sites in various parts of Asia outlined above. Any further evidence of the presence of early hominids that South Asia holds is still to be discovered. Artefacts were found some years ago by the Geological Survey of India in the Indian Siwaliks in a context dated to 2.5 my (Verma, 1991), but unfortunately these have not so far been illustrated or put on display. In view of recent discoveries in other parts of Asia it seems probable that more will shortly be forthcoming. It is to be hoped that the search will continue for physical remains and further cultural remains of the earliest South Asians. The maxim 'absence of evidence is not evidence of absence' is one no archaeologist can afford to forget, especially in situations of this kind.

THE BEGINNING OF CULTURE

Before going further we must say a little about the archaeological or cultural aspects of the hominid finds from Asia and Africa that we have been discussing. This after all is what distinguishes hominids and humans from other primates such as gorillas or chimpanzees. There has always been discussion regarding the definition of the human race. When do tool-making hominids become human? The question involves either making a physical distinction on the basis of the scarce and fragmentary fossil skeletal remains available, or alternatively using the evidence provided by artefacts, i.e. making a

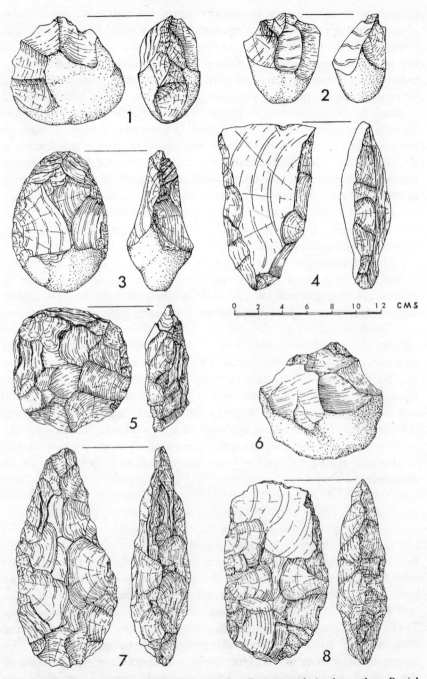

Fig. 2. *Lower Palaeolithic stone tools from early collections made in the northern Punjab (Nos. 1 to 4) and Madras (Nos. 5 to 8). Nos. 1, 2 & 6, chopping tools; Nos. 3 & 7, hand-axes; Nos. 4 & 8, cleavers.*

cultural definition of mankind. The latter seems the more satisfactory from the point of the archaeologist, but the problem is that from the distant times we are considering, artefacts of stone are virtually all that survive. The occasional examples of bone and wood, preserved in exceptional conditions, are so rare that although they are exciting they cannot be regarded as representative. They do, however, support the commonsense view that it is highly probable that many more tools were made of wood, bone and other organic materials than were ever actually made of stone. This is also supported by ethnographic records of people who made and used stone tools in recent times, such as the aboriginal population of the interior of Australia when first visited by administrators and anthropologists during the nineteenth century. They were found to produce a limited number of skillfully made, highly finished stone tools, such as spear heads, knives and adze blades. In addition, large quantities of roughly-shaped stone artefacts were briefly used and quickly discarded in the process of making many useful, often ornamented objects, ranging from dugout canoes to barbed wooden harpoons and string bags, made from wood, fibre, mastics, bone and other materials. Some recorded communities in South-east Asia used neither metal nor stone, but made their heavy-duty tools and cutting tools from hard bamboo at the time they were studied.

All this shows that the absence of well-finished stone artefacts of recognizable form at a hominid site, or indeed the total absence of surviving artefacts of any kind, cannot be taken as an indication of the absence of manual skills, nor of the activities and cultural features that are normally assumed to go with them. This situation emphasizes that there are many unanswered, and for the time being unanswerable, questions regarding what our ancestors were like and how they lived. The distinction between hominids and humans, although useful in some ways, has led to much discussion. The dilemma as to where in the evolutionary record humanness begins has been resolved for the time being, for practical purposes, by discussion among experts in the fields concerned. The details of the arguments need not concern us here, or distract us from attempting to follow the development of early human culture in South Asia.

One point, however, deserves to be borne in mind when considering this question, and that is that stone artefacts are extremely difficult to make. Many prehistorians who have experimented have learnt this to their cost. First of all, it requires a great deal of knowledge and experience to select a suitable kind of stone which will fracture in a regular manner when struck, and so can be worked

42 *Origins of a Civilization*

to a predetermined shape. Given the best of raw material, to make even the simplest of stone artefacts, let alone a well-finished hand-axe or cleaver (*Fig. 2*), requires a great deal of strength and control, and a very high level of sheer expertise. All recognizable stone artefacts are the product of highly-developed craft traditions that must have been passed on from generation to generation, in some cases for thousands of years. The social and economic implications of this are far-ranging, and deserve to be considered when defining the limits of humanness.

The Significance of Stone Artefacts

On account of their survivability stone artefacts have received a great deal of attention from archaeologists and others. Something made hundreds of thousands of years ago has tremendous impact, especially if, when held, it fits and balances in the hand. Found in a known and fully studied and recorded context, a stone artefact is a valuable piece of evidence: divorced from that context it is merely an object of antiquarian interest. Much has been written in the past about the technology and methods of making stone artefacts, and about detailed distinctions in their form. More recently, archaeologists have put greater emphasis upon understanding the cultures that artefacts represent and the ways in which they relate to the environment of their time, and upon following cultural adaptions and developments within changing environmental contexts.

For the purpose of this book we shall tend to follow the recent trend, only discussing the nature of stone and other artefacts where this is of importance to wider issues. But at the same time we must remember the recurring tendency for traditions of making artefacts according to certain patterns or types to become established, and to continue and develop for thousands of years. This has not been universal, so each area and period must be considered individually. Certain traditional 'type tools' such as hand-axes are easy to recognize and, partly for this reason, have acquired a special importance for archaeologists as cultural or chronological markers. As such they are very useful markers, but they have to be treated with caution because, as we shall see, the use of similar stone artefacts does not mean that people were necessarily similar in other ways: nor does the use of different kinds of stone tools necessarily mean that people are profoundly different in more general cultural respects, although the implications of all such differences have to be carefully considered.

Roots: Ancestors of Mankind and the Beginning of Culture

Some sort of typological/chronological system of classification of stone artefacts is essential in order to study them effectively, and such systems have been employed almost universally. The problem is that they tend to become traditions in themselves, sometimes to the extent of being accorded almost the significance of dogma, which is unfortunate as it leads to new material being forced into categories that do not fit. A system can all too easily become a tyranny instead of an aid to understanding.

With these reservations in mind we can look at the situation in South Asia where, as in much of the Old World, there is a long established division between the Old Stone Age or Palaeolithic and the New Stone Age or Neolithic. In the following part of this chapter and beginning of the next we shall be dealing with the Palaeolithic, which covers an immensely long period of time during which hominids and early humans lived mainly by hunting and gathering natural foods, and were learning to utilize an ever-widening range of environments with the aid of increasingly effective tool-kits. Later, we shall come on to the Neolithic which, in very general terms, is considered to begin with the advent of settled life, pastoralism and agriculture, and is often marked by the presence of ground stone axes *(Figs 10 & 11)*.

A threefold division of the Palaeolithic into Lower, Middle and Upper Palaeolithic, based on typology and technology and generally on a relative chronology provided by geological stratigraphy, has been widely used in South Asia, and is increasingly being clarified by independent physical dating. The Lower Palaeolithic includes everything up to and including the hand-axe tradition, i.e. to around 100,000 years ago; the Middle Palaeolithic covers a variety of flake industries which generally developed from and superseded the hand-axe tradition; the Upper Palaeolithic represents a further level of technological development first in evidence c. 40,000 years ago. There are many exceptions to the system and in practice there are no hard and fast lines between the main categories. However, it provides a useful working basis for dealing with large assemblages of material.

The concept of an additional typo-chronological phase, the Mesolithic (beginning c. 10,000 years ago with the beginning of the Holocene) was introduced in an attempt to cover the transition period between Palaeolithic and Neolithic. As we shall see, this is one of the most complex and interesting phases of cultural development in the subcontinent. We shall use all these terms from time to time, where appropriate, while concentrating primarily on more

44   *Origins of a Civilization*

fundamental cultural developments wherever possible.

The Pre-Hand-Axe Tradition. The earliest stone artefacts or tools recorded in association with hominids in both Asia and Africa are pebbles of quartz, or other hard rock, chipped to produce a strong sharp edge for chopping and hacking hard materials such as wood or bone. They are known as chopping tools *(Fig. 2, nos. 1,2 & 6)*, and with them are often smaller tools made from the flakes struck off the pebbles. In Africa, the artefacts are generally made from rather small pebbles: in Asia, the material used tends sometimes to be larger. Such artefacts are not always easy to recognize, and as they continued to be made through to Neolithic and later times they are not, as such, cultural or chronological markers. Therefore, unless they are discovered in a datable context, in a group with other more culturally or chronologically distinct artefacts, or in association with hominid or human skeletal remains or other evidence, they cannot be taken as an indication of great antiquity. The finds from Riwat are meaningful primarily on account of their character as a group of artefacts, and of their dated context. Their authenticity is supported in a broad contextual sense by the discovery of increasing numbers of hominid skeletal remains and artefacts of comparable dates in various parts of Asia, as already pointed out. Continuity with later stone industries within the Potwar region is provided by chopping tools and flake tools found in Siwalik deposits in the Pabbi hills which fall sequentially and chronologically between the Riwat finds and the hand-axe industries discussed below. Elsewhere in the subcontinent, few pre-hand-axe artefacts have been identified in dated or datable contexts.

The Hand-Axe Tradition. In early Pleistocene contexts in East Africa, tools with a more definite and consistent form begin to appear in the archaeological record. Roughly pear-shaped, they have a point at one end with a strong sharp cutting-edge on either side produced by knocking off flakes systematically from several directions *(Fig. 2, nos. 3 & 7)*. They are not unlike the artefact from Riwat illustrated above. They are known as hand-axes and the tradition of making them appears to have persisted in Africa for almost one and a half million years, gradually achieving a high level of technological refinement and variety of size and form. This is by far the longest tool-making tradition known. Hand-axes have come to be regarded as a 'type tool', forming part of an industry that included other closely related tools such as cleavers *(Fig. 2, nos. 4 & 8)* and much larger quantities

Roots: Ancestors of Mankind and the Beginning of Culture   45

of less obviously distinct kinds of tools made on flakes and smaller pieces of stone which seem to have been used for cutting, splitting, scraping and smoothing wood, bone, hides and other substances.

Hand-axes appear in Europe about half a million years ago, perhaps taken there by their makers who were moving north during an inter-glacial period. In much of Asia hand-axes and similar tools occur only sporadically, not as a constant tool type or a regular feature of stone industries, which tend to consist only of less distinct artefact forms.

In South Asia hand-axe industries are found very widely, many of them, for reasons that we shall go into below, at surface sites. Following publication about the discovery of hand-axes in Madras in the 1860s (only three years after they were first recognized in Europe) and then in Sindh, many collections began to be made and recorded by amateur and professional archaeologists. As with early archaeological discoveries everywhere, most finds were quite inadequately documented, according to more recent archaeological practice, but they provide a record of distribution, much of which might otherwise have been lost. Collections were made and put on record from the Las Bela district and the Bugti hills of Baluchistan and elsewhere in the mountain valleys to the north-west of the Indus plains.

As time went on hand-axes and other stone artefacts steadily continued to be discovered at surface sites and in river gravels in Himalayan foothill valleys from that of the Beas (an eastern tributary of the Indus) to tributaries of the Brahmaputra system in Assam. None have been recorded on the surface of the alluvial plains of the Indus or the Ganges, but they have been found on outlying rocky hills within the plains, such as the Rohri hills in Upper Sindh, and along the southern margins of the Ganges plains where they meet the first escarpment of the Vindhyas. Both the last-mentioned localities are of great interest, and we shall have more to say about them shortly.

Around the margins of the Rajasthan desert, and also in the more arid central part, small groups of hand-axes and related Lower Palaeolithic artefacts are frequently found near the foot of rocky hills, on which they were perhaps made, and obviously were left by their makers. They are sometimes on the surface, and also incorporated into slope wash debris which is interdigitated with the calcified windborne sand of an old sand sheet *(Fig. 6, p. 64)*, (Allchin et all, 1978). During the eighties, a team from Deccan College, Pune, excavated Acheulean artefacts, including hand-axes, from calcareous

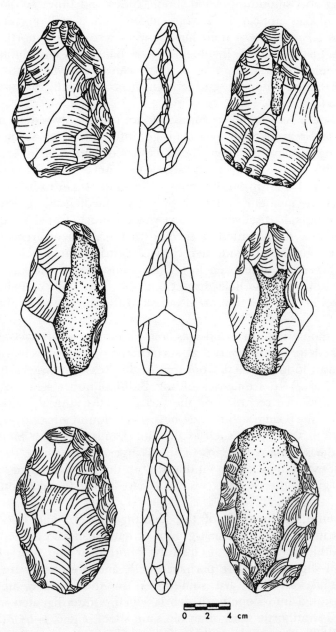

Fig. 3. Hand-axes from dated contexts (c. 500,000 BP) from Jalalpur and Dina, Jhelum valley, northern Punjab, Pakistan.

Roots: Ancestors of Mankind and the Beginning of Culture

loam in old stratified sand-dunes near Didwana. The layers immediately above were dated to c. 40,000 years ago (Misra, 1995). Some of the finely made artefacts are clearly Acheulean, while others are more crudely made, and might prove to belong to an earlier phase of the Lower Palaeolithic. Much of the Lower Palaeolithic material in the Thar appears to have been incorporated into or covered by the sand of a climatic phase considerably more arid than the present, and therefore probably belongs to preceding phases and to the beginning of the arid phase. On the Saurashtra coast Acheulean tools were found in gravels beneath a miliolite or beach rock for which two thermoluminescent dates of c. 95,000 and 67,000 years ago were obtained.

Hand-axe industries are found throughout Central and much of peninsular India, but so far, for reasons that are unclear at present but are probably connected with the environment, none have been reported in the Western Ghats, or south of the river Kaveri (i.e. in the extreme south of the peninsula) or in Sri Lanka. Many sites and groups of artefacts have been found on the surface, and in or immediately below the topsoil in situations where the ground has remained relatively undisturbed. Sites tend to be in river valleys, often in close proximity to rivers and streams where both water and stone (in the form of river gravels) were available, and where game animals coming to drink could be secured. In some cases the artefacts are associated with, or are on the surface of, colluvial fans, i.e. spreads of gravel and boulders brought down by tributary streams and deposited at the side of the main valley.

Sometimes Lower Palaeolithic artefacts appear to have been associated with older land surfaces at higher levels which have been reduced by deflation (i.e. the gradual erosion of lighter materials such as soil, silt or disintegrating rock) leaving the heavier material and stone artefacts approximately where they were originally, but at a lower level. All such sites are difficult to date scientifically, but in recent years methods of studying them have been developed.

Chronology and Dating

In a limited number of places hand-axes and associated artefacts have been found in geologically stratified contexts to which their relationship is clear. One of these is the site in Rajasthan mentioned above. At two sites, Dina and Jalalpur in the Jhelum basin, in the Pakistan Punjab, a total of fifteen artefacts including three hand-axes were found by members of the British Potwar Project in conglomerates previously dated by palaeomagnetism to 500,000 to 700,000 years ago (Rendell & Dennell, 1985). Their alignment in relation to the rest of the deposit indicated that they had been incorporated into it at the time it was laid down *(Fig. 3 & Plate 2)*.

Hand-axe industries and later Stone Age material have been regularly noted and put on record by geologists and archaeologists for well over a century, from gravels within the alluvial deposits laid down by many major rivers of northern, western and Central India and the northern Deccan at times when climatic conditions clearly differed from those of the present. Rivers where depositional sequences incorporating artefacts have been recorded include the Narbada in Central India; the Mahi and other rivers in northern Gujarat; the Pravara in northern Maharashtra; the Son and Belan (both southern tributaries of the Ganges) on the borders of Uttar Pradesh and Madhya Pradesh. Subsequent changes and the establishment of the present climatic regime have resulted in rivers cutting their channels down into the alluvium, and in places cutting steep cliffs in which sequences of layers of deposition can be clearly seen. These usually show two, three or four gravels, progressively decreasing in size, separated by deep layers of sand and fine silt. The lowest gravel normally includes Lower Palaeolithic artefacts, the second Middle Palaeolithic artefacts and the third and fourth, where present, respectively Upper Palaeolithic and Mesolithic material.

Several problems are raised by the complexeties underlying this apparently simple pattern, for while in general terms it is fairly consistent, closer observation indicates that the sequences do not correspond precisely on different rivers, which makes interrelating the sequences difficult. The extent of rolling and abrasion due to being carried along by the main river or by tributary streams also varies considerably. In some cases the artefacts are in the same condition as the gravels, indicating that they have been carried some distance from the point where their owners left them; in others they are virtually unworn, indicating that they were probably made after the gravel was approximately in its present position. Then there is the question of interpreting the sequences in terms of past climates and environments. This is complicated by considerations of the effect of Himalayan uplift. During periods of rapid uplift, such as those in the Middle to Late Pleistocene, the rate of erosion and consequent deposition and accumulation of silt must have been greatly accelerated, especially in the Ganges system which centres on the trough or foredeep in front of the Himalayas. How much of the gravel and silt is due to this, how much to climatic factors stemming from Himalayan

Roots: Ancestors of Mankind and the Beginning of Culture   49

uplift, and how much to more general world climatic change, is therefore an open question.

An attempt to solve some of these problems on the Son and Belan rivers, both southern tributaries of the Ganges, was made during the seventies by a joint team from the Universities of Allahabad and Berkeley, California (Clark and Sharma, 1983). They made a comprehensive survey of the valleys covering all periods of the Stone Age, to which we shall refer again from time to time. The survey showed that the Son river in its middle course, flowing through Vindhyas before emerging into the Ganges, scoured and incised its valley down to bedrock during a time of arid climatic conditions and marked seasonal spates. Colluvial gravel and shale, brought down the side of the valleys by tributary streams and slope wash, covered the valley floor. Lower Palaeolithic artefacts, including Acheulean hand-axes, appear both to have come down with this material and to have been made from it after it had been deposited. As the extreme climate modified, the river flowed more regularly and deposited the finer sands and silts which overlie the gravel. Deposits of this cycle in the Middle Son valley are named Sehawal. The finer element of the Sehawal formation was dated by the thermoluminescent method to around 100,000 years ago (Clarke & Williams, 1986). This is interesting, but does not date the Acheulean context as such. The Sehawal formation was followed by three further cycles of a similar kind, including respectively Middle Palaeolithic, Upper Palaeolithic and Neolithic material.

It is suggested that the reason for the absence in the Middle Son valley of anything earlier than the Sehawal gravel may be that the valley itself, and the tectonic fault in the Vindhyas in which it flows, may not have existed in their present form before the time when the valley was scoured out and the Sehawal gravels began to accumulate on its floor. This would mean that the tectonic events of the Middle to Late Pleistocene radically altered the drainage of the region, and as a result the catchment and flow of the Son river were greatly increased and the valley swept clean. During this period the uplift of the Himalayas is considered to have progressively increased the intensity of the monsoon, and therefore must have effected the climate and environment of the Ganges plains and Central India in a number of ways. Precisely how the Middle Son and other river valley sequences reflect the effects of both the climatic and tectonic factors at work throughout the Pleistocene may be shown by future research.

Moving up the section and forward in time, with each cycle the initial gravel becomes both smaller and of a somewhat different

50 *Origins of a Civilization*

character and contains successively later artefacts conforming to the general pattern described earlier. The Son and the adjacent Belan valleys each provide a sequence of alluvial deposits, with artefacts and surface sites of various periods, which together provide a continuous record from the Acheulean to the Neolithic. We shall return to the later phases of the sequence in the following chapter.

Surface Sites

The South Asian environment is essentially one of erosion and deposition, as pointed out in the previous chapter. Therefore, Early Stone Age artefact assemblages have tended either to be covered by massive deposits of alluvium, as just described, or to have remained on or near the surface. Furthermore, for reasons that are not clear at present, artefacts of the Lower and Middle Palaeolithic are only very rarely found in caves or rock shelters, in contrast to Europe and eastern Asia and to some extent Africa. On account of this situation archaeologists have been forced to develop ways of understanding Stone Age cultures by studying surface material.

Some of the most interesting and obviously archaeologically rewarding surface sites are factory or work sites where stone tools were made and other activities were carried on. These are usually places where suitable stone was available, to which people came and made tools. They left quantities of debris and unfinished or broken artefacts which are of great interest to archaeologists as a means of understanding how the tools were made. Stone Age sites of all periods vary greatly in nature and extent, and in the range of artefacts and debris they yield. They include multiple-activity living or camping places, more specialized sites and small clusters of artefacts which presumably their owners lost or abandoned after using them for some purpose. No two sites are ever exactly alike. This is part of the interest of prehistoric studies, and we shall try to convey something of this interest by giving brief accounts of some sites of different kinds that have been put on record. First a few words must be said about methods of studying surface sites.

One of the problems in studying surface sites is that so much must have been disturbed by floods, general erosion, deflation, the feet of passing animals and people over the course of time, or by cultivation. Fortunately, traditional Indian ploughs do not turn over the soil, but merely cut through the surface, so cultivation causes only minimum disturbance. Recent research has shown that even when artefact groups have been locally disturbed by any of these agents or simply by a general tendency to move downhill, as the great majority we see today probably have, they tend to stay together and retain their group character and much of their interest for the archaeologist. This situation is known as spot provenance, and is a fairly common one in the case of Lower Palaeolithic sites. By contrast, point provenance means that objects have remained precisely where their owners or users left them, allowing us thereby to see how they relate to each other and to make more detailed inferences regarding their use. This situation is more commonly found at sites of later periods, as we shall see in the next chapter.

A notable example of a surface study is Hunsgi in the southern Deccan, where an extensive group of Lower Palaeolithic sites in the valleys of two small headwater streams of the eastward flowing Krishna river system have been investigated over a period of nearly twenty years by K. Paddayya (of Deccan College, Pune), latterly in collaboration with M.D. Petraglia (Paddaya & Pedraglia, 1995). Groups of hand-axes and related tools were found at a range of sites on the valley sides and on the surrounding ridges. Close investigation has shown that virtually all had been effected to a greater or lesser degree by the erosion processes described above. Therefore, these are spot provenance artefact groups within each of which the artefacts relate to one another and collectively represent the character of the site.

A few of the Hunsgi sites are quite large, up to two hectares in extent, located on rocky outcrops, ridges and other higher ground, where there were many different artefact types and accumulations of debris from their manufacture and other activities. These could be considered as places where groups regularly came together, lived and made tools, and which probably formed group bases at certain times of year. There is evidence that they were used at intervals over quite long periods of time. There were also much smaller sites which appear to have been temporary camping places; and others with more limited ranges of artefacts where specific activities such as killing or dismembering game, making wooden tools or hunting equipment, curing hides, etc., probably took place; and there were caches of finished tools stored away for future use but never reclaimed. Some of these sites were associated with springs or places where water had accumulated to form ponds.

Tools were made chiefly from hard limestone, but also from dolorite and other kinds of stone that were available close at hand. There is no indication that tools or stone were carried far within the valleys, nor that they were brought in from outside. This and other

52 *Origins of a Civilization*

factors lead the investigators to the conclusion that one or more local groups lived in the locality, moving round and living on different sources of food such as large and small game, fruit, roots, seeds and so on that were available at different times of year. Some of the artefact groups appear to be more developed than others, suggesting that the Hunsgi area was occupied by hand-axe makers over a long period of time, either periodically or continuously.

There are other Lower Palaeolithic sites in the peninsular which have been studied and are of great interest, but the Hunsgi area, by virtue of the detailed survey and the study it has received over a long period, probably provides a fuller picture than any other site group so far described.

The Lower Palaeolithic sites that we shall look at next are in Sindh. These sites and their localities have not yet been studied in the kind of detail that either Hunsgi in the Deccan or the Son and Belan valleys on the southern edge of the Ganges plains have, for over two decades. But being in a very different environmental situation and each having their own individual character, they add another dimension to the overall picture of the South Asian Lower Palaeolithic, and also raise a number of new and interesting questions.

The first site, a stone tool factory in Lower Sindh, on a flat-topped limestone hill overlooking the Indus plains from the north-west, opposite Hyderabad, is known as Milestone 101 (*Plate 3*). This is an area of very low rainfall, but which is slightly higher and more regular than that of Upper Sindh or the central Thar desert. Prior to our visit in 1975, the site had been visited and put on record by an officer of the Pakistan Government Archaeological Department, but had not been otherwise studied. It was only possible for us to spend a few hours there, so the observations we published (*Allchin, B., 1976*) were accordingly limited and of a preliminary nature. The hill is topped by a layer of flint nodules, extending over an area of two hectares or more, which had been used during virtually every technological phase of the Palaeolithic. When we visited it, we found overlapping working areas of different periods which appeared to have been virtually untouched since the Stone Age craftsmen departed. As far as we were able to observe in the course of a few hours, Lower, Middle and Upper Palaeolithic tools and stone technology were all represented, and probably also Early Harappan, but we did not see any Mature Harappan material. The most striking feature was the quantity of Lower Palaeolithic material, especially hand-axes, in various stages of manufacture from roughouts to virtually finished pieces. A high proportion of the material appeared to belong to the Lower Palaeolithic, including hand-axes and cleavers, and seemed

Roots: Ancestors of Mankind and the Beginning of Culture 53

to be predominantly Acheulean. Of course, a brief survey of this kind would not preclude the possibility of earlier material being overlooked.

Another Lower Palaeolithic site was recently discovered in the Rohri hills of Upper Sindh, an area we shall be looking at in more detail in the following section and later chapters, as it is also rich in artefacts and factory sites of later periods. These hills too are of limestone, flat-topped, many of them capped by a layer of large flint nodules, which provide ideal material for making artefacts. These were used extensively during many phases of the Stone Age. Today the rainfall is virtually nil, but there is evidence that during Middle and Upper Palaeolithic times, and to some extent also during Early and Mature Harappan times, conditions were somewhat less arid. As pointed out earlier, a hand-axe was reported from Sukkur, where the Indus passes through the hills, in the 1860s; another is illustrated by de Terra and Patterson (1939). In 1994, a group of Italian and Pakistani archaeologists working in the Rohri hills discovered an early hand-axe factory site at Ziarat Pir Shaban (Biagi et at, 1996). Broken and unfinished hand-axes and other tools and debris from their manufacture, including hammer stones, leave no doubt that this was a Lower Palaeolithic, probably Chellean, factory site.

Lower Palaeolithic artefacts appear on present evidence to be more plentiful in Lower Sindh where the rainfall is marginally higher than in the extremely arid Rohri hills of Upper Sindh. Both Sindh sites are located at sources of high quality flint, on limestone hills, one on the edge of the Indus plain and the other surrounded by it. Flint of this quality is a relatively rare resource even in a limestone region, as is emphasized by the way in which in each case the site was used at virtually all periods of the Stone Age. The artefacts must have been carried away and used in the surrounding alluvial plains and other areas where good stone was not available. Only much more thorough investigations in the future can give any clear indication of the extent of the area these factory sites served at different times throughout the Stone Age.

The difference between the situation in the arid north-west and in peninsular India during the Lower Palaeolithic is interesting. At Hunsgi the evidence pointed to local self-sufficiency and reliance upon stone available within the immediate locality of the Lower Palaeolithic sites. In Sindh, on the other hand, we see large factory sites at places where good stone is to be found. The situation in the Son and Belan valleys is not quite so clear-cut.

The South Asian Lower Palaeolithic, as we have seen has much in common with that of Africa and Europe, especially in the character of the widespread Acheulean industries that are found in many different contexts. In one respect, however, the region differs radically from either, and this is in its involvement with the ongoing collision of the Indian and Asian plates which was particularly active during the Middle and Late Pleistocene. The profound disturbance this caused has left its mark on many aspects of the environment. At present there is only a small amount of evidence of hominid activity before this time, but the few examples of groups of artefacts of greater antiquity suggests that more may be found. At present we do not know in what kind of situations to search for them. From Acheulean times onwards tectonic disturbance appears to have decreased, and artefacts occur regularly in some profusion in predictable situations, so it is not difficult to find more sites.

Because of the special aspects of the South Asian environmental situation in Lower Palaeolithic times, we have devoted considerable space to this period. During the remainder of the Stone Age environmental conditions in South Asia seem to settle down, and the evidence suggests that changes continue to take place, but in a less violent manner. In the following chapters we shall be looking at some of the same localities. This is partly because they have sources of good stone, and therefore tend to have had continuous traditions of using it for tool-making. It is also because, for various reasons, Stone Age sites seem to have survived in these localities, and because research has been concentrated there.

So far most of the hand-axe industries recorded in South Asia have been considered to belong to the later, more developed part of the tradition, as it is known in Africa and Europe, generally termed Acheulean, and only a few examples corresponding to the earlier phase (Chellean) have been recorded. If we assume that the hand-axe tradition had a single origin, it would indicate that the technique arrived in the subcontinent at an early stage of its development, but only flourished extensively there later. This might indicate either that advanced Acheulean technology was brought in by later incoming peoples, or that it was passed on at a certain stage from group to group as technological knowhow. Analogy with recorded stone-using societies such as those of Australia or New Guinea suggests that the latter was the most probable process by which manufacture and use of advanced forms of this singular 'type tool' reached South Asia. However, the question of the origin of the technique of making hand-axes, if indeed there is a single origin, is one on which it is probably advisable to keep an open mind for the time being. The claim that the earlier developmental phases of the hand-axe tradition are totally absent from the South Asian archaeological record seems no longer sustainable, although examples of early hand-axes are still rare.

Chapter 4

The Long Climb: The Middle and Upper Palaeolithic

The Middle Palaeolithic

Wherever the Middle Palaeolithic has been studied in Africa, Europe, western Asia or Central Asia, it has been found to be characterized by marked regional diversity. South Asia is no exception. These regions correspond generally to those in which, during Lower Palaeolithic times, the hand-axe industries flourished, and in some of which a constant tradition of tool-making was maintained for hundreds of thousands of years, as we have seen. The makers of Middle Palaeolithic artefacts, however, penetrated further north in Europe and Central Asia than their predecessors had done; and what was more, they continued to live there during the last glacial phase, living in caves and dwellings of various kinds, rather than retreating to warmer latitudes. The use of technology to sustain life in a cold environment was a significant development, and opened up a whole lot of new possibilities for mankind. Regional differences in stone technology indicate that adaptions to changing environments were being made throughout. The tendency to change appears perhaps to have begun before the onset of the last glaciation; so what actually triggered the developments in stone technology and in the actual stone tool-kit we do not yet know.

A New Tradition: The Nevasan in Peninsular India

In much of South Asia the overall change at first sight appears to be a negative one. The hand-axes and related forms, so carefully crafted using long-developed skills, ceased to dominate the tool assemblages. In some regions they continued to be made in small numbers and on a much reduced scale: in others they seem to have disappeared

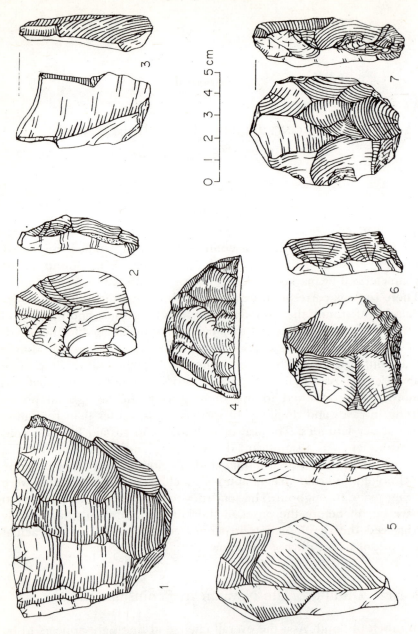

Figs. 4a and 4b Middle Palaeolithic artefacts from the surface of the red fossil soil at Hokra, near Budha Pushkar.
a. nos. 1, unidirectional core; 2 & 5, flakes struck from prepared cores; 3, burin; 4, carinated scraper; 6, scraper made on a flake; 7, discoidal core.
b. (facing page) nos. 1, utilized flake or adze blade; 2, broken palette stone; 3, tip of a broken hand-axe; 4, core; 5, hammer stone.

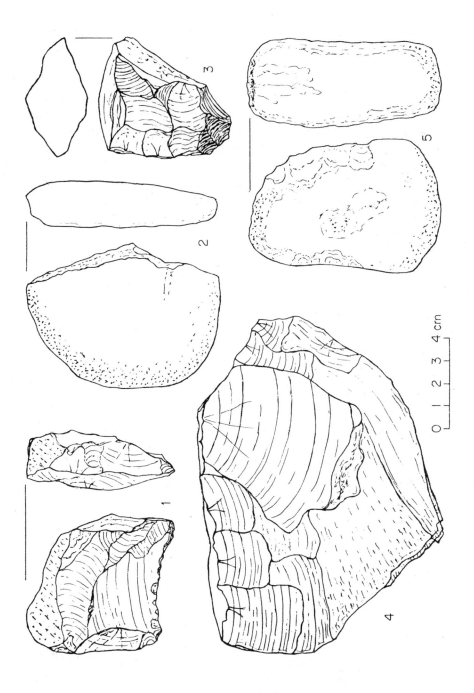

58 *Origins of a Civilization*

altogether. The emphasis in tool technology shifted to smaller, lighter tools made on flakes struck from various kinds of cores. Some cores were carefully prepared by trimming into shape so that when the final flake was removed it was of the outline and thickness needed (*Fig. 4a*). This process demanded forethought and a thorough understanding of the kind of stone selected, and it meant that a lot of time and thought was put into achieving the end result which was a single artefact. Flake tools of this sort had been present as part of the hand-axe industries, but with the Middle Palaeolithic they appear to have become the focus of more thought and care, and to be the 'type tools' or markers of the industry. Clearly, all sorts of things were being done in new ways, and done with a much lighter stone component in the material culture as a whole.

The emphasis in Middle Stone Age assemblages as a whole, and especially the Nevasan assemblages, is on scrapers which are relatively light and are not obviously suited to grasping in the hand, as opposed to hand-axes and cleavers which are large and weighty and do tend to fit and balance in the hand—so much so in some cases that they appear to be intended specifically for either the right or the left hand.

Ethnographic and archaeological studies both suggest that scrapers were used for woodworking, and other work for which an edge that was sharp but was also tough and would not shatter easily was needed. This seems to indicate that what we are looking at is a changing concept regarding the use of stone artefacts, perhaps a change towards combining them with hand grips or shafts of other materials.

Ethnographic evidence points towards the use of natural mastics such as resin for this purpose, together with wood and possibly bone. But until we have some more specific evidence to go on, it would be foolish to attempt to be too specific. The climatic evidence from the Thar desert which indicates a long period of more humid conditions with considerably more vegetation than at present is compatible with an increasing emphasis on wood-working tools. Some examples of hafted stone artefacts of comparable size to Nevasan scrapers, made and used by indigenous Australian craftsmen in the last century and recorded by anthropologists and ethnographers, are illustrated below (*Fig. 5*).

Middle Palaeolithic artefacts are almost as numerous and widespread in South Asia as those of the Lower Palaeolithic, and for similar reasons are also found largely at surface sites, which are often deflated, and in river gravels. Throughout much of the subcontinent

The Long Climb 59

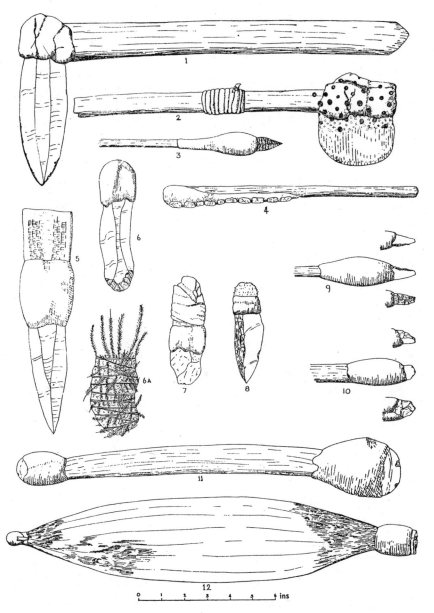

Fig. 5. Hafted stone artefacts from Australia in their original mounts of wood and resin or other masti (from the British Museum collection, now in the Museum of Mankind).

Middle Palaeolithic assemblages consist almost exclusively of cores and flakes, and tools made from flakes by trimming one or more of the peripheral edges to produce a strong sharp working edge that can withstand pressure. A certain proportion of carefully prepared cores are present throughout, but there also seems to have been a tendency to make whatever was available into something that would serve the purpose for the job in hand, rather than to produce a tool according to a predetermined model as had been the case in the hand-axe industries, and as was the case in some Middle Palaeolithic industries in Africa and Eurasia. There are exceptions to this, as we shall see, but what we have said applies to the great majority of Middle Palaeolithic industries found in peninsular, Central and eastern India. As yet little research, of the kind that can give an insight into the lives of the communities who made them, has been done on the nature of Middle Palaeolithic sites in the peninsular and Central India. There is a need for studies that analyze the site types and relate them to a locality and to sources of raw material, such as we have for the Hunsgi Lower Palaeolithic sites. It is clear from the work that has been done that with time both cores and flakes tended to become smaller and more finely made; but everywhere both factors were necessarily controlled by the quality and maximum size of the pieces of raw material available. In some cases, for example, it was available only in the form of small river pebbles.

The apparent amorphousness of the tools of the Nevasan industries, due to the lack of 'type tools', is perhaps the principal reason why the Indian Middle Paleolithic was only recognized as a significant technological and cultural phase in the period following the First World War. Hand-axe industries and what were classified as Neolithic industries (consisting of microliths and ground or polished stone axes), both of which include easily recognizable, visually attractive stone artefacts of consistent form, were regarded from the 1860s as representing the two distinct techno-cultural phases of the Stone Age (Foot, 1916). The position of the Middle Palaeolithic in the Stone Age sequence was only established in the 1960s (Allchin, B., 1963). H.D. Sankalia named the Middle Palaeolithic of peninsular and Central India, Nevasan, after the site where he first recognized the Middle Palaeolithic tools in a stratified river gravel (Sankalia, 1964).

Sri Lankan and South Indian Shore-Dwellers: Quartz. Recent research in Sri Lanka has lead to the discovery of artefacts in the Ratnapura beds, geological formations in the southern wet zone which, on the basis chiefly of faunal remains, are considered to date from

The Long Climb 61

c. 200,000 to c. 40,000 years ago (Deraniyagala, 1992). The artefacts appear to represent a stone industry related to the Late Acheulean tradition, and in process of development into a local Middle Palaeolithic industry. Along the north-west coast, in the northern dry zone, a series of sites have been found related to old shore lines and sealed by partially fixed coastal dunes. The sites are considered to be living or camping places and the artefacts appear to cover a period of development and miniaturization, paralleling to some extent that seen in the Indian Middle Palaeolithic and Upper Palaeolithic *(see p. 81)*. Thermoluminescent dates indicate a time range of c. 74,000 BP to c. 28,000 BP for the levels with which these sites are associated. We have here an extensive group of coastal sites created by communities using coastal resources, and representing a long tradition: probably the only example of coastal living dated to such an early period so far recorded in South Asia. It also indicates a possible time-frame for a similar group of sites, know as terri sites, recorded in the last century but never independently dated, on the south-east coast of India.

North India: Changing Environments. As we saw in the previous chapter, in the alluvial sequences recorded from river valleys of North and Central India and the Deccan, the Middle Palaeolithic is generally associated with the gravels that mark the beginning of the second, Patpara, cycle of aggregation. The cycles are interpreted as representing, in each case, first a period of aridity with torrential seasonal storms causing a greater or lesser degree of down-cutting and scouring of the valley, accompanied by the accumulation on the valley floor of gravels brought down by the river and its local tributaries. During the next phase of each cycle, sands and silts carried in suspension by the river and its tributaries were laid down over the gravels, and represent increasingly more equable climatic conditions. This finer material sometimes includes loess or fine windborne dust, which may be carried by the wind for long distances and is indicative of arid conditions at certain seasons, accompanied by dust-storms. The initial phase of each cycle appears to have been progressively less violent in its effect *(Plate 4)*.

In the Son valley the deposits forming the Patpara cycle conform to this pattern, and its initial gravels include both Late Acheulean and Middle Palaeolithic artefacts. Taking all factors into consideration, it is estimated that the Middle Palaeolithic in this area may have lasted from c. 100,000 to c. 40,000 years ago (Clarke & Sharma, 1983). In the middle Narbada valley, at Marble Rocks near Jabalpur,

62   *Origins of a Civilization*

in the same environmental region, the second gravel includes only Middle Palaeolithic artefacts of a more developed kind, suggesting a later phase and a later date than the Patpara gravels of the Son sequence. Whatever the eventual interpretation of this and many other differences in the pattern may prove to be, it illustrates the problems involved in attempting to use alluvial/colluvial sequences of this kind to establish anything beyond the most general interrelationships between different river systems. However, as a result of these same differences, an overview of the sequences noted in different river systems provides many overlaps which taken together support the view that the Middle Palaeolithic industries of peninsular, Central and eastern India developed primarily out of the Acheulean tradition of the region. The situation in the Thar desert and the north-west generally is somewhat different, as we shall see shortly.

The cycles of climatic change represented by the alternating deposits of silts and gravels laid down by North Indian rivers have been considered to reflect in general terms worldwide climatic changes (i.e. major glacial and inter-glacial phases). In view of the differences between cycles even on rivers in the same region, much like that noted in the previous paragraph, the relationship to the world pattern of any particular river valley sequence will require detailed investigation in the future. The effects of world-wide glacial advances and retreats on the climate and environment of middle latitudes generally is beginning to be worked out. Throughout South Asia, as we have already seen, the rapid rise of the Himalayas had a significant effect upon the intensity and pattern of the monsoon and on the climate as a whole. This must have influenced environmental conditions across North India, and in the Ganges valley in particular, and must have brought about all kinds of regional and local modifications of the overall world pattern. This is something that has to be taken into consideration in interpreting evidence of Quaternary climatic change.

The changes brought about world-wide by the last major glacial advance (maximum c. 18,000 years ago) and its decline, and the transition to the warmer conditions of the Holocene are rather clearer, and have also been studied in more detail in some regions of South Asia. We shall indicate briefly what these were in at least some regions at appropriate points as we go on. While this provides a model that give some indication of what may have taken place during the earlier glacial phases and the transition to warmer conditions in each case, it is also probable that there were differences both in the world pattern and the regional one.

The Long Climb

Although Middle Palaeolithic artefacts have been recorded throughout most of peninsular and Central India, there is no detailed study of sites of different types in relation to an ancient landscape or environmental context, such as we have for the Acheulean in the Hunsgi area. All that can be said is that sites and groups of sites of different size and character have been reported, many of the larger ones in close association with sources of raw material. A frequent source of raw material seems to have been river gravels which include material both of local and more distant origin, from among which suitable kinds of stone were selected for tool-making. Middle Stone Age craftsmen seem to have used the gravels where they were, on gravel beds which were covered when the river was in flood, but exposed for much of the year, as we see in many Indian rivers today; and also in some cases to have carried selected pebbles a short distance to higher ground overlooking the river, and made the tools there. A number of Middle Palaeolithic factory sites of this kind have been reported from river valleys in Central India and the Deccan. What appear to be larger factory sites and/or living and general purpose sites used by groups of people over periods of time have also been reported, but it is not always clear how they relate to the landscape and to sources of water and stone.

A Stone Age factory site means primarily a place where we have clear evidence that recognizable stone artefacts and tools were made. The evidence is practically always limited to stone (viz. unfinished artefacts and characteristic debris from their manufacture). We have to infer from this and from the context what was done there. If we consider the situation from a practical point of view, and in the light of what has been put on record about hunter/fisher/gatherers observed over recent centuries, we must assume that other things also were done at the same place or very close by. Whenever the preparation and use of stone tools have been observed, as in Australia, the smaller and more carefully finished ones have formed component parts of tools and equipment. In many cases they were mounted in resin or other natural mastics on wood or bone shafts or handles to act as the cutting edges of knives, adzes and planing tools; or as the points and barbs of spears and harpoons. This is the kind of function the smaller Middle Palaeolithic stone artefacts probably served (*see Fig. 5*). Further stages in the process of tool construction, incorporating the stone components as parts of composite tools, probably took place at or near larger stone artefact factories.

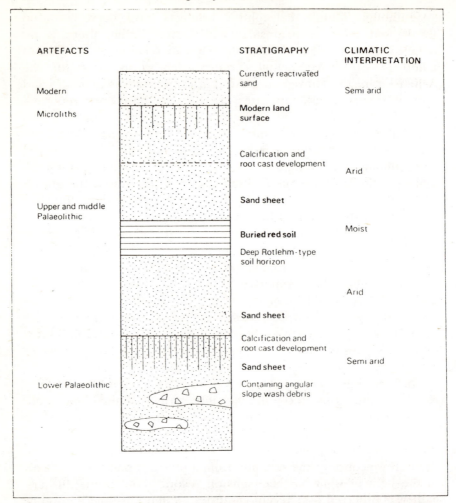

Fig. 6. A schematic interpretation of the Late Pleistocene to Early Holocene stratigraphic and cultural sequence at Pushkar.

Western India: The Thar, an environment for hunters. In and around the Thar desert the Middle Palaeolithic is associated with deep reddish brown soil (*Fig. 6*), which formed on the surface of the sand sheet with which the hand-axe industries are associated. It indicates a marked change of climatic and environmental conditions. Termed as a fossil soil, it must have been formed during a period when climatic conditions were markedly different both from what went before and from those of the present. For such a soil to form there would need to have been plenty of vegetation, grass and probably bushes and forest in places, implying a long period of cooler, more humid conditions when for at least part of the year the rate of evaporation must have been considerably less than at present and the rainfall may have been somewhat higher. For such a situation to exist there must have been significant winter rain in the Thar, which presumably meant a southward shift of the winter rainfall belt such as occurred in the Holocene (*Chapters 5 & 6*). This would have meant a rich environment for large herbivorous animals such as deer and antelope of many kinds, elephant, rhinoceros, buffalo, wild cattle and pig; many smaller animals, birds and reptiles; and predatory animals such as lions, tigers, leopards, wild dogs, jackals and hyenas. It would have been a rich environment for hunter-gatherers too. The small size and relative frequency of the sites indicates that groups of hunter-gatherers were constantly on the move, probably moving within limited group territories which could supply all their needs including stone for tool-making.

Another indication of more humid conditions over this period in the southern Thar is the fully-developed drainage system formed by the Luni river and its tributaries which today is virtually dead. Stretches of the old river and stream beds carry water for a few days following the rare heavy rains that fall when the south-west monsoon reaches the desert, but much of the system is blocked or submerged by sand-dunes. The northern Thar is considered to have been watered, during this period, by a river originating in the Himalayas which at times flowed with sufficient force to carry a considerable load of gravel and deposit it in its bed. It is believed that due to tectonic movements in the Himalayas and the Indo-Gangetic divide the river was later captured by either the Indus or Ganges system, and subsequently its course too was largely submerged by silt and sand. Thus, the northern Thar was left without a source of water from outside, or a system of drainage to carry off the small amount of rain water it now receives, which in consequence accumulates in hollows and between lines of sand-dunes where it evaporates and forms salt pans and further silt accumulates.

Middle Palaeolithic artefacts are found in the Thar and its eastern margins at factory sites associated with spreads of gravel or outcrops of rock which provide suitable stone for tool-making. Sometimes, these are the same hills at the foot of which Lower Palaeolithic artefacts are found in slope wash mixed with the sand of the earlier dry phase. Factory sites are seldom large, usually covering a few square metres. There are also numerous small surface sites in the open plains, temporary camping places, consisting of a few tools and sometimes a small quantity of debris. Many of them are in areas

66 *Origins of a Civilization*

of the desert where today there is no water and people can only live by sinking deep wells; and many are on the banks of dead streams once part of the old drainage system. The indications are that at times during the Middle Stone Age, perhaps continuously over a long period, people were able to live and find adequate water, and supply themselves with stone tools from local sources in what are today some of the most arid parts of the desert. This reconstruction fits in with the evidence for a fairly long period of somewhat cooler damper conditions than those of today with which the Middle Palaeolithic is associated.

Budha Pushkar. Water is always the prime necessity for animal and human life. For Stone Age communities good quality stone was also a high priority. Some of the factory sites in the desert are a considerable distance from former stream beds or other places where water might have been available, and no doubt people visited them briefly to supply themselves with tools and suitable stone. To find both permanent sweet water and good stone in close proximity is rare, and must always have been unusual except along the courses of major permanent rivers. Budha Pushkar lake on the eastern margin of the Thar is such a place (*Plate 5*). Due to its unusual geological situation the lake has never been known to run dry. The truth of this is demonstrated by the immense size of its fish, which clearly must have lived and thriven there for many years. It lies a few kilometers up the valley from Pushkar Raj, the great pilgrimage centre and scene of the famous annual camel fair, situated around another lake that is probably also partly natural.

The special nature of the Budha Pushkar lake is further emphasized by the extraordinary profusion of Stone Age sites from the Middle Palaeolithic period onwards situated all around it. Lower Palaeolithic material is also to be found there but, due to its being generally submerged by sand and slope wash and only visible where it happens to have been exposed by local erosion, it is difficult to estimate how much there is. Clearly, this was a very special place to which people came, and perhaps it was already regarded as holy during the Stone Age.

The Luni Industry. Some of the Middle Stone Age artefact assemblages in the present desert and dry zone resemble the Nevasan, as we have described it. The majority, however, show a wider range of stone tool types than those commonly seen in the Nevasan industries of the regions discussed so far in this section. It appears that when more humid conditions set in, allowing the formation of the deep soil profile we have described, the makers of this stone industry came into the region bringing with them a somewhat different concept of the kind of artefacts they needed. Their range of artefacts included a number of rather more constant predetermined forms, particularly points, carinated scrapers and denticulated or saw-edged tools, in addition to small hand-axes and cleavers and other forms, and a range of scrapers made on flakes (*Fig. 4*). The assemblage is reminiscent in some respects of Central Asian Middle Palaeolithic industries. V.N. Misra who first discovered and put on record Middle Palaeolithic industries in the southern Thar recognized their distinct character, and named them the Luni industry after the dead river system with which they are associated (Misra, 1968).

Archaeological and climatic evidence indicate that the Thar region was a difficult if not impossible place for human habitation during the arid phase following the Acheulean. When it again became more hospitable, Middle Palaeolithic communities with differing equipment appear to have moved in (*Fig. 6*). Those with a characteristic Nevasan assembly of artefacts no doubt came from adjacent areas to the south or east, but where the makers of the Luni industry came from we do not know at present. There are indications, as we shall see in a later section, that when more humid conditions prevailed in the Thar, they probably did so in the Indus valley too, so the makers of the Luni industry could have come from almost anywhere to the north. It is also possible that they came from the north-west via Lower Sindh where the rainfall is relatively a little higher, and a slight increase in precipitation would make the Indus delta and Rann of Kacch attractive hunting grounds. This hypothesis can only be tested when more is known about the Middle Stone Age of Baluchistan and particularly Las Bela District. So far no Middle Palaeolithic sites have been reported in the regions intervening between south/central Rajasthan, which we have been discussing, and the rather different Middle Palaeolithic tradition of the regions to the north and north-west which we are going on to.

The Potwar Plateau. Moving north to the Potwar Plateau, in the northern Punjab province of Pakistan, where some of the earliest artefacts were discovered, Middle Palaeolithic sites have a rather different character. Between the wide valleys of the Indus and Jhelum, in the piedmont zone, the Siwalik hills and Potwar plateau are deeply cut by the steep valleys of local streams and *nallas*. On the intervening ridges and plateaux there are extensive spreads of quartzite

68 *Origins of a Civilization*

pebbles, cobbles and small boulders, brought there by former streams in earlier phases of the turbulent geological history of the region (*Plate 6*). They lie on an old eroded and probably deflated land surface, sometimes exposed and sometimes, particularly in valleys and hollows, covered by loess to a depth of anything from a few centimetres to several metres.

Many of the cobbles are of limestone and these are largely untouched, but there are areas, sometimes several hectares in extent, where they are of quartzite, a material which is very suitable for tool-making. Here just about every stone except the smallest has received some attention from tool-makers. There are many cores, flakes and chopping tools, but few other finished tools. The greater part of the material appears to be the debris of Middle Palaeolithic technology. Some Acheulean material has been reported from the Potwar, but it is not clear whether this was made from the same spreads of quartzite cobbles as the Middle Palaeolithic. No comprehensive study of the Potwar surface sites as such has been made. At present it appears that most of the Lower Palaeolithic material is derived from deeper levels in the Siwalik stratigraphy, like the two million year old tools found in the Potwar plateau in 1983. There are undoubtedly some Early Upper Palaeolithic working areas, as we shall see below.

Whether the loess ever covered the tops of the ridges is not clear, but it came some way up the valley sides from which today it is in the process of being washed off by every monsoon. A series of thermoluminescent dates have been obtained for the loess in the locality, ranging from 75,000 to 18,000 years ago. The loess immediately over an Upper Palaeolithic site (site 55), near the present edge of the loess sheet, gave a date of 45,000 years ago (Rendell, Dennell and Halim, 1989). This means that the site is marginally older than the loess which was being deposited just before it was abandoned. Site 55 has been classified by the excavator as Upper Palaeolithic on the basis of the technology of the production of parallel-sided blades from prepared cores and other factors. There can be little doubt that the industry is a development of the Middle Palaeolithic tradition so widely represented at the Potwar surface sites. While the thermoluminéscent dates give a *terminus ante quem* for site 55, only further investigation can give a clear indication of the time-span of the Middle Palaeolithic.

The interpretation of these extensive sites in terms of the part they played in the lives of those who used them is difficult at present. The general rarity of unbroken finished tools in relation to the frequency of discarded cores from which flakes and blades had been struck, and the quantity of split pebbles and other debris seem to indicate that people came to these areas to make stone tools, and took most of the finished products away with them. The Early Upper Palaeolithic site excavated from under the loess has been identified as primarily a work-site, where stone artefacts were made, and also used on the site for other purposes, probably the curing and preparation of hides. This suggests that, in addition to making stone tools for use elsewhere, people came to the area for more complex purposes, perhaps a range of purposes, in which stone artefacts played an important role; and that they are likely to have been doing this during Middle Palaeolithic as well as Early Upper Palaeolithic times.

The quantity of utilized material at the Potwar sites, alone, shows that many people must have made use of the quartz cobbles over a considerable period of time. That period probably began before the deposition of the loess which overlies (and is currently being eroded off) many factory areas. It seems unlikely that all the factory areas were ever totally covered. The accumulation of loess indicates a dry, dusty, inhospitable environment, which could have been one of the reasons why people gave up using the sites. A further possible reason for their abandonment is that throughout the subcontinent, with the development of Upper Palaeolithic technology and the decreasing size of stone artefacts, there was a tendency to select more fine-grained stone in favour of quartzite.

The Rohri Hills of Upper Sindh. The Rohri hills in Upper Sindh (*Plate 7*) collectively provide the richest and most complete sequence of factory sites for the manufacture of stone tools known anywhere in South Asia, extending from the hand-axe industries (viz. at latest 50,000 years ago, and perhaps much longer) to the end of the Mature Harappan (c. 1500 BC), and probably until the beginning of the Iron Age (c. 1000 BC). We have already mentioned the Chellean factory site recently found there, and earlier isolated finds of hand-axes, and we shall be discussing later material in the appropriate sections. Many of the hills, as we saw earlier, are capped by layers of large nodules of flint (Allchin, B., 1976). These lie on and in a layer of red soil a half to one metre thick which was formed under more moist conditions than those of the present, probably at the same time as the fossil soil of the Thar desert (*see Fig. 6*). The flint nodules have a dark brown crust, or cortex, on the outside, due to weathering, and inside the flint is light grey or buff, sometimes slightly mottled, and of extremely good quality with few cracks or flaws. Many nodules are of a long and roughly oval shape, and

Origins of a Civilization

some of these have had successive flakes removed, starting from one end, each taken off by a single hard, carefully placed blow. Each flake retains a rim of cortex round the edge so that they look like slices of bread cut off a loaf. In some cases flakes found lying within a small area could be fitted together, and part of the original nodule reconstructed. Some flakes of this kind had been chipped irregularly around part of the edge, and appeared to have been used on the spot, as they were, for cutting or trimming purposes. This technique seemed to be a speciality of the Rohri hills, and it was difficult to link it positively to a particular phase of the Stone Age. However, cores and flakes of this kind were often associated with Middle Stone Age material. Although the flint was similar at Milestone 101 we did not see any 'sliced bread loaf' cores or flakes there.

On several of the Rohri hills with flat tops a hectare or more in extent, there were large quantities of Middle Stone Age cores, flakes and other debris, plus the 'sliced loaf' artefacts just described. It would take a careful survey, of a kind we had not time to carry out, even to make an approximate estimate of the range and quantity of stone artefacts and debris of all periods on the tops and sides of all the hills of the group. Much early material had been thrown down the hillsides by later stone workers (*see Chapter 8*). There can be little doubt, even on the basis of a prefunctory survey such as ours was in 1975, that the Middle Stone Age predominates. As in the case of the Potwar surface sites described above it is difficult to interpret what we saw. It seems an inescapable conclusion that so many large factory sites must have served a considerable area beyond the environs of the Rohri hills, in one way or another. The communities who lived in and around the hills may have specialized in making stone artefacts, and traded them over quite long distances to people based in the alluvial plains of the Indus where there was no stone at all, and elsewhere where there was little or no good-quality stone for tool-making. Alternatively, or in addition, people may have come to the Rohri hills from far and near to make and take away stone artefacts, and also to stay a while and carry out other processes for which stone tools were essential.

THE UPPER PALAEOLITHIC

The Upper Palaeolithic was a time of innovation, and it was also a stage of human development which, looking back, we begin to see in sharper focus than was the case with any earlier period. No longer do we have to make an effort to visualise stone tools and such other

The Long Climb

71

evidence that can be found as parts of living cultures. Upper Palaeolithic culture projects itself through living places that look like living places; rock art in which a major element is skilfully drawn pictures of animals which we can instantly identify; and living parallels provided by studies of hunter-gatherers and other communities with relatively simple life-styles in various parts of South Asia.

For the archaeologist, in Europe and Western and Central Asia the Upper Palaeolithic is marked by a tool-kit based on innovations in stone technology, and by increasing numbers of small bone tools, some of which were probably used for making clothing from animal skins, necessary to sustain life in the cold conditions of the latter part of the last glacial phase. It is also the time of magnificent rock art in the limestone caves of France and Spain, which depict many of the animals of the cold Tundra environment that prevailed there. In South Asia the climate at this time was dry and windy and cooler than at present, but there were not such extremes of cold as further north. Here too, adaptions were made and human migrations of people appear to have taken place in response to changing conditions. The Upper Palaeolithic is marked by changes and developments in the character of the stone artefact assemblage, based upon a general reduction in the size and weight of artefacts, and by new methods of stoneworking closely comparable to those taking place in Europe and western Asia. In its later stages, it is associated with the beginning of the distinctive rock art of Central India, of which we shall have more to say later.

Responses to New Demands. The changes in stone tools and in methods of making them which characterize the Upper Palaeolithic coincide with the last phases of the Pleistocene, when the last glaciation was coming to an end and sea levels were rising. This was not just a simple process of rising temperatures: the melting ice from the polar ice-caps kept the sea cold and, as a result, for a considerable period winds were strong and rainfall low. Deserts tended to expand, new sand-dunes were formed and old ones rejuvenated, and the dust and sand blown off arid areas were deposited in many regions. In terms of environment this must have involved progressive changes: the Thar which had been a savannah region during Middle Palaeolithic times, reverted to desert (Allchin el al, 1978); regions of marshland and thick forest, like parts of the Ganges valley and Central India, changed to grass and open woodland, and larger trees retreated to river valleys and the margins of major rivers (Blumenschine and Chattopadhaya, 1983). Grazing animals must have moved with the

72 *Origins of a Civilization*

environments that suited them into new regions of the subcontinent, and communities of hunter-gatherers must have done the same. Changes in the stone tool assemblage probably reflect adaptions of groups of hunter-gatherers to the changing environment. Drier conditions would probably have meant a greater dependence upon meat, as opposed to vegetable foods, and must have called for movement over longer distances.

Blade-Making: Lighter More Versatile Tools. The new developments in stone technology were based on making long parallel-sided blades from carefully prepared cores. It was both a development of the Middle Palaeolithic technique of striking flakes from previously prepared cores (*Fig. 4*) and a move towards mass production (*Plate 9*). This is because, once the core had been prepared, many more blades could be obtained, before it had to be abandoned or rejuvenated, than was the case when using the Middle Palaeolithic method of striking flakes from prepared cores of various kinds which had to be rejuvenated frequently.

The change was made possible by increased control over the way in which force was applied when removing flakes or blades, both when preparing the core and when striking off the blades which were the end product of the operation. With the help of experimentation and observation of traditional Australian practice, archaeologists have found this could be achieved by applying force indirectly. One way in which this was done was by placing a strong point made of bone or hard wood on the precise spot where the blow was intended to fall, and either hitting it with a hammer of stone or wood, or simply pressing on it very hard. Blades removed by this process were parallel-sided, and of a remarkably regular breadth and thickness throughout most of their length (*Fig. 7*). Each one could be trimmed to make the operative part of a tool such as the blade of a knife, or a spearhead; or it could be further divided and used as one or more of the component parts of a wide range of tools, including barbs for arrow and harpoon heads and barbs and composite blades for knives and sickles (*Fig. 5*) (Allchin,B., 1966). Ethnographic parallels from nineteenth-century Australia and South Africa cannot show us exactly how stone artefacts were used in South Asia in the Late Pleistocene but, together with the accounts of ethnographers who saw them made and used by hunter-gatherers in various, mainly arid, environments, they demonstrate how effective stone artefacts were. They also show how the artefacts we collect from ancient sites could be used for a whole range of purposes,

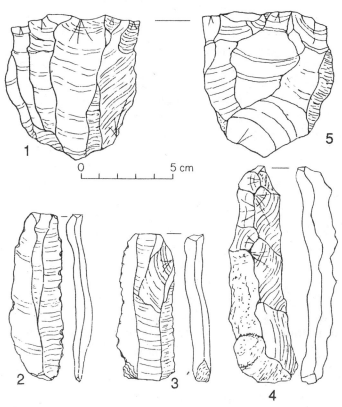

Fig. 7. Upper Palaeolithic artefacts from the site in the Rohri Hills, shown in Plate 9. Nos. 1, blade core; 2 & 3, blades; 4, blade core trimming flake—a characteristic by-product of core preparation.

many of them quite different from those traditionally ascribed to them by archaeologists. It is interesting that a factor common to Australian and South African stone tools, and one also shared by Neolithic artefacts found at Mehrgarh in Pakistan and at Mesolithic sites in Europe, has been the use of mastics (i.e. resin, bitumen etc.) to mount the stone components on or in wooden or bone shafts and handles.

Blade-making continued to be developed and refined in South Asia during the later phases of the Stone Age and Chalcolithic, and was used up to and beyond the beginning of the Iron Age in c. 1000 BC. In its later development metal points were used, as they are in the Cambay bead industry today, to apply force to a precise spot on the agate core in the early stages of blocking out a bead. The

74   *Origins of a Civilization*

bead-maker fixes the point in the ground and holds the bead against it, striking the other side with a buffalo-horn-headed hammer (*Plate 10*). The Australian method of applying indirect pressure when making a finely worked spearhead was different, and no doubt there have been many ways of using the same principle to achieve a very precise result.

One great advantage of blades made by these techniques was their lightness; they provided straight, sharp edges with a minimum weight of stone behind them. Frequently, they were made of fine glass-like rock, such as flint or chert, which provided a razor-sharp edge but shattered easily in use. This was counterbalanced by the practice of mounting them on wood or bone, embedded in a strong mastic such as resin or bitumen with only the cutting edge exposed; and sometimes also by slotting them into grooves. The use of these techniques resulted in a very light and versatile tool-kit. Supplies of whole blades or selected pieces which weigh very little could be carried for long distances, if necessary far from the source of supply, and used when needed as replacements for broken or lost parts, or for assembling new knives, missile heads, etc.

Such equipment was suited to people constantly on the move, whether as hunters in search of game, or for other reasons, but it included nothing suitable for heavy work such as woodcutting or digging. This was supplied by chopping tools, made from cobbles, like those of the Lower and Middle Palaeolithic, which are frequently to be found at Upper Palaeolithic and later sites, but have often been ignored by archaeologists because they are so different from the delicate blade tools. Generally they were made of coarser rocks, probably locally obtained, and discarded after use.

The new light equipment was adapted to the increasingly arid conditions prevailing in western and northern India towards the end of the last glaciation, which would have meant that game animals and human hunters could only move into regions like the present margins of the Thar desert during and immediately after rain, and that they would have to leave when the last pools of drinkable water dried up or became brackish. Then hunters and animals alike would have had to move to sources of permanent water, which ultimately would have meant the nearest major river. If this was fed by sources outside the region, like the Indus and the Ganges and many of their tributaries, it would be probably still be flowing. Rivers with a regional catchment would probably have ceased to flow, and only deep pools would remain in places in their beds, like some of the smaller rivers of the peninsula today. Such a regime would mean

Riwat artefact.

The deposit at Dina in which one of the hand-axes illustrated in Fig 3 was found in 1983 by members of the British Archaeological Mission to Pakistan. The way in which the artefacts became incorporated in a conglomerate of this kind and are later exposed is shown in Fig 2.

Milestone 101, a Stone Age factory site where many hand-axes were made, overlooking the Indus plains in Lower Sindh.

The Belan river, 1973, with a party from Allahabad University. The coarse conglomerate below the path includes Lower Palaeolithic artefacts, the gravels halfway up the section Middle Palaeolithic and those near the top Upper Palaeolithic. Mesolithic material is located below the topsoil.

Budha Pushkar Lake, Rajasthan, with the permanent lake in the foreground and the lake basin which fills occasionally after rain ringed by trees behind it.

The Potwar Plateau, northern Punjab, Pakistan, near the village of Aurangzeb, showing a spread of cobbles and pebbles, most of which are artefacts or debris from tool-making.

The Rohri hills, Upper Sindh (1975), showing the old red soil with flint nodules capping the flat tops, and a man leading a camel loaded with firewood in the foreground.

The Rohri hills, Upper Sindh (1975), view along the tops of the hills, with flint worked at many periods. The hill in the middle distance were being quarried to obtain limestone for cement-making.

An Upper Palaeolithic workplace in the Rohri hills with cores, blades and debris.

A bead maker in Cambay (1968), blocking out agate beads by the traditional method using a hammer with a buffalo-horn head and flexible, cane handle and an iron spike fixed in the ground.

Sangao Cave, North West Frontier Province, Pakistan, 1963.

Excavated trench Sangao Cave, as it was in 1963. The man on the right was over six feet tall.

Kitugala, a mountain cave in south-west Sri Lanka formerly occupied by the makers of stone artefacts of the kind shown in Fig 8.

A Vedda family in a rock shelter in south-western Sri Lanka, photographed by the Seligmans at the beginning of this century.

An excavation in progress (1983) at Alu Lena cave, currently part of a Buddhist residential complex.

Fisherman with traditional sea-going catamarans on the south-east coast of India, south of Madras.

Baghe Kor, a Central Indian rock shelter formed in Vindhyan sandstone.

Outline drawing of a female Sambar deer.

Outline drawing of a rhinoceros in red ochre in Lekhahiya rock shelter in the Vindhyas.

Bhimbetka, a hunting scene showing two hunters killing a buffalo bull superimposed on & surrounded by pictures of other animals.

Nawishta, Baluchistan: an ibex with two goats.

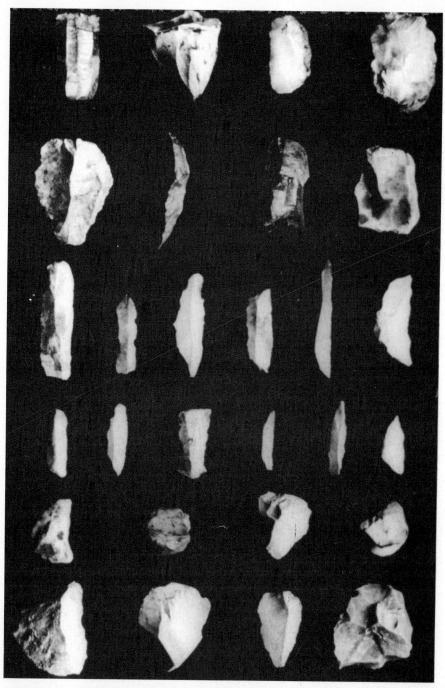

Microlithic artefacts from Barkaccha, a factory site on the edge of the Vindhyas from which tools were exported to sites in the Ganges plains, made of grey agate. Line 1, cores; lines 2,5,&6, flakes; lines 3&4, sections of microlithic blades & 'geometric' microlithic.

Yanadis fishing in the Mallemadugu lake near Renigunta. Such nets and other fishing gear are mentioned in the late medieval literature.

Yerukula Giddanna laying a multiple noose trap near a water pan for birds, near Betamcherla.

Neolithic living & field terraces, Tekkalakota, Karnataka, South India.

Modern houses on a terraced hillside at Tekkalakota, Karnataka, built in a similar way to those of Neolithic times.

A rock bruising of a bull from the Neolithic site of Maski, Raichure District, South India.

A hoof impression in vitrified cowdung from Utnur, an 'ash mound' or Neolithic cattle pen.

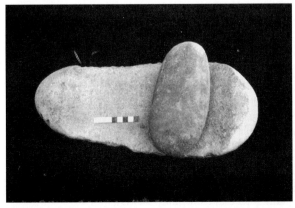

A large saddle quern from Tarakai Qila, a settlement of the early Harappan period, NWFP Pakistan; similar to those in use from Neolithic times forward, those from Mesolithic contexts being smaller.

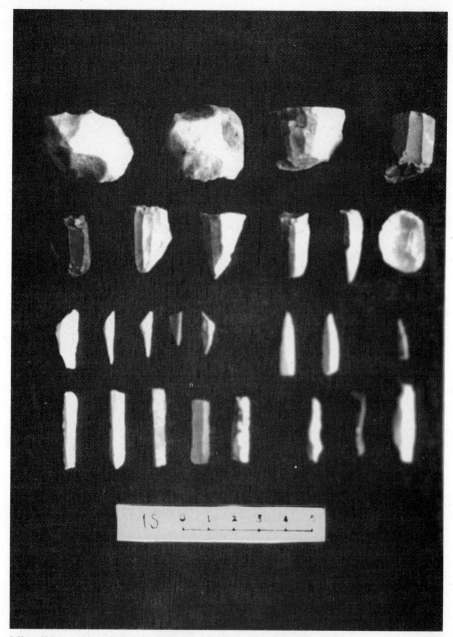

Microliths made of fine grained quartzite, chert and crystal from a site on the surface of the final sand sheet at Pushkar.
Row 1, a carinated scraper and three broken blade cores.
Row 2, five blade cores and a carefully trimmed crystal;
Row 3, five triangular microliths, probably arrow barbs, and three small points, probably drill heads;
Row 4, sections of small parallel side/blades each trimmed and blunted along one edge, perhaps parts for composite knife blades.

yearly migrations, and perhaps long periods spent out of reach of sources of good stone, so supplies would have had to be taken along.

Innovation and Continuity: the New Beside the Old. The distribution of Upper Palaeolithic sites in South Asia appears to be more limited than that of the preceding Lower and Middle Palaeolithic, or of the Mesolithic that followed. This is no doubt partly due to the general increase in aridity, and partly because we have as yet only a few independent dates for the period as a whole, and often do not know which other stone industries are contemporary with the distinctive Upper Palaeolithic blade industries. The change described in the basic tool-kit does not appear to have been a complete or sudden one. This is characteristic of South Asia: often where the new blade technology appeared the older methods of preparing flake cores of various kinds continued alongside it in a reduced or miniature form. The extent to which the new technology took over varied from region to region, and in some it had little impact beyond a reduction in size. (Allchin et al, 1978; Allchin and Allchin, 1982). In parts of South India and in Sri Lanka, an additional method of fracturing stone was used. This situation brings home to us forcefully that we still have to rely largely on artefact types to place an assemblage in the chronological sequence, when South Asian prehistory has clearly reached a point where more precise dating is needed in order to understand what was going on.

In view of all this diversity we must assume that, in the widely varying environments of South Asia, different life-styles coexisted side by side in the past, much as they do today. As we begin to see the past in sharper focus, from Upper Palaeolithic times forward, diversity emerges as a distinct element of South Asian culture. The picture is clearly a complicated one, more so because some research has been done in certain areas and none in others, and we still have not got enough information to allow a general overview. Therefore we shall concentrate, as before, on certain interesting sites and localities which can give a feeling of the nature of the new cultural developments and of the dynamics of change.

Northern Punjab: A Palaeolithic Work Place. The earliest dated Upper Palaeolithic site we know of in South Asia, and featuring the production of large parallel-sided blades, is site 55 at Riwat in the Potwar plateau of northern Pakistan, (Rendell, Dennell & Halim, 1989). Loess had been accumulating at the time the site was abandoned, and later covered it completely, protecting it from

76 *Origins of a Civilization*

disturbance and providing a means of dating. The excavator carefully removed the loess and made a detailed study of the site, plotting every feature, including each piece of stone. He has shown it to be a single period site where he considers hides were cured in the shelter of a windbreak, and stone tools made for use at the site and perhaps also to carry away. The stone used was quartzite, and the blades large and thick when compared to those from some other Upper Palaeolithic sites discussed here. Increasing aridity was a feature of the end of the Pleistocene, as we have seen, but this site has been dated by the thermoluminescent dating of the overlying loess to c. 45,000 years ago or earlier (meaning that it was occupied at that time or marginally later). This is well before the height of the last glaciation which is considered to be c. 18,000 years ago, let alone the following period of arid conditions. In world terms it is among the earliest dates for an Upper Palaeolithic tool assemblage. How the Riwat material relates to the Upper Palaeolithic of the subcontinent as a whole remains to be seen. Both from a technological point of view and from its early date it can probably best be regarded as transitional from Middle to Upper Palaeolithic.

Caves in the Northwest Frontier and Afghanistan. Any discussion of the South Asian Upper Palaeolithic would be incomplete without reference to Sanghao cave in a remote mountain valley in the North West Frontier Province of Pakistan (*Plates 11 & 12.*). Since the 1960s when it was discovered, it has been excavated on at least three occasions, but little has been published. When visited by the writers in 1963 it contained an occupation deposit at least three metres deep, including stone artefacts and debris characteristic of both the Middle and Upper Palaeolithic traditions. Hearths and numerous animal bones and what appeared to be burials could be seen in the sides of the excavation trenches, but sadly everything excavated, with the exception of a few small pieces of stone, had been discarded and no records kept. The discarded artefacts and debris (almost all milky quartz) showed some affinities with the Middle and Upper Palaeolithic industries of the Thar, and also with those from sites in mountain valleys in Afghanistan.

Several Afghan caves, both north and south of the Hindu Kush, were excavated during the 1950s and 60s (Davis, 1978). They were found to contain stone industries of both Middle and Upper Palaeolithic character, somewhat confused stratigraphically, followed by so-called Epi-Palaeolithic and finally microlithic material. The artefacts were made chiefly of good-quality local flint, and in some

The Long Climb 77

places where flint was available there were also large surface factory sites. A number of Carbon 14 dates were obtained from various levels in some of the caves which give a range c. 32,000 to c. 10,000 for the whole complex. At one of them, Aq Kupruk, in north Afghanistan, animal bones stratified with Upper Palaeolithic artefacts were found to be almost exclusively those of sheep and goats which formed 90 per cent of the total. The remaining 10 per cent included bones of gazelle, aurochs, onager or wild ass, red deer and wolf. This was taken to indicate that sheep and goats were domesticated, and formed a regular part of the diet of the occupants of the cave, while the other species were hunted. The layer was dated by Carbon 14 to c. 16,000 years ago, a date considered early for domestication at that time, but not without parallels in western Asia.

Sindh: the Hilltop Factory Sites. In the Rohri hills, in Upper Sindh, and also at the Stone Age factory site at Milestone 101 in Lower Sindh, Upper Palaeolithic working areas have been identified, but only briefly studied (Allchin, B., 1976). These sources of good-quality flint were used to make Upper Palaeolithic blades which are of unusual quality, but which can be distinguished from blades of later periods by their proportions and details of their manufacture (*Fig. 6*). The Upper Palaeolithic industries from Sindh seem to have much in common with those of both Afghanistan and the Thar: a detailed study of them would be of great interest.

Budha Pushkar, a Lake in the Thar Desert. In the Thar desert during the arid phase in the latter part of the Pleistocene, much of the upper layer of the deep red-brown soil, formed during the preceding phase and with which the Middle Palaeolithic is associated, was eroded and blown away and the dunes were rejuvenated with new light-coloured sand. Upper Palaeolithic sites are found around the lake at Budha Pushkar and at other places on the present margins of the Thar but, with the exception of such favoured places, are generally much less frequent than Middle Stone Age sites and scarcely seem to penetrate the central arid areas.

At Budha Pushkar there is a strong element of continuity between the Middle and Upper Palaeolithic sites that cluster around the lake, which is seen in aspects of the technology, in some of the artefact types, and in the choice of material which is predominantly fine-grained quartzite in both cases. At the same time there is an overall reduction in size in the Upper Palaeolithic stone tool assemblage; parallel-sided blades, of the kind described above, are a significant

78 *Origins of a Civilization*

feature, and small flake cores and flakes, like those of earlier times but reduced in size, continue in use alongside them. There is no break between industries based on the flake tradition and those based on the new blade technology, such as appears to be the case in some parts of the world. Geometric microliths made from blades are also part of the tool-kit, but are not so numerous or finely worked as in some of the later Mesolithic industries.

Different kinds of stone, such as chert and crystalline quartz which both have a smooth concoidal fracture that makes them suited to the production of fine blades, and milky (crypto-crystalline) quartz which is difficult to flake regularly but has qualities of toughness, began to be used at this stage also. Milky quartz was used particularly for making burins, or engraving tools, which had been present earlier but come into prominence as part of the Upper Palaeolithic tool-kit of which they are a characteristic feature. Burins are considered to have been used among other things for making grooves in wooden or bone handles and shafts in which to fix sections of blades to form composite knife and sickle blades, and in which to insert the points and barbs of arrow and harpoon heads.

At Budha Pushkar, as with the Middle Palaeolithic, Upper Palaeolithic artefacts are found in clusters on the dunes around the lake, and there are more in the valley below the lake. They appear to represent small living and multi-activity sites, where family groups camped for a time, probably during the dry season, to take advantage of the freshwater lake. In view of the increased aridity of Upper Palaeolithic times, and the removal of the upper layer of the red soil profile formed earlier, these sites must be regarded as examples of spot provenance rather than point provenance (*see p. 51*): i.e. while they retain their integrity and cultural interest as a related group, their precise functional relationship to one another has probably been disturbed. The majority of the artefacts relate to the process of blade-making. They sometimes include hammer stones and small anvil or grinding stones made from flat oval pebbles, slightly shaped by hammer dressing like those in Middle Palaeolithic assemblages (*Fig. 4*). Some are pitted in the centre, perhaps as a result of being used as anvils or for fire drilling. One found by one of the writers in 1972 was heavily stained with red ochre in the centre of the concave side. It is interesting to speculate what the ochre was used for. The distribution of sites suggests a situation something like the great traditional annual fair held at Pushkar Raj a few kilometres down the valley, but on a much smaller scale. During the fair many families camp near the pilgrimage centre with their animals, and camels and other livestock are bought and sold.

The Central Ganges Valley and the Vindhyas. Further to the east, in the Belan and Son Valleys, a series of research programmes initiated by Prof G.R. Sharma during the 1960s and 70s, in addition to investigating earlier periods, have gone some way in tracing cultural developments from the Upper Palaeolithic onwards (Sharma et al, 1980; Clarke and Sharma, 1983). In both valleys Upper Palaeolithic artefacts are associated with gravels at the beginning of the third cycle of deposition which, in the Belan sequence (*Plate 4*), are dated by Carbon 14 to between c. 25,000 and c. 19,000 years ago (Possehl, 1994), and in the Son sequence to c. 10,000 years ago (Mandal, 1983). As in the case of the Afghan caves these are isolated dates, and they cover a time range extending from the height of the last glaciation to the beginning of the Holocene. But the Afghan and North Indian sets of dates generally parallel one another to a remarkable degree which considerably strengthens them both.

In the Son and Belan valleys a number of Upper Palaeolithic and later sites were recorded. In the cold dry windy conditions of the time, the sheltered valleys of rivers emerging from the Vindhyas onto the Ganges plain would have been desirable places to live, especially in winter. Chopani-Mando in the Belan valley, excavated in the 1970s (Sharma et al, 1980) showed a sequence of occupation from Upper Palaeolithic to Neolithic. The lowest level, lying on disintegrating bed rock, contained Upper Palaeolithic (termed by the excavators Epi-Palaeolithic) artefacts made from chert locally available in the Vindhya hills. The range of artefacts is similar to those described from the Upper Palaeolithic of Pushkar in Rajasthan, but they have a more delicate appearance due to the finer-grained stone. This being the lowest level of the excavation, only a small area was exposed, but the disposition of artefacts suggests a multi-activity/living site, with possible post holes of a hut or windbreak.

At Chopani-Mando animal bones were found throughout the excavation, but those in the lower levels unfortunately were too decayed to be identifiable. However, fossil bones have been identified in the gravels of all four depositional cycles of the Belan river. Bones of wild cattle of at least two kinds and several other species were present in gravels one to four, but sheep and goats were only present in the third gravel (with Upper Palaeolithic artefacts) and the fourth (with Neolithic remains) (Sharma et al, 1980). It has been pointed out that sheep and goats were not indigenous to the region, and the nearest wild populations were located in the Himalayas 250 miles to the north and in the mountains of the western borderlands c. 1000 miles to the west. It, therefore, appears that they must have been brought to the southern

80   *Origins of a Civilization*

side of the central Ganges plain by migrant human groups (Possehl, 1992). It also seems possible that there were wild sheep somewhat nearer at hand in the Punjab hills as there were in the last century.

Assuming that all this is substantially correct, it means that sometime between c. 25,000 and c. 19,000 years ago not only had sheep and goats been successfully domesticated within their own environment by Upper Palaeolithic hunter-pastoralists in Afghanistan, as we have seen, but they had also been taken out of their original environment and successfully maintained in a different one, again by people with an Upper Palaeolithic stone tool-kit. The general time correspondence of an Upper Palaeolithic stone industry with the appearance of sheep and goats in north India, and with the increasingly arid conditions of the later stages of the Pleistocene, seem to lead to the conclusion that human groups with Upper Palaeolithic equipment and domesticated sheep and goats came into the middle Ganges valley and Central India, bringing their flocks with them, at a time when an environment of dry open forest and grassland prevailed there. The interesting question is where did they come from: from the north, seeking refuge from low temperatures, due to climatic change and the increasing height of the Himalayas, or from the west, escaping from the increasing aridity of the Thar?

If the latter is the case, we must ask whether the Upper Palaeolithic communities of the desert margins, such as those who camped around the lake at Budha Pushkar, kept sheep and goats, and whether sheep and goat husbandry was an established way of life in environmentally suitable regions of the subcontinent in Upper Palaeolithic times. In Afghanistan and the mountainous regions of Central Asia sheep and goats were indigenous and, whether hunted or domesticated, had a long tradition of association with mankind. Their horns were placed on Middle Palaeolithic graves; and they were widely represented in rock art. In Central India on the other hand the animals represented in early rock art included a whole range of wild species, and sheep and goats which were sometimes represented always appeared to be domesticated, which would go with their having been brought into the region as domestic animals.

Vindhya Caves and Rock Shelters

Towards the end of the Upper Palaeolithic a change in favour of living in caves and rock shelters where these were available took place in Central and peninsular India. Most such rock shelters consist of a shallow cave or an area protected from the weather by overhanging rocks; and many have bare rock floors, often sloping, where all that has accumulated is a thin spread of stone artefacts, debris and dust. A small proportion have deeper deposits and some of these have been excavated, and generally show either Mesolithic artefacts only, or an upward gradation from late Upper Palaeolithic to Mesolithic and later material. We do not know why the change took place at this time, nor why it did not take place earlier. Possibly, it is connected with the ability to evict and prevent the re-entry of large carnivores such as tigers and leopards, and reflects improvements in equipment and in group organization.

The first discovery of Upper Palaeolithic artefacts in a cave in the subcontinent was at Reniguntur in southern Andhra Pradesh, and further material was found in stratified gravels in a nearby river valley, suggesting a comparable environmental situation to that in the Ganges valley *(Murty, 1969)*. They have since been found at a number of surface sites of various kinds in western, Central and peninsular India, many of which are interesting in themselves but add little to the main cultural story except in terms of distribution.

Quartz for Choice: South India and Sri Lanka. In the extreme south of India and in Sri Lanka there seems to have been a local tradition from the end of the Middle Palaeolithic forward, of making a high proportion of stone artefacts from milky quartz. The later stages of the sequence of coastal sites of north-west Sri Lanka, described in the last section, and dated to between c. 74,000 and c. 28,000 years ago, are generally contemporary with the early stages of the Upper Palaeolithic of the north and north-west. The tools are made of quartz and chert, and throughout show only minimal influence of blade technology: they seem to represent a continuous coastal tradition and a development of Middle Palaeolithic technology. A similar situation seems to exist at a series of coastal sites in South-east India, known as the terri sites, which have not so far been dated.

In south-western Sri Lanka there is another group of Stone Age sites that have been known since the end of the last century. They include caves, rock shelters and surface sites in the mountains of the interior *(Plate 13 & Fig. 8)* and the coastal lowlands. At the time of their discovery some of the caves were inhabited at certain seasons of the year by people known as Veddas or Vaddas, generally regarded as a surviving remnant of the indigenous population who inhabited southern Sri Lanka prior to the arrival of north Indian settlers in the first half of the first millennium BC. Sri Lanka's rich ethnographic

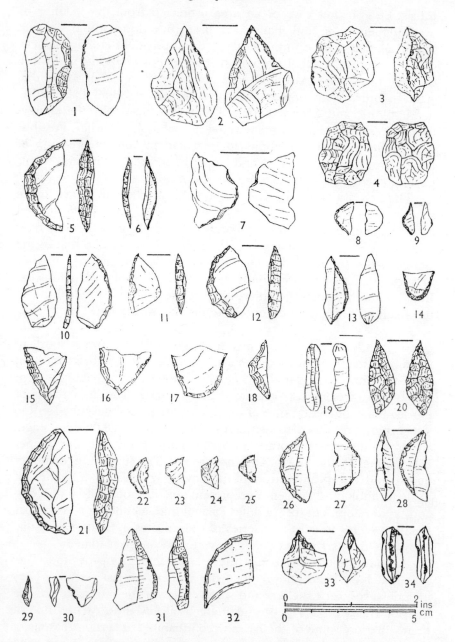

Figs. 8a. Sri Lankan quartz artefacts from the factory site of Bandarawela, southwest Highlands.

a. Nos. 1 & 2, scrapers; 3 & 4, small discoidal cores; 5 to 8 & 21 to 30, a range of 'microliths' characteristic of the later quartz industry of Sri Lankan; 31 & 33, awls or borers; 34, a quartz crystal.

The Long Climb

record provides accounts of the Veddas who, in the late nineteenth century still maintained many aspects of their hunting and gathering life-style, hunting with bows and arrows and moving to different parts of their group territories at appropriate seasons of the year to utilize the resources of the forest environment (*Plate 14*). Like all such communities in South Asia they also maintained ongoing relationships with neighbouring agricultural and village communities. In addition to hunting deer and other animals they gathered honey and a wide range of plant foods, and sold honey and forest produce, and sometimes worked as labourers. In this way they earned enough money to buy iron axes, knives and arrowheads, and small quantities of rice, cloth and other items. Other caves had been taken over by Buddhists.

Caves of both groups have been excavated (*Plate 15*), and they all show a long tradition of cultural and technological continuity. The main feature throughout is a stone industry made chiefly of quartz, and small quantities of quartz crystal. As already pointed out, quartz is a very difficult material from which to make delicate artefacts. However, blades of a sort were produced from small quartz cores, and small flakes and flake cores are found alongside them as elsewhere in India. But a considerable proportion of the artefacts appear to be made from slivers of quartz produced by shattering pebbles or blocks, rather than by striking off individual flakes (*Fig. 8*). It seems probable that this process included heating the pieces of quartz and then either pouring cold water on them and striking them, or both. A wide range of small artefacts were made, the most common types being small points, triangles and lunates (so called geometric forms) made by trimming slivers of quartz along one or more edges, and D-shaped forms which have a sharp straight edge and are trimmed round the curve. They also included a small proportion of delicately worked points made by careful pressure flaking on both surfaces.

In some of the caves there are occupation deposits several metres in depth. Along with the microliths are found heavy stone artefacts including hammers and small anvil or pallet stones, sometimes pitted in a way that suggests they were used for cracking nuts and perhaps for fire drilling and other purposes; artefacts of shell; bone points; animal bones, charcoal and other organic remains. There is virtually no rock art associated with the occupied caves. There is little change in the cultural material from bottom to top, and no evidence of major climatic or environmental change, which is to be expected in such close proximity to the equator. A range of Carbon 14 dates have

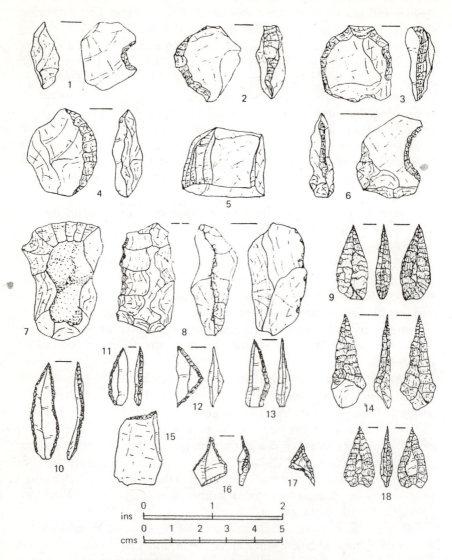

Fig. 8b. Sri Lankan quartz artefacts from the factory site of Bandarawela, southwest Highlands.
Nos. 1 & 6, concave scrapers; 2, 3, 4 & 8, convex scrapers or adze blades; 5 & 7, carinated scrapers; 9, 4 & 18, bifacial points; 0 to 3 microliths; 5, burin; 17, tanged point.

been obtained for occupation layers in a number of caves, and for one of the most thoroughly investigated, Batadomba-lena, there is a

The Long Climb

sequence of occupation starting from the lowest layer which is dated to over 27,000 years ago. It is remarkable that the artefacts described include microliths of a range of forms, made almost entirely of milky quartz and some quartz crystal, such as are generally associated elsewhere with the Mesolithic; and that they show little or no change from bottom to top. At the top, in all cases where the upper levels have not been disturbed, the quartz industry gives way to iron, without a significant transition period, at 900 to 600 BC (Deraniyagala, 1992). The surprisingly early date for the earliest appearance of what appears on typological grounds to be a Mesolithic industry, raises the question whether such a long-lived and apparently unchanging culture should be considered part of the Upper Palaeolithic on account of its early beginning, or as part of the Mesolithic on account of its artefact types and late survival.

Around the coast of South Asia, virtually wherever a systematic search has been made, Stone Age sites have been found on headlands, islands and coastal dunes associated with the present shoreline, and sometimes with earlier and somewhat higher shorelines which date from times when the world climate was warmer and the sea level higher than at present. In all probability, further sites dating from times of lower sea level and cooler world climates, such as prevailed during the last glaciation, have been largely submerged as the sea level rose during the Holocene. At many coastal Stone Age sites such as those recorded around Bombay and those from the coast of South India and Sri Lanka mentioned earlier, which are close to the present shore, in situations much like those used by present fishing communities, microlithic artefacts are found and miniaturized Middle Palaeolithic techniques are strongly represented. Little systematic research has been done on coastal archaeology of this kind, apart from that in Sri Lanka and South India already cited, but there are indications that there was a continuous tradition of coastal living and the use of fish and shellfish from late Middle Palaeolithic times foreward in many coastal areas. At the present time traditional fishing communities all round the coast employ a wide range of craft, ranging from simple canoes and catamarans (Katamarans) made from tree trunks (*Plate 16*) to much more elaborately built boats with parallels in many parts of the ancient and the modern world.

Rock Art

Central India is particularly rich in caves and rock shelters formed in the Vindhyan sandstone, many of which were inhabited, and their walls and ceilings provided surfaces for drawing or painting

(*Plate 17*). A large part of the rock art of Central India would be most accurately described as crayon drawing, and in such situations, protected from the weather, it has tended to survive. Thanks to this combination of factors Central India is very rich in prehistoric art. Everywhere animals predominate, accurately and sensitively drawn with deftness and assurance, and frequently in attitudes that reflect close observation of their natural behaviour (*Plates 18 & 19*). Pictures of people appear less frequently, and generally relate in terms of style and content to Late Prehistoric or Early Historic times. Many of the animals are drawn in outline, sometimes stippled, hatched or completely filled in colour. The most common substance used is ochre of various shades from brown, orange and pink to scarlet and deep, purplish red. Small pieces of ochre, often worn smooth at one corner and in corresponding colours to the pictures at hand, have been found in some of the rock shelters. Occasionally, black and greenish-blue were also used.

Attempts have been made to define different stylistic groups and to place them in chronological order, the most comprehensive being the work of the late V. S. Wakankar (Brooks & Wakankar, 1976). In general, naturalistic drawings of animals seem to be the earliest, while various kinds of stylisation, representations of people, and events such as dances, hunting scenes, ambushes and battles appear to be newer. All the rock art is difficult to date or to relate to a specific level or archaeological phase. Those considered to be the earliest, on the basis of their state of preservation and the superimposition of pictures in other styles, are representations of wild animals of many different species some of which, like spotted deer, wild pig, monkeys and various large birds, are still found in Central India, while others like the Indian rhinoceros are now extinct or threatened. There are also many drawings with an identifiably later content, such as people with distinctive clothing and headgear, domestic animals being guarded, armaments, horse-drawn chariots or caparisoned elephants, which sometimes link them to identifiable Early Historic periods or actual events. Others again equally clearly continue the rock art tradition into medieval and modern times. Altogether, rock art in Central India has a long history which relates to other artistic and craft traditions in different communities in the past and today; and to various styles of folk painting and painting on the walls of houses for decorative and religious purposes. The tradition of making pictures on rock, like that of making stone artefacts, is a long one, spanning many periods of prehistory and history.

Where there are no suitable rocks there can be no rock art, and we must assume that people found other means of artistic expression. In most regions where there are suitable rocks there is an indigenous tradition of rock art, as in Central India. In the southern Deccan there is a tradition, mainly associated with the Neolithic, of hammering or bruising pictures, usually of humped cattle *(Bos indicus)* and sometimes of other animals or people, on the exposed granite rocks of which many of the hills are formed; and sometimes painting or drawing also *(Plate 26)*. In Baluchistan rock bruising and drawing go side by side, again on exposed rocky hills, and the subjects are often elaborate scenes including both animals and people, and are probably of religious or mythological significance. In the Karakoram ranges there is a strong tradition of indigenous art, mainly focused on long-horned sheep and goats; and along the route of the Karakoram Highway there is a more sophisticated kind of traveller's art which includes symbols of a number of religions and inscriptions in many languages. Further east, in some of the Himalayan valleys and in Tibet, there are related traditions.

Both in Baluchistan and in Central India there are what appear to be centres where complexes of suitable rock formations were available, and where rock art was practiced with great intensity. Nawishta in northern Baluchistan, and Bhimbetka in Central India are both outstanding examples of such centres *(Plates 20 & 21)*. Each is situated on a rocky hill, and each has an extensive range of styles, subjects and probably periods of art. What the precise significance of such centres was we do not know. Presumably, it must have been both religious and social. It is interesting that Sanchi, the great Buddhist centre believed to have been founded by Ashoka, is sited near Bhimbetka.

The animal art of the Vindhyan rock shelters was done by people who were acutely observant, imaginative and had complete control of their media. We do not know what their precise objective was in portraying animals. Clearly the animals played an important part in their lives, and they felt very close to them. Did they perhaps seek through portraying them to control and manage them to some extent, or to propitiate them and ensure that they multiplied and provided a continuing source of food? These are questions we cannot answer. What we can say is that this art is an expression of the Stone Age hunters' view of the natural world, upon which they were still immediately dependent, at the period in time when they were beginning to experiment with ways to gain more control over that world. The long climb, for better or worse, was bringing them into a world not very far removed from our own.

Chapter 5

PATHWAYS TO SETTLED LIFE: THE MESOLITHIC AND EARLY NEOLITHIC

THE MESOLITHIC

In South Asia the cultural developments that followed from the Upper Palaeolithic are hard to define. We have seen that in the tropical forests of southern Sri Lanka a life-style established in Upper Palaeolithic times continued, apparently without a break, until the arrival of settlers from north India in the first millennium BC. Thereafter, the same life-style had the added dimension of contact and communication with a more advanced agricultural and urban culture. Part of the indigenous population was obviously absorbed by the new culture, and part was encapsulated upon its fringes and became part of a wider cultural web, with an urban core with which it had contact, albeit often remote and intermittent, through trade and labour relations.

Something like this, but generally less sudden and dramatic, and rarely so well-documented by historical tradition and early ethnographic accounts, is what happened at some time to most hunting and gathering communities in the subcontinent. Many Mesolithic societies were, in fact, communities maintaining many of the aspects of earlier life-styles but in contact with more advanced cultures. In some cases their role was that of a minor satellite culture, supplying raw materials, goods or labour to a more powerful neighbour; and at the other end of the scale they could have been receiving only the remotest ripples of events taking place in far away centres. Cultural change has been a continuous process, as we have seen, sometimes very slow and sometimes more rapid and radical. The changes that initiated the Mesolithic seem to have been of the slower developmental kind, made as a response to environmental change at the beginning of the Holocene. Some of them however must have laid the foundations for the more fundamental changes of the Neolithic.

Pathways to Settled Life

What appears to have happened in South Asia, as in much of the Eurasian world, was that with the end of the Pleistocene and the establishment of climatic conditions much like the present, new environmental situations were created. These changes were more marked in the north and north-west than in the south and east of the subcontinent. As warmer and more humid conditions began to prevail in what is now Pakistan and western, northern and Central India, new resources must have become available and the population must have expanded. People experimenting with different ways of using the new environmental resources must have adapted their ways of living, resulting in a whole range of new life-styles emerging at the beginning of the Holocene, some of which were to prove enormously and unimaginably successful. Once the process of change had started it seems to have had a knock-on effect, with the result that no society remained totally unaffected.

The term Microlithic is often used instead of Mesolithic, but looking carefully at the evidence we see that the two are not always synonymous. It is important to remember that Microlithic is a general technological term, while Mesolithic is a cultural term describing a way of life. From the traditional archaeological point of view a decrease in the size of stone artefacts and the presence of a higher proportion of 'geometric' microliths are regarded as the hallmark of the Mesolithic. Generally, this seems to hold good, but whether the change was primarily due to practical considerations i.e. producing a light and more flexible tool-kit, or was more a matter of fashion, or a combination of the two, is uncertain. It was certainly a change of style, much like the changes in pottery and other artefacts that have been used as markers in later prehistory: like them it is useful, but must not be allowed to become confused with the complex evidence of more profound cultural change.

Frequently, the decrease in artefact size was accompanied by an increasing use of crypto-crystalline rocks such as flint, chert or agate which occured widely in the form of small nodules, often as river pebbles. From Neolithic times forward we know that the nodules were heated to improve both workability and colour, and it is quite likely that this practice began during the Mesolithic, and was one of the factors that made possible the manufacture of much smaller tools from small nodules of high quality material. What the relationship was between this practice and that of heating milky quartz to facilitate shattering it, which appears to have been used in Sri Lanka, is not clear at present. The use of flint and semi-precious stones, and the practice of heating them, continued into later

90   *Origins of a Civilization*

times and was the basis of the Chalcolithic craft of bead-making.

Cultural Change in the Central Ganges Valley and Vindhyas. What is more significant than the change in stone technology is the evidence of a more settled way of life that we find at some Mesolithic sites. Examples of the process of change and development from an Upper Palaeolithic to a Mesolithic and then to a Neolithic life-style, in a changing environmental context, have been recorded in the central Ganges valley/Vindhyan region, studied over many years and described by the late G.R. Sharma and others.

Mesolithic sites of several different kinds have been recorded in the plains north and south of the Ganges, in the Belan, Son and other tributary valleys, and in the Central Indian hills. The last group consists chiefly of rock shelters, as described in the previous chapter. A number of them have been excavated from the 1960s onwards, and the results confirm the developmental sequence of stone blade industries from late Upper Palaeolithic onward. Several were also found to contain burials, generally with the body extended with an east-west orientation, and many sites contained microliths evidently put in as grave goods.

In the southern plain and the tributary valleys Mesolithic and early Neolithic sites have been recorded virtually wherever surveys have been made. The Mesolithic stone-blade industry is much like that of the Upper Palaeolithic, and made of similar fine-grained stone, but considerably smaller in every respect. The reduction in size has been quantified by the excavators, and is consistent throughout (Sharma et al, 1980), as is the higher proportion of geometric microliths. Artefacts closely comparable to those found at Mesolithic surface sites (*Plate 22, & Fig. 9*) and excavations in the locality have been found in gravel lenses in the silts of the third cycle of deposition in the Belan valley, and one of the earliest is dated by Carbon 14 to c. 11,000 years ago.

Several Mesolithic sites have been excavated, and a picture emerges of small permanent or semi-permanent settlements, each consisting of a few clusters of small huts supported by wooden posts let into the ground, and with walls of wattle and daub, burnt pieces of which were found in the excavations. They had consolidated earthen floors, hearths and a number of relatively heavy stone artefacts including roughly-shaped upper and lower grinding stones, or querns, suitable for grinding wild grains and softer substances (*Plates 28 & Figs. 12a & b*); pallet or anvil stones like those of the Upper Palaeolithic; hammer stones of various shapes; stone balls assumed to be used as

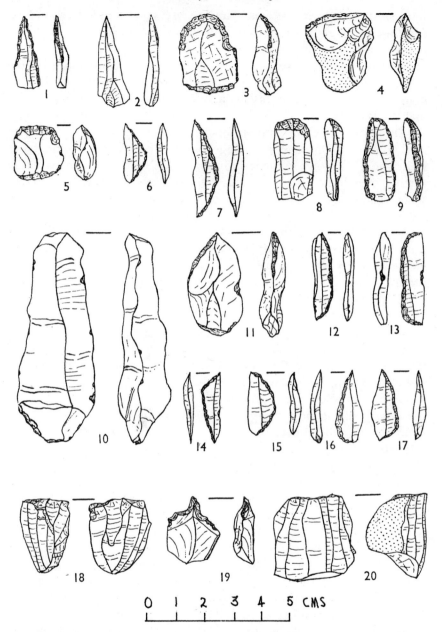

Fig. 9. Artefacts from Barasimla, an Upper Palaeolithic/Microlithic factory site in Central India recorded in the 1930s. Nos. 1 & 19, awls or borers; Nos. 3, 4, 5 & 8, scrapers; Nos. 6 & 4, triangles; Nos. 6, 7 & 12 – 17, 'geometric' microliths all made from sections of small parallel-sided blades struck from cores resembling Nos. 18 & 20; No. 10, blade struck from a large Upper Palaeolithic type core; No. 18, very small microlithic blade core; No. 20, top part of a somewhat large microlithic blade core.

92   *Origins of a Civilization*

sling stones; and ring stones. The last are approximately round or discoidal cobbles in which two hollows or pits have been made by hammering from opposite sides, and deepened until they meet in the middle. As far as we know ring stones were used as mace heads, and as weights for digging sticks and bolases, and probably also for many other purposes as much labour must have been involved in making them.

Dwellings, together with so much heavy equipment, would argue in favour of a life-style revolving round a permanent home base; while the light, delicate blade industry is clearly suited to being easily carried over long distances. Together, as they are here, they would seem to represent a way of life with various options. But they are not always found together: many more sites with microliths have been recorded in this region, and indeed throughout the subcontinent, than have those either with heavy stone artefacts alone or with both elements. This seems to indicate that many communities pursued a life of hunting, fishing and gathering edible plant foods which involved being often on the move, while some, like those with home bases in our region, were able to lead a more settled life. A probable explanation for this is provided by the charred and carbonized grains of wild rice which are found in the burnt clay remains of wattle and daub walls of huts of the later Mesolithic levels at Chopani-Mando. Other Mesolithic sites excavated included Mahadaha and Damdama. Wild rice is indigenous to the region, and this, taken together with the querns of the carbonized grains suggests that it was an important element of subsistence for these communities, whether actually harvested from the wild or deliberately sown but not as yet selectively bred to change it significantly.

In the Vindhyas there are a number of factory sites where artefacts from Upper Palaeolithic times forward were made from locally available stone. Barkaccha, about five miles south of Mirzapur is one of these (Allchin, 1974). On both banks of a small river, where it emerges into the plain, are a number of large concentrations of small blade cores, broken blades and debris made from pebbles of light grey agate. Altogether, the site covers several hundred square metres, and appears to have been used in Mesolithic and later times. This is one of a number of sources which supplied stone artefacts to settlements in the plains. Areas supplied can be identified by the colour of the stone which varies from source to source, showing that there were regular ongoing relationships along established routes between certain localities in the hills and communities in specific areas in the plains from this time onward. (Sharma et al, 1980). It

Pathways to Settled Life

seems probable that artefacts used in the rock shelters might also be traced to their point of origin, as a means of identifying a further set of contacts and relationships.

Mesolithic sites on the northern Ganges plains have a somewhat different character to those on the south. Associated with old lakes, now in many cases dry, which appear to be cut off meanders of former streams, most of these sites seem to have been temporary camping places. Some, like Mahadaha excavated by the Department of Archaeology, University of Allahabad, appear to have been regularly inhabited. The sites investigated had occupation areas with hearths in large oval pits, traces of huts in some cases, and burials within the living areas. There was no suitable stone for tool-making available in the Ganges plains, and the blade tools of the northern plains Mesolithic were made at the sites from nodules of chert and other materials originating in various parts of the Vindhyas, and presumably carried across by their makers or obtained through contact and exchange. All the artefacts are extremely small, and the cores used to the maximum, presumably because of the need for economy. Heavy stone artefacts are present, but largely as broken fragments, probably for the same reason. But they include pieces of querns, and some complete hammers and sling-balls which are closely similar to those from Chopani-Mando and other sites south of the Ganges. The number of bone artefacts is very limited.

Numerous animal bones have been found, and at Mahadaha there appears to have been a large butchering area where meat and bones had been chopped up, and an area where bone tools were made. Cattle bones predominated and no signs of domestication appeared to be present in these from the Mesolithic levels; sheep and goat bones showed indications of domestication throughout; there were also bones of a number of further species of wild animals and birds. Large quantities of bones had also apparently been thrown into the lake. In many ways these sites have the character of seasonal hunting camps, and one feels that their occupants spent part of their time elsewhere: the question is, where?

The burials were extended and mostly east-west oriented like those in the Vindhyan rock shelters, but the skeletons were those of considerably larger, more robust people. Subsequent studies have confirmed this and have shown a lesser degree of sex-differentiation in height and bone structure in the skeletons from the northern sites than in those from the Vindhyas. This raises further interesting questions as to the relationship of the two communities to one another. Were the Mesolithic inhabitants of the northern plains part of a

94 *Origins of a Civilization*

population whose habitat extended into the Himalayan foothills, and who perhaps moved in a yearly cycle between the hills and the plains, possibly following seasonal movements of the animals they hunted? Was there at that time a cultural and perhaps an ethnic interface between those whose roots were in the south, and those who had connection with the Himalayan foothills to the north? If so, a certain amount of contact and exchange of goods evidently took place between the two groups which perhaps had differing ethnic and/or cultural histories.

THE NEOLITHIC

The Neolithic is easier than the Mesolithic to define as a way of life, as it has been generally taken to involve settled life, crop cultivation and animal husbandry. However, we still have to remember that other older ways of life continued, and new ways arose alongside them. Communities of many different kinds were evidently living in close proximity to one another in South Asia in the past, much as they do today, and following their development and interaction is what much of the archaeology of Later Prehistoric times is about.

The Central Gangetic and Vindhyan Region. The Neolithic of this region appears to have developed out of the Mesolithic, retaining many features such as the microlithic blade industry and the range of heavy stone tools; but it was distinguished by certain important new features including domesticated cattle, whose bones are found increasingly alongside those of wild cattle; larger huts grouped round small cattle pens in which the actual hoofprints of cattle were found (*Plate 27*); and, most important, a form of cultivated rice. All these features were found at Mahagara, near Chopani-Mando, on the right bank of the Belan river, which is one of the most important sites of this kind. Further Neolithic sites of the same type were found in the Belan and Son valleys, and in the Ganges plains, and excavations were also carried out at Koldihwa and Kunjhun. Kunjhun proved to be a specialist industrial site with a number of areas where selected stone for blade-making was heated to improve its colour and workability (Clarke and Khanna, 1989). Carbon 14 dates indicate a period of occupation between 4000 and 2500 BC (Possehl, 1994b).

An important new feature of the Neolithic is hand-made pottery

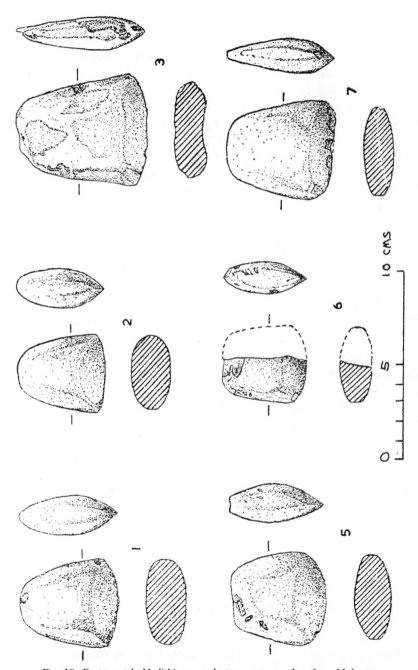

Fig. 10. Eastern style Neolithic ground stone axes or adzes from Mahagara

of several types, cord-impressed ware, plain red and plain black ware, and a type with a deliberately roughened outer surface known as rusticated ware. A further feature of this group of sites is the small, flat, ground stone axes, round or square in outline (*Fig. 10, p. 95*). In the extreme west of the region we have been discussing, in Banda district, stone axes of a different kind, longer, more cylindrical in section and triangular in outline, and characteristic of the Neolithic of the western side of the the subcontinent, are found. Both the small square axes and the cord-impressed pottery are characteristic of eastern Central India, Assam and South-east Asia. The rusticated ware, on the other hand, recalls pottery from some of the earliest settlements on the Indus system, found along with the Hakra ware in Cholistan on the Punjab-Rajasthan border and at Jalilpur, and dating from the fourth millennium BC (see below chapter 7). Thus, it seems that this region formed the frontier of a rice-producing Neolithic culture, with eastern affinities which are further demonstrated by its material culture and the western Neolithic.

Undoubtedly, the area we have been discussing forms a western extension of this distinctive eastern Neolithic culture. Sites, some on the banks of major rivers, have been reported over the last two or three decades from Bihar, Bengal and Orissa, which form part of a rice-based eastern Indian Neolithic culture. The few dates available suggest a time range of c. 8500 to c. 4500 years ago (6500 - 2500 BC). The far-reaching implications of the relationship of the rice-based agricultural society of the east to the wheat-based Indus civilization of the north-west, will be discussed further in a later chapter.

The Ganges Basin is one of the major zones in South Asia in which a Neolithic culture emerged, based on the agricultural potential of the region. We have outlined the process of development from the Mesolithic of the central southern Ganges plain, the tributary valleys of the Belan and Son rivers, and the Vindhyan hinterland as far as is possible on the basis of the evidence available. Now, we shall look at some of its further distinctive features and aspects of its character which differentiate it particularly from the Neolithic of the Indus region, and are important to later developments.

The Neolithic of this region has been demonstrated to have developed out of the local Mesolithic context, but it also appears as a western relative of the rice-based Neolithic of eastern India, South-east Asia and beyond, and in its wider aspects may be referred to as the Eastern Neolithic. The earliest evidence of the use of rice here, as we have seen, comes from the later stages of the Mesolithic in the form of charred grains of wild rice embedded in burnt clay from hut debris. Evidence from both Neolithic and Chalcolithic sites in the middle Ganges region, such as Chirand, Senuwa, Khairadih, Narhan, Imlidih and Sohgaura, points towards rice being the principal cereal. It is commonly found embedded in charred clay lamps and pottery segments by the close of the third millennium BC.

In view of the great interest and importance of the sequence covered by the central Gangetic and Vindhyan Mesolithic and Neolithic, with their evidence for early exploitation of rice in South Asia, it is a pity that a more substantial number of radiocarbon dates have not been obtained. This is an area where more research is called for.

At this point it may be helpful to digress briefly to look at the wider context of the early use of wild rice, and of its cultivation. Following T.T. Chang (1977) and Shastri and Sharma (1974), we believe that rice was a wild perennial plant, the distribution of which extended from East Asia to West Africa. More particularly, its Asian distribution extended from South China and South-east Asia through eastern India to the Ganges valley, and southward down the eastern coastal strip. In all these areas wild rice is still to be found. The original plant was perennial, with shattering panicles so that the seed was naturally shed. From it, an annual form of wild rice developed, known by the name *Oryza nivara*, from *nivara*, a Sanskrit name for wild rice. Like the perennial form, this had a very wide distribution and retained its shattering panicles. The development of the cultivated variety of rice, *Oryza sativa*, involved the selection of varieties having non-shattering panicles and seeds capable of rapid germination. We have currently no idea how often, where or when this selective process may have been carried out. We have to recognize that there may have been long periods when people collected and consumed the seeds of wild rice along with seeds of other grasses, before satisfactory cultivated varieties were selected.

In China there is evidence that the cultivation of rice goes back to c. 6000 BC; and we may expect the Indian evidence to be somewhat similar, when a greater body of controlled evidence is available. A very hopeful line of future research is a recent development of Carbon 14 dating (AMS) which allows individual grains extracted from pottery or clay to be dated (Bellwood et al, 1992). At Chopani-Mando the earliest occurrence of wild rice is said to be in the final stage of the Mesolithic, dated to c. 6000 BC; and cultivated rice occurs first at Neolithic sites such as Koldihwa and Mahagara (sixth to third millennium BC), on the basis of a very

98 *Origins of a Civilization*

limited number of samples (Sharma et al, 1980). Until a greater body of Carbon 14 dates from carefully controlled samples is available, these have to be accepted with some reservation as providing an approximate chronology.

The Archaeological Past and the Ethnographic Present

The Ganges valley itself is today a region of intensive agriculture, largely inhabited by orthodox Hindu village communities. The hill and forest region of Central India, on the other hand, is still inhabited by many different communities with a whole range of distinctive life-styles. Some of these are complex communities, like the Gonds of eastern Central India for example, with well-defined ethnic and cultural identities, and their own systems of agriculture, commerce and relations with the outside world.

Others have a distinct identity but are scattered among other groups, like the Baiga who were described by Verrier Elwin (1939). Others again are more in the nature of occupational groups. To all of these have been added from time to time remnants of displaced or defeated groups of people from the plains who have sought refuge in the remote and less densely populated hills. Many of these forest people of Central India have a long established balance between traditional ways of life which they still maintain, living in their own villages, hunting, fishing and practising small-scale agriculture, and the extent to which they participate in the outside world through trading; working for other communities away from home for periods of time; becoming through permanent employment or education part of the urban society of India.

The traditional life of these people, their hunting and fishing, their dances and other activities, the designs they paint on their houses, and many other things find echoes in the rock art of the region, as do the two following examples of artistic continuity from further west. The Worlis of the Western Ghats and western coastal lowlands near Bombay paint elaborate scenes embodying traditional religion and mythology in white on the mud and cowdung-plastered walls of their houses on special occasions such as marriages. Their pictures done on brown paper are now quite well-known (Dalmia, 1988). The wall paintings of the Rathva Bhils of western Central India, representing their community's creation myth, are done in vivid colours on the mud-plastered walls of rooms or verandas of their houses by a local pujari who goes into a trance (Jain, 1984).

Numerous microlithic sites have been found throughout most regions of Central and peninsular India. They vary in size, but the vast majority seem to be fairly small living and multi-purpose sites; nearly always they are on small hills or rising ground, often overlooking a stream or a major river. Within easy reach of water, these sites must have provided good positions for sighting game animals coming to drink. There are also some larger factory sites, usually near rivers with gravel beds exposed during much of the year, which include pebbles of suitable materials for tool-making, sometimes carried by the river for many miles from sources outside the region. Caves and sites of any kind with evidence of Mesolithic occupation that might throw light on diet, subsistence strategies or life-style are rare in peninsular India. However, there are many accounts of communities living primarily on the natural resources of their environment, particularly in the Eastern and Western Ghats which provide ethnographic parallels for the kind of site distribution just described. The Haimendorfs' account of the Chenchu in the Nallamalai hills of eastern Andhra Pradesh describes a group who in the 1940s still depended primarily on hunting, fishing and collecting vegetable foods and honey, and had limited contacts with the outside world (Von Furer-Haimendorf, 1943). They lived for part of the year in places similar to those used by the microlith makers for the reasons we have already inferred and because, they said, there were fewer mosquitoes on the tops of hills; and at times they also used rock shelters, as the Veddas did in Sri Lanka. Among the vegetable foods they used were roots and yam-like tubers, and the seeds of wild grasses.

M.L.K. Murty's accounts of the forest peoples of many different environmental zones of eastern peninsular India demonstrate the varied ways of life and means of subsistence of such communities (M.L.K. Murty, 1994). He analyzes the methods of subsistence of communities dependent on different combinations of fishing, hunting and collecting in various environmental belts ranging from the shore and the lagoons of coastal Andhra through the foothills to the high ranges of the Eastern Ghats. The inhabitants of each environmental belt have long-established traditions of utilizing the resources of their own territory. An enormous range of wild foods are recorded, and the methods of obtaining them are numerous and highly skillful (*Plate 23*). This provides an insight into the probable life-style and means of subsistence of early Mesolithic communities at the beginning of the Holocene, when they were still untouched by the influence of agricultural communities. No study of forest people today can give a complete picture of what they were like, but it can, as this one does, show something of their profound and detailed knowledge of the natural world, and the skill with which they utilize its potential while conserving its resources, rather than constantly trying to change it as agriculturalists do. The seasonal movements of an extended family group within its territory, utilizing different resources, for example, can indicate how we might interpret the distribution of Mesolithic sites; to different resources, by considering their proximity to permanent water in the dry season, to other areas when fruits and seeds were ripe or when game animals frequented them, and to sources of stone for tool-making.

Another aspect of this approach is that it demonstrates how today each group has well-established relationships to other more complex, economically advanced communities. These relationships and the ways in which some of them were created are shown by historical records to extend back to the early centuries BC; and it seems they must have begun much earlier, with the appearance of the first pastoral or agricultural communities in the region. The links are so close, and the communities so finely integrated, that the various groups of forest people could be described as forming parts of a single complex society. The history of their relations with the early South Indian kingdoms shows that the goodwill and collaboration of the forest people were sought and highly valued by princes and their officials. As Murty points out, any attempt to portray the Stone Age culture of South India is incomplete and unbalanced if it does not take account of the ethnography and history of the forest peoples who are its heirs.

The history of relations between hunter-gatherers and agricultural peoples in South India extends back a long way, especially in the Krishna-Tungabhadra basin where there are numerous Neolithic settlements, the earliest of which go back to the beginning of the third millennium BC. The Neolithic settlements seem to appear rather suddenly around 3000 BC, as though their inhabitants had arrived as settlers from elsewhere. This is unlike the situation in North India where there appears to have been a process of local progression from one scenario to the other.

The South Indian Neolithic

The southern Neolithic offers a distinctive picture. It is considerably later than the Neolithic of either the Ganges or the Indus system, and its origin is in some ways mysterious. Throughout the Deccan Mesolithic cultures were widespread, but we have few firm dates to fix any of them chronologically. The South Indian Neolithic was based primarily upon cattle-keeping and to some extent on the cultivation of a range of millets and perhaps some other crops. The settlements are located on the southern Deccan plateau, and are more often associated with minor streams than major rivers. The earliest are stockaded cattle pens, situated in open country; the

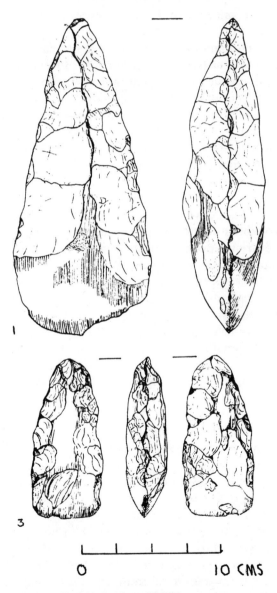

Fig. 11. *Southern Neolithic stone axes.*

102 *Origins of a Civilization*

earliest dates obtained so far range between 2900 and 2400 BC, coming from Kodekal, Utnur and Pallavoy, which have been excavated. Others which appear to be somewhat later, dating from c. 2000 onwards, are on the granite hills which rise out of the plateau. The hill settlements consist of round huts made of wattle and daub supported by wooden posts, with earthen floors, situated on artificially made terraces on and around the granite hills of the region (*Plates 24 & 25*).

The domestic equipment includes a range of heavy stone artefacts similar to those found at Neolithic settlements in North India, except that there do not appear to have been any ring stones. The axes are all of the western Neolithic form (i.e. an elongated triangular outline with a cylindrical section), and are numerous and very finely made (*Fig. 11*). They and a number of other tools are made from basalt, available in the form of intrusive dykes which are a feature of the region. Saddle querns, hammer stones of various kinds, and sling-balls, all made from different kinds of stone, are also a regular part of household equipment (*see below Figs. 12a & b*). There is a fine blade industry with large, regular blades made from blocks of chert which were probably obtained from Salvadgi and Hegragi in south-west Gulbarga district. Copper appears in small quantities at quite an early stage, and although never plentiful becomes steadily more common until the beginning of the Iron Age (c. 1000 BC), when stone and copper tools are displaced by iron. Throughout the Neolithic period, there is a range of ceramic wares, mainly made on a turntable: in particular grey, buff or brown burnished pottery predominates, with smaller quantities of red or black slipped wares, some with painted designs. A number of burials have been found in the habitation areas, which contain grave goods in the form of stone axes, chert blades and pots. The skeletons are those of tall large-boned people.

It is clear that from the beginning the southern Neolithic economy was centred around cattle-keeping: not only are cattle pens a prominent feature of the settlements, but in addition to cattle bones, there are also terracotta figurines of humped cattle and many rock bruisings of cattle on the rocks around the settlements (*Plates 26*). Many cattle bones had been deliberately hacked and broken, as meat and bones are today throughout South Asia when being prepared for cooking. There were also a small proportion of bones of wild animals, which it has been suggested come from meat obtained by purchase or barter from traditional hunters, as is the current practice among agricultural communities in South India. The earliest South

Pathways to Settled Life 103

Indian cattle known, both from the study of bones and from the representations of cattle in rock art and as terracotta figurines, are lightly built, long-horned, humped animals which are clearly *Bos indicus*, but seem to have little in common with the heavier breeds depicted from the Indus region. The late Prof. Alur who made a study of their bones was of the opinion that they were probably at that time recently domesticated in the locality. As the earliest dates available are from the early third millennium BC, it seems that the cattle, and perhaps also the human population, have a different genesis to those of the Indus region.

The quantity of cattle bones and the size of the stockaded cattle pens throughout much of the region cause us to consider whether the cattle were being exported from the region, or used for some other specific purpose; or whether perhaps large herds were maintained as symbols of wealth and status. In this connection we must remember that in Karnataka gold mining probably goes back to quite early Neolithic times, although it was only later carried on at great depths. As the earlier phases of the South Indian Neolithic overlap both the Early and Mature Indus Civilization, it seems probable that gold may have been exported either to the Indus world, or direct to those with whom the Indus merchants were in contact, for example, in Mesopotamia and Egypt.

At all southern Neolithic sites, including the earliest, the many saddle querns found indicate that grain, such as perhaps *kodon* (*Paspalum scrobiculatum*), either collected from the wild or cultivated, or other wild grasses then available in the Deccan, must have been an important item of diet (*Plate 28*). It is unlikely to have been rice, as that grows wild in more humid environments, and domestic rice was probably only introduced into the Deccan plateau later with the advent of tank irrigation. It is also unlikely that wheat and barley were cultivated then in this environment, although they too make their appearance in the region in later times. Millet, if available, would probably be the most suitable crop as it is today in much of the Deccan plateau where irrigation is not available.

Factors which support the latter possibility are the range of millets cultivated in this region in more recent times, and a distinctive kind of terracotta headrest which is unknown elsewhere in the subcontinent but closely parallels some Egyptian headrests. So far no attempt has been made to find settlements or ports on the west coast through which contacts with the outside world might have been made, and this remains a tantalizing question.

There has been a lengthy discussion regarding the origin of the

104   *Origins of a Civilization*

several main types of millet, and the evidence now seems almost incontrovertible that all were of African origin (Hutchinson, 1977; Weber, 1991, Possehl, in press). A study of their South Asia find-spots suggests that the oldest introduction to South Asia was *Ragi (Eleusine coracana)*, which occurs first in Gujarat and Saurashtra in the period 2500-2000 BC, and in Maharashtra and the south only after this date. A reported early occurrence at Hallur (c. 1900 BC) has been questioned. *Bajra (Pennisetum typhoideum)* has a somewhat similar history, occurring first in Gujarat and Saurashtra in the same early period; and *Jawar (Sorghum bicolor)* only after 2000 BC. This suggests that the millets were introduced to western India by sea, and that thereafter they spread far and wide. It is also possible that they were introduced by sea traders, independently, to the South Indian Neolithic farmers and to other communities through ports on the west coast.

On the basis of the available evidence it seems probable that the southern Neolithic originally developed as a predominantly pastoral economy supported by the collection of wild grains, until millets made their appearance sometime in the course of the third millennium BC. This would help to explain why the earliest sites so far dated are ash mounds, that is cattle pens; while the hill settlements with terraced fields appear to belong to the second phase of the culture, from c. 2000 BC onward. Whatever the details of its development may prove to be, the southern Neolithic at its height represents a subsistence pattern based on millets and suitably adapted to the lower rainfall areas of South India.

THE HOLOCENE IN THE NORTH-WEST

The Thar Inhabited Once More. Climatic conditions improved around the beginning of the Holocene and something like the present monsoon pattern was established, but bringing considerably more rain than today. The winter rains too reached the Indus plains and north-west India, with the result that many marginal arid regions became habitable once more for animals and for human communities (Bryson and Swain, 1981). In western India microlithic sites of all kinds abound everywhere except in the most arid central parts of the desert. As in peninsular India they take the form of small camping places, semi-permanent settlements and multi-activity sites, usually on old fixed dunes or small hills; and quite large factory sites to which nodules of chert and agate must have been carried many kilometres from their sources. The brilliant colours and delicate workmanship both tell us that the stone was heat-treated (*Plate 29*). The microliths achieved such regularity and elegance of form that we seem to be looking at things made for aesthetic rather than utilitarian purposes; the vast quantities however show that they must have been intended for use. We do not know whether they were used primarily by hunters, by herdsmen who came into the desert following the monsoon, or by merchants carrying goods between urban centres. Probably, many different communities came and went using the region in different ways, as is the case in Rajasthan today. A few sites have been excavated and one, Bagor in eastern Rajasthan, has shown a cultural sequence from Mesolithic to Chalcolithic, with Carbon 14 dates ranging from c. 7000 years ago forward. During this time the site changed from a Mesolithic camping place to a small Neolithic/ Chalcolithic settlement, and in the upper levels there were copper arrowheads closely similar both to those of the Mature Indus civilization, and those from the chalcolithic site of Ganeshwar in Rajasthan.

Kashmir. An interesting Neolithic development from what appears to be a local Mesolithic base was discovered in the Kashmir valley, at the sites of Burzahom and Gufkral. This begins at the latter site around 2900 BC with an Aceramic phase, where hunting formed a mainstay of subsistence, with domesticated sheep and goats, and there is evidence of the cultivation of wheat and barley. The inhabitants appear to have lived in pit dwellings dug into the loess, and used a range of bone tools as well as ground stone axes and distinctive 'harvest knives' whose nearest comparisons come from far to the north, in China and Mongolia. Another unusual feature is the presence of animal burials, of dogs, wolves and ibex. From around 2500 BC the sequence continues with the introduction of domesticated cattle and fowls, although hunting remains important. In the final phase of the Neolithic, domestic sheep, goats, cattle and pigs are present, and the hunting element in the diet is markedly reduced.

The Northwestern Borderlands. In the Bannu Basin, in the North West Frontier Province of Pakistan, divided from the Indus plains by only a low range of hills, microliths have been reported from a number of sites. These include small sites of unknown date associated with sand-dunes, and settlements of the fourth and third millennium BC (Khan, Knox and Thomas, 1991). Close to a village called Lewan stands a stone artefact factory area where stone artefacts of many

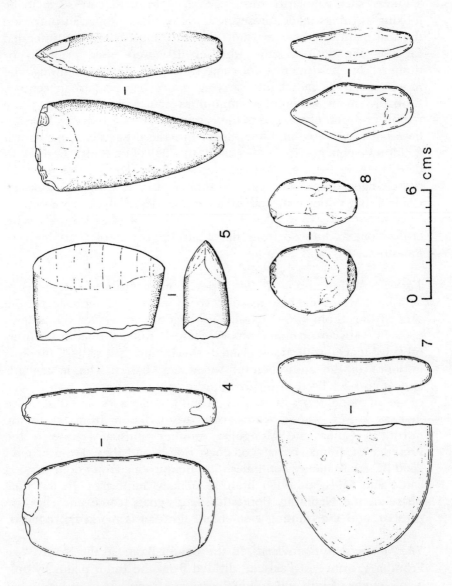

*Figs. 12 a & b (facing page). Heavy stone artefacts from Lewan factory site.
a. No. 1, hammer; 2, broken blade of an axe; 3, axe, hammer dressed with ground blade; part of a broken palette stone; small hammer/sling-ball; pointed stone dressing hammer.*

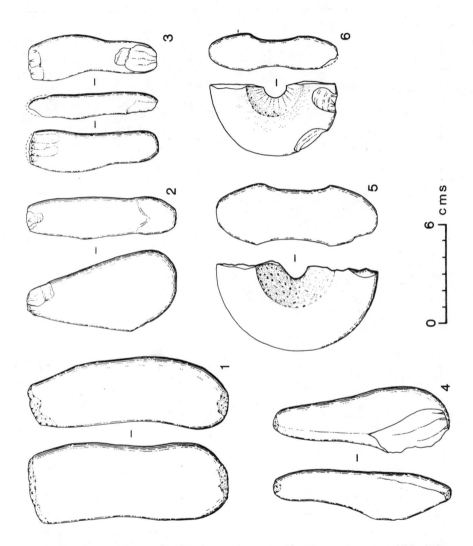

b. No. 1, natural cylindrical pebble used at both ends as a hammer; 2 – 4, natural pebbles used as stone dressing hammers, all showing wear &/or shattering the ends characteristic of this group of tools; broken ring stones probably made with stone dressing hammers similar to those illustrated here.

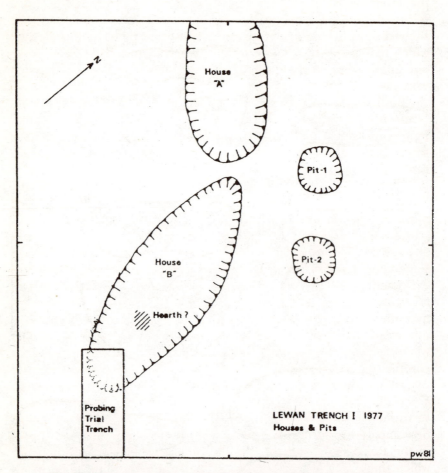

Fig. 13. Lewan excavations; outline-plans of huts or houses of c. 3000 BC.

kinds were produced. They include microliths closely similar to those of Rajasthan, the Vindhyas and the Central Ganges plains, made largely from chert which appears to have been heat treated (Allchin and Allchin, 1993). A wide range of heavy stone artefacts, closely similar to that found at Mesolithic sites in the Central Ganges valley, were also made there in large numbers. They included querns of several kinds (*Plate 28*), stone balls and the long triangular western

Pathways to Settled Life 109

type of stone axes recorded in the western part of that region, (but not the smaller eastern type). There were also many ring stones of the kind described earlier in various stages of preparation, and a series of pointed hammer stones made from river pebbles which showed signs of very heavy use and a consistent pattern of shattering, which had clearly been used in their manufacture (*Fig. 12 a & b*). In one limited area beads and bead-making material area were integrated with the rest.

Both the main factory site, which measured c. 450 x 325 m, (*Plate 30*) and a smaller site nearby where microliths predominated, had been subject to deflation and to degrading by the Tochi river which had subsequently changed its course and moved away. As a result, finds, most of which lay on the surface, and localities, such as that where the bead-making equipment was found, within virtually the entire site, had all been somewhat disturbed or displaced, and must be regarded as placed with a fairly accurate degree of spot provenance rather than point provenance (as described in chapter 2). The one exception to this was the remains of a small settlement, (*Fig. 13*) on a limited area of the main site, which was excavated and dated by the pottery and other objects to the late fourth to early third millennium BC. How long before and after this time the stone artefact factory was in use we do not know. Temporary houses of a similar kind are being built today by nomadic people when settling down for a few months to work for farmers or contractors in Pakistan, and by refugees (*Plate 31*). What is clear is that the production of both microliths and heavy stone artefacts, especially rings stones, was on such a scale that it suggests that surrounding areas were being supplied. In this respect Lewan could be compared to the stone artefact factories in Sindh, at Site 101 and in the Rohri Hills; and to sites like Barkaccha in North India from which there are clear indications of material being distributed along identifiable routes.

The Indus Plains. No microlithic sites have been found in the Lower Indus valley (i.e. Sindh) nor in the Punjab, possibly because many minor archaeological sites have been submerged in alluvial silt. What is surprising is that microliths have not been reported at the extensive stone procuring and factory localities in the Rohri Hills or at Milestone 101 in Sindh, both of which were used at virtually every other stage of the Stone Age. It is possible that they are present and have been overlooked, or that both sources of flint were submerged in sand during the arid conditions prevailing at the end of the

110   *Origins of a Civilization*

Pleistocene: both seem unlikely. No microliths have been reported from Early or Mature Indus sites although they are found in profusion at contemporary sites such as Bagor, in Rajasthan, and at Lewan and other early sites in Bannu, and during the early Neolithic phases at Mehrgarh, so it appears that they were not part of the Early or Mature Indus culture as such. It is possible that the sources of high-quality flint in both Upper and Lower Sindh were easily available to the major urban centres, even perhaps under their control, and therefore they were able to go on making larger blades and flake tools, to serve the purposes required, and did not to change to miniaturization.

There may well be Mesolithic sites along the south-eastern margin of the Indus plains, in both Sindh and Punjab, that have not been recorded as few of these areas have been fully surveyed from this point of view. No microlithic sites have been reported from the northern Punjab, although some attempts have been made by archaeologists to find them. It seems therefore that while microliths do not appear to have been part of the culture of the Indus world itself, they were used contemporarily in many surrounding areas which were to a greater or lesser extent under its influence. Microliths were used as parts of tools and weapons for hunting and fighting, and for many of the routine purposes served by metal knives today. They were an essential part of life for many communities in South Asia for thousands of years. Their use continued in regions outside the Indus system during the entire period of the Indus civilization, and in many regions until the beginning of the Iron Age.

The Indus Neolithic: the Kachi Plain. Further south, Mehrgarh, on the borders of Sindh and Baluchistan, is the earliest settlement of Neolithic character so far known in the South Asia. It is situated in the Kachi plain which is a northerly extension of the Indus plain formed in the tributary valley of the Bolan river. The story of cultural development that has been traced in this locality, from the seventh millennium to the Mature Indus urban period, will be discussed in chapter 7. Certain aspects of the earlier phases of settlement, however, form part of the overall picture of South Asian Mesolithic and early Neolithic cultures, and as such deserve consideration here. First, it must it be said that while the Kachi plain has been thoroughly surveyed and much has been discovered about its prehistory, finds made in the course of more general surveys of Las Bela district to the south-west indicate that further early settlements are probably located there. From a number of early sites excavated in Iran and the

Pathways to Settled Life

Middle East we get the impression that Mehrgarh in the sixth or seventh millennium has parallels in western Asia. Therefore, it is not an isolated phenomenon, but an outstanding, fully-studied example of the culture of a particular locale the full extent and affiliations of which are not yet known.

Mehrgarh is situated near the point where the Bolan River comes out of the Brahui hills and enters the Kachi plain. Today a road into the hills follows the course of the river, probably an ancient route between the Indus valley and the Iranian plateau, and perhaps one of the paths followed by herds of grazing animals moving between the hills and the plain in the days before permanent human settlement. It is an area where one of the wild ancestors of cultivated barley grows. Emerging from the hills, the Bolan river spreads out and in times of flood deposits its load of gravel and silt, providing a fertile if volatile environment. As we have already indicated, a feature of the early levels at Mehrgarh is a microlithic industry, not dissimilar from those from other regions surrounding the Indus plains that we have been discussing, but made largely from grey flint which was presumably locally available. (In the later levels, the stone industry is more like that of other Early and Mature Indus sites.) There is also a range of heavy stone tools which appear to be much like those from Lewan.

Whether this Neolithic culture, which we shall refer to as the Indus Neolithic, emerged from a locally-established Mesolithic substratum or came into the region from elsewhere is not at present clear. Nor is it clear what was the earlier history of the domestic plants and animals on which its agriculture was based. Animal remains from the early levels include small quantities of bones of a number of wild species, including cattle and several species of deer; and larger quantities of bones of sheep and goat which appear to have long been exploited, if not fully domesticated in the region, as we have seen. Cattle bones, by contrast, only become a regular occurrence during the course of the first millennium of the site's existence, suggesting that they were domesticated locally. The earliest food grains at Mehrgarh appear to be locally domesticated wild varieties of barley and wheat which in time were augmented or replaced by other varieties probably derived from long distance interaction with Iran, and with western and Central Asia. What we must stress is that already between 6000 and 5000 BC a pattern of subsistence had emerged, based upon wheat and to some extent barely, sheep, goats and cattle, which has remained largely unchanged throughout the Indus system until the present, albeit with certain modifications and additions from time to time.

112 *Origins of a Civilization*

From the outset the subsistence pattern of Mehrgarh and the Indus system, which is discussed in more detail in chapter 7, shows affinities with contemporary systems in Iran, Mesopotamia, and even Asia Minor. It differs fundamentally from the Neolithic system of the central and eastern Ganges valley, and from that of the southern Neolithic: but with each of these, at later stages, links were formed which led to the emergence of more complex and diverse systems adjusted to the environments of various parts of the subcontinent.

Conclusion. This chapter has looked at some examples of the many and varied Mesolithic cultures of the subcontinent, and briefly considered three distinct regional Neolithic subsistence patterns that were seen to be emerging from them in widely separated regions of South Asia. The three centres were located in the Indus system, the Ganges system and the southern Deccan; and their agriculture was based respectively on different groups of cereals, wheat/barley, rice and millet. All three depended on the same three principal domestic animals, sheep, goats and cattle, with the addition sometimes of other domestic animals such as the buffalo. Their diet was augmented to varying degrees by fish, game, wild plants and honey. Their material culture varied somewhat, as we have already seen, the Ganges valley or eastern Neolithic being the most distinct in this respect. These three highly successful Neolithic life-styles were to influence one another in the changing environmental situations of the periods that followed, as we shall see, and the regional agricultural patterns that resulted form the basis of South Asian agriculture today. In the following chapters, we shall be focussing on the culture of the Indus system and its remarkable early urban development which has been the subject of a considerable amount of research. In doing so we shall try not to lose sight of events elsewhere in the subcontinent. In the final chapters we shall discuss the process of mutual influence and cultural integration that eventually took place.

Chapter 6

THE INDUS WORLD: THE CONTEXT OF THE FIRST SOUTH ASIAN TOWNS AND CITIES

The next three chapters are concerned with the development and flowering of the Harappan civilization, and the development of an agricultural system which, with certain minor modifications, has remained to the present day the basis of life in a large part of South Asia. Our attention will be focussed primarily upon the area comprising the Indus system, as described in chapter 2, and the Indus or Harappan culture that is associated with it; and to some extent also upon other regions in South Asia and outside, into which the Indus culture extended, or with which it had significant contacts. The upper courses of the Indus and its four major tributaries through the Himalayas and Karakoram do not really come into the story, except that the rivers bring all important water from melting snow and silt resulting from the erosion of the rapidly rising mountains into the plain *(Plate 32)*. Therefore, the term Greater Indus System, as it is sometimes used, means essentially the Indus plains and the surrounding hills and valleys; and includes the ancient courses of the Sarasvati river which, as we have seen, in former times flowed either into the Indus or into the sea via the Hakra channel, and the somewhat similar Drishadvati river. The main features of the Indus system, as we saw in chapter 2, are first of all the extent of its catchment area and the wide range of climatic regimes from which it draws its water *(Map 1)*. Secondly, the Indus flows for the last five hundred miles of its course through desert and virtual desert, receiving little or no water from local sources, as streams from the north-western hills become lost in the plain before they can join the main river. Drainage from the Thar, such as it is, is into the Hakra (see below).

Early River Valley Civilizations. In many respects the Indus closely resembles two other great river systems, the Nile and the Tigris-Euphrates. All three flow through deserts in their lower courses, and provide comparable environments. In each of their valleys one of the

114   *Origins of a Civilization*

early civilizations of the world came into being. Hot, dry, arid conditions in which little grew for most of the year, but having a plentiful supply of water in the form of an annual inundation, when flood water spread over the plains or was available for canal irrigation, provided ideal conditions for growing cereals and other crops without undue clearing and preparation of the land. This made it possible for early communities who had stone, wood and copper tools, but no iron, to practise comparatively intensive agriculture and produce enough food to support complex urban societies, with highly specialized arts and crafts and, in the case of each of the three we are considering, its own system of writing. Apart from these basic similarities, so important to early human settlement, the Nile, Tigris-Euphrates and Indus river systems were very different in other ways, and each civilization had its own unique character which developed out of the way its inhabitants utilized the potential of their own environment. Other early cultures, notably those of China and Central America, developed in parallel but different ways.

The Nile has its principal source in the great lakes of equatorial Africa, and flows northward through the Sahara to the Mediterranean. Throughout its lower course through Egypt it flows in a narrow valley cut down into the desert between steep cliffs which confine the spread of flood water and rich alluvial soil largely to the valley. The result is a long corridor of intensely cultivated land running through the desert without any significant fertile side valleys or piedmont zone. Mesopotamia presents a different picture, with a shorter, wider alluvial plain formed by the twin rivers Tigris and Euphrates. The valley is bounded by the Arabian desert and plateau on the south-west; and on the north-west, north and north-east by the mountains of Syria, Turkey and Iran, which provide the main catchment area, well within the northern winter rainfall zone. The Tigris receives a number of tributaries which flow from the mountains of Iran on the north-east through the relatively well-watered piedmont country *(Map 1)*. Ancient Mesopotamia had a system of irrigation canals from an early stage. The Lower Indus valley resembles that of the Tigris-Euphrates in many respects, having a desert plateau on the south-east and mountains on the north-west, north and north-east. Today, its tributary mountain valleys and piedmont zone are more arid than those of Mesopotamia, but this may have been somewhat different in the past. Agriculture in the Indus plains seems to have depended throughout for a varying amount of its production, upon inundation or natural flooding of the river. There also seems to have been some dry cultivation of certain crops, and local irrigation systems appear to

The Indus World 115

have been constructed, from early times in the north-western valleys, using the water of smaller streams.

On account of their similarities the three regions are sometimes discussed collectively, as by Gordon Childe in his monumental work, *New Light on the Most Ancient East.* This could be taken to imply that the three centres had some sort of collective development. As we shall see this is partly true, but throughout their early developmental stages only in a very general and indirect sense. In their later stages, in addition to overland trade with their own extensive and varied hinterlands and beyond, they traded with one another by sea and land, as already indicated at the end of the last chapter; and they undoubtedly influenced each other and came to depend on their trade connections. As time went on Egypt built up a network of trade contacts in the Mediterranean and western Asia, and so to some extent did Mesopotamia which had a relatively short land route via the upper Euphrates to the eastern Mediterranean, and also many other land contacts to the north and east. The Indus civilization too had a wide range of land contacts, particularly with Central Asia and Iran. But its sea contacts were relatively limited, Mesopotamia and the Arabian Gulf being the main ones, and direct contact with Egypt via ports on the Red Sea not being ruled out. In this respect the Indus civilization contrasts with the later civilization of the Ganges valley which had a direct outlet to the sea on the east, and thence the Far East; in addition to well-established land routes to a series of west coast ports giving access to the Arabian Gulf, Red Sea and Mediterranean; and the land routes to central and western Asia. This is a subject which we shall discuss further in the following chapters. For the present we need only note the proximity to the Indus of the Tigirs-Euphrates valley in particular, and the awareness of the other early centres of civilization as part of the wider context of the Indus culture.

Indus Agriculture. The Indus valley culture at its height, like the other two early cultures, was based on an agricultural system that was efficient enough to support a sophisticated urban civilization with all that that implies. In its earlier stages, the agriculture of the region, like that of Mesopotamia, was based upon utilizing the water of tributary streams that emerged from the foothills to the north-west, rather than on the plain itself. The system which was based on the plain, and partly upon utilizing the flood water of the Indus for growing cereals and other crops on the rich alluvial soil, appears to have been a further development. Intensive growth of crops must have been possible, as it is today, following the inundation, because

116 *Origins of a Civilization*

the hot climate and the water left in the soil by the retreating flood provided ideal conditions for the rapid growth of crops; and because the silt carried down in suspension by the river and deposited as the flood water slowly spread out over the plain renewed the fertility of the soil *(Plate 33)*. There can be little doubt that, as in Mesopotamia and to a lesser extent in Egypt, the immediate hinterland also provided grazing for animals and opportunities for dry cultivation of certain crops at appropriate seasons of the year, for hunting and for gathering wild foods. Such activities were probably in the hands of communities which had established relationships with the towns and cities, and later perhaps came under the control of the state authority. These aspects of subsistence must have played a major role in the early stages, and continued to be part of the economic base on which the cities relied. Archaeologists are beginning to work out what part various methods of food production played in later stages, and in different regions within the Indus system.

The Indus Environment. We have already briefly described in chapter 2 the overall instability of the Indus system and its environment, which is due to two principal sets of physical factors. The first of these stems from its proximity to the Indo-Asian collision zone, corresponding approximately to the Hindu Kush and Himalayan mountain arcs. The pressures and tensions within the earth's crust that the collision generates are the cause of earthquakes throughout the region; landslides in the mountains which block valleys and cause rivers to change their courses; changes in levels in the plains which also have effects upon the course of rivers, and on every aspect of natural drainage. Such events are interrelated, and when one takes place others tend to follow. Any one of them, or any combination, can devastate large areas, as we sometimes see today, and could all too easily undermine the viability of a large city with a complex infrastructure. When a mountain valley or gorge in which a major river flows, like that shown in Plate 32, is blocked by a landslide, depending on the terrain, the river will eventually either break through or overflow the barrier, or it will find a new outlet and join another stream. In the first case when the river breaks though it is likely to cause great devastation and the force of the torrent, on reaching the plains, may cause it to adopt a new channel, as Burns records the Ravi did in the 1830s. The second case is likely to lead to the river becoming part of another river system, in the way that the Upper Sarasvati is thought to have joined the Jamuna and become part of the Ganges-Jamuna system (Wilhelmy, 1969). Either

The Indus World

way the effects upon human communities can be devastating and are likely to call for radical adjustments in life-style and movements of centres of population.

Recent studies of the Indus system (Flam 1993, and others) indicate that during the period from 4000 to 2000 BC, (i.e. the Mature Indus urban period) the Lower Indus flowed through Sindh in a somewhat different course to that of the present day, which is known as the Sindhu Nadi. In northern Sindh it flowed to the west of the Rohri hills, instead of through the Sukkur gap as it does today. Further down, it flowed some distance to the south-east of its present course, at a distance of some 25 km from Mohenjo-daro; whereas today it flows so close that the site is in danger of being seriously eroded. During the same period, the Hakra appears to have been an active river, fed by both the Sarasvati and the Sutlej, both of which were later captured, the former by the Jamuna and the latter by the Indus. It is thought that the capture of the Sutlej, and the consequent increase in volume of flood water carried by the Indus, took place towards the end of this period, and may have precipitated the movement of the Indus channel towards Mohenjo-daro. This would have both endangered the site and caused the loss of much valuable agricultural land, and was probably a major factor in the abandonment of the site *(Plates 34 & 35)*.

As pointed out earlier, in addition to causing rivers to change their courses within the mountains, mountain uplift due to the collision of the Indian and Asian plates has accelerated the rate and increased the scale of erosion and deposition of silts and gravels which have contributed to the building up of the Indus plains and surrounding foothills, processes that have been going on before, during and since the early Harappan period. The large quantities of silt carried by the Indus and its major tributaries, and progressively dropped as they enter the plains and flow more slowly, causes them to build up their beds. As a result they flow in shallow channels from which they frequently spill out and change their courses, again contributing to the build-up of silt in the Indus plains as a whole. Following the end of the last glacial period and the beginning of the Holocene, the rising sea level (caused by release of water from the melting polar ice-caps) has caused the river to flow more slowly in its lower course and further increased the rate of build-up of the plain.

Even a minor change in the course of a large river, such as these factors cause from time to time, can ruin the agricultural productivity of an area which has no other source of water, and cause settlements to be abandoned, as they were progressively along the former course

118 *Origins of a Civilization*

of the Sarasvati and the Hakra during Harappan and later times, and along the inland distributaries of the Drishadvati, and elsewhere. Another effect of the steady build-up of the plain of the Lower Indus valley is that settlement sites have tended to become engulfed by rising deposits of silt. This has happened to some extent in the case of Amri, an early Harappan settlement of moderate size on the right bank of the Indus, on the edge of the plain *(Map 4, p. 124)*, which was excavated first in 1929, and again in the early 1960s, and where the occupation layers were found to extend below the modern surface of the plain. At Mohenjo-daro not only is the earlier occupation now below the level of the plain, but much of the site is below the present water table and therefore cannot be investigated by archaeologists. This must indicate, among other things, a widespread rise in the level of the plain.

The increasing depth of silt in the Lower Indus valley is general, and has been the principal mechanism whereby the plain has been built up at such a constant level, but the depth today obviously must vary according to what lies beneath. Tectonic movements along fault lines approximately at right angles to the course of the river have caused changes in the relative levels of the underlying rocks. This means that sections of the valley floor have dropped or risen in relation to one another, causing greater accumulation of silt in the low-lying sections.

At places along the plain's margins, outlying hills and rocky promontories extend out into it. The Rohri hills in Upper Sindh virtually block the valley, forcing the present Indus to cut its way through. A number of sites like Mohenjo-daro and Amri are situated near the present margin, or like Kot Diji at the foot of the Rohri hills, and appear to have been founded on hard ground before the silt had risen to its present level. It follows from this that smaller sites and those originally located at somewhat lower levels will have been totally submerged. This may in part account for the absence of smaller settlement sites on much of the plain.

Such events as we have described on the upper courses of the major rivers have had knock-on effects lower down, and conversely changes in the Indus delta area have had widespread effects upon the level of the plain. An example of this is the Allah Band, a fault scarp 10 to 18 feet high and c. fifty miles long, created by the earthquake of 1819, mentioned in chapter 2, which altered the drainage pattern of a large area of the delta and for some years blocked one of the distributaries of the Indus. At the same time as the Allah Band was formed a large area of the floor of the Rann of

The Indus World   119

Kacch dropped by some twenty feet (Oldham, 1926).

These are a few examples of the evidence of changes in the Indus system that appear to be due directly or indirectly to tectonic causes, and there are many others, some of which will be referred to at relevant places in the following chapters. The Indus valley differs from those of both the Nile and the Tigris-Euphrates with regard to the extent to which it has been subject to such tectonic events, both the other river systems having suffered rather less from such disturbances during the Holocene.

The other set of factors which render the Indus system generally, and the Lower Indus valley in particular an unstable environment, are climatic. The position of the Lower Indus valley between the path of rain-bearing winter storms on the north, and that of the south-west monsoon on the south means that today it has a very low rainfall, and in some years none at all. As in all marginal areas a slight increase or decrease of average rainfall over a period of a few years could make a crucial difference to the vegetation, and consequently to the amount of food available from areas immediately surrounding the Indus plain. Gurdip Singh and others found during the 1970s that on the basis of evidence from the Rajasthan lakes there was a significant increase in overall precipitation during the Early and Mature Indus period which must have meant a similar increase in the Indus region also (eg Singh et al 1974). Bryson and Swain (1981) were later able to show that monsoon precipitation between c. 5000 and 3500 years ago (3000 and 1500 BC) in the Indus region was at least double that of the present. However, they pointed out it had been at a similar level to that of the present during the preceding period. What differentiated the climate of the Indus period from that of earlier times was that:

> The winter rains appear to have been at maximum during Indus times, decreasing the winter dessication that now characterizes the region and increasing the overall precipitation efficiency (Bryson & Swain, 1981).

This change in rainfall pattern they considered important to the history of Indus agriculture, as indeed it must be. A change of this kind, involving not only approximately double the present summer rainfall, but also a significant winter rainfall in an area that previously (and subsequently) had virtually none would make the Lower Indus valley a considerably different place. There would be more natural vegetation for grazing, both on the plain and in surrounding hilly

120 *Origins of a Civilization*

regions; more potential for dry cultivation (i.e. without irrigation) of cereals and other crops. Having more vegetation in the tributary valleys, there would be less massive, sudden floods, the rivers would tend to incise their channels into the plain somewhat more, and would therefore be more stable. If inundation took place beyond a regular flood plain (such as we see on the lower Narbada today), it would probably be generally more predictable than it is now. These factors together with the absence of water from the Sutlej would have made the Lower Indus valley both more stable and a more productive agricultural environment.

When these factors all began to change towards the present situation the agricultural basis of the cities must have been seriously undermined. A decrease in rainfall could cause the civilization of the Lower Indus valley to have become almost totally dependent upon food produced on the plain with the help of the flood waters of the Indus, while lacking major alternative food sources previously available in the adjacent foothills and on areas of the plain not subject to inundation. Both aspects of the agricultural system, the wet and the dry, must always have been there, as we have already pointed out, but even a slight deterioration in the climate could seriously reduce dry crop production and put a society with a large urban population into a dangerous state of over-dependence on one aspect, namely inundation agriculture. If this too was disturbed by the movement and increased flow of the Indus, there would be little left even to support the rural population adequately, let alone provide food for a city.

Another important factor in any marginal climatic situation is human pressure on the environment *(Plate 36)*. This is something of which we have ample evidence throughout South Asia today. Over-grazing, too frequent cropping, too much cutting of small trees and bushes for firewood, felling of large trees for timber—all can cause deterioration and loss of productivity of the land and loss of other resources. This comes about through flash floods and other forms of erosion and loss of soil. When forests are reduced a decrease of rainfall tends to follow.

The plains of Sindh as we see them today have little natural vegetation, even where they are uncultivated, except for the narrow ribbon of gallery forest along the banks of the Indus channel which still remains in places *(Plate 36)*. The hills along the margin too are sparsely covered with very small, thorny bushes and occasional patches or tufts of coarse grass and other plants. Near the edge of the plain, within reach of villages, they are regularly grazed by goats which are herded and kept constantly on the move within quite a wide radius of their home villages. More remote areas appear to be somewhat less heavily grazed and to have rather more vegetation.

Historical records leave no doubt that the interior valleys of the North West Frontier Province and Baluchistan previously had many more trees than they have today. It is recorded that when the Khyber railway was built from Peshawar to the Afghan frontier and Landikotal in the 1920s, a band of forest had to be cut down on each side so as to remove possible places of concealment for brigands. By the early 1950s, when the writers first saw it, the line crossed a bare, treeless plain to the pass. Large trees are still being felled and sent out from some of the valleys. As a result water retention is reduced and flash floods occur more frequently, washing away fields within the valleys and doing further damage downstream, and less water is available throughout the dry season. Trees are generally not replaced, as when self-sown saplings appear they tend to be eaten by grazing animals, greatly reducing the possibility of natural regeneration of forests.

These are some of the most obvious effects of over-exploitation of the environment today. What we do not know, and archaeologists need to try to find out, is to what extent these pressures were felt already in Harappan times, both along the edge of the plain, in the immediate hinterland of the settlements; and more generally and widely due to timber felling, which we know must have taken place in the Mature Indus period. The question for the archaeologist is to what extent human activity was a factor in past change and particularly in deterioration of the environment. This is one of the many questions about the environment of the ancient Indus world and its culture that currently need to be addressed. Such questions are important because the answers will help greatly in understanding a major and extremely interesting formative period of South Asia's past, including the reasons for the collapse of the Indus cities in the second millennium BC. Furthermore, such questions are of profound relevance to understanding the problems of the present day.

The environment of the Indus culture is more complex and more difficult to reconstruct than at first appears. On the one hand we have the Indus system with the wide range of sources from which it draws its water that in turn help to ensure its perennial flow through the desert, and provide the seasonal flooding or inundation which makes possible an abundant harvest. But on the other hand, today the whole of the Lower Indus valley is never flooded in any one season. The main channel may shift on account of tectonic instability, as we have seen, and even if this does not happen, other factors may cause the floods to break the river banks in new places

122   *Origins of a Civilization*

with the result that the flow of flood water will follow a different
path. This means that a settlement can be quite suddenly deprived,
temporarily or permanently, of its water and its main source of food.

In our attempts to build up a picture of the environment in
which the civilization of the Indus region developed, flourished and
finally apparently virtually disappeared, we have looked at some of
the changes that are known to have taken place during Harappan
times, and discussed the causes of change, some peculiar to the
region and some more general. It must have become clear that the
situation is fraught with uncertainties. We know that changes and
events took place, but we rarely know exactly when, and often we do
not know the underlying causes: for instance, how far the drying up
of the Sarasvati was due to a change of course following events in the
Himalayas, and how far to more general climatic change.

Regions

The Lower Indus Valley. Up to this point we have been discussing the
Indus system as a whole, and in so far as we have focussed on any
particular region it has been on the Lower Indus valley, that is to say the
province of Sindh, through which the old course of the Hakra also
passes. This is where many of the towns and cities of the early and
mature phases of the Harappan culture, including Mohenjo-daro, its
principal city, are situated. On its north-western margin, near the
present border of Baluchistan, sites have been found which belong to
the earliest known culture directly ancestral to it. Sindh and the hilly
region to the north-west therefore have some claim to be regarded as
the heartland of the Indus culture. Enough has already been said about
the geography and general character of the region, so we shall now look
briefly at some of other regions that formed part of the Indus world.

The Punjab and Northern Rajasthan. Punjab means land of the five
rivers, i.e. the Indus and its four major tributaries, the Jhelum,
Chenab, Ravi and Sutlej. In the past the most easterly of these, the
Sutlej, and a sixth river, the Sarasvati, flowed into the Hakra which
followed a parallel course through Sindh to the sea. Conditions
become progressively less arid upstream from the Sindh border, as
we move north-eastward. In the recent past, prior to the creation of
a number of major dams and irrigation projects which have greatly
increased the area of productive agricultural land, the countryside of
the southern Punjab would have looked considerably more arid than

The Indus World   123

it does today. It was largely a region inhabited by nomadic pastoralists, with a fairly broad corridor of better-watered land, suited to agriculture, along the piedmont zone and outer valleys and foothills of the northern mountains. Through this fertile corridor passed one of the major routes of passage and communication between the Indian subcontinent and Central Asia and the world beyond.

Today, the northern Punjab presents a contrast to Sindh. It is fairly intensely cultivated, and its natural vegetation, where it can be seen, consists of grassland and thorn forest or jungle. The Indian tiger was found here in considerable numbers a century and a half ago. Babur recorded in the *Baburnama*, in the early sixteenth century, that his son, the young Humayun, fell off his horse because he laughed so much on seeing an Indian rhinoceros for the first time on the way down from Peshawar. Neither tigers nor rhinoceroses are to be found in the Punjab today, but there are still quite large areas of thorn forest where cattle are herded and some wildlife can be found. Most of the forest has been cleared and the land used for the cultivation of cereals and other crops, with or without some canal irrigation. In Harappan times there must have been a comparable difference to that we see today between Sindh and the Punjab.

Northern Gujarat, Saurashtra and the Makran Coast. These regions are not strictly part of the Indus system in the sense that in none of them is there a major tributary of the Indus to which its principal Harappan settlements relate. In terms of environment, northern Gujarat and Saurashtra are in many ways like an extension southward, down the coastal plain, of the environment of the Lower Indus valley and the delta. The climate is similar but today the rainfall is a little higher and more regular than in Sindh, with the result that the countryside is less barren and dry cultivation of cereals is possible. The principal sites are located either on the estuaries of minor streams or on rocky hills or uplands. In the latter case they also differ from the tradition of both the regions discussed above, in that the settlements were largely built in stone rather than burnt and unburnt mud brick. Research shows that many of the same crops were grown as in Sindh and Punjab, and considerable quantities of wild foods similar to those available in the region today were also used.

In spite of close similarities to the heartland there are indications that these sites served as gateways to the outside world: to sea trade with the Arabian Gulf and Mesopotamia; to overland trade with the Ahar copper miners of southern Rajasthan and the agate miners of central Gujarat; and perhaps also trade with other communities in the subcon-

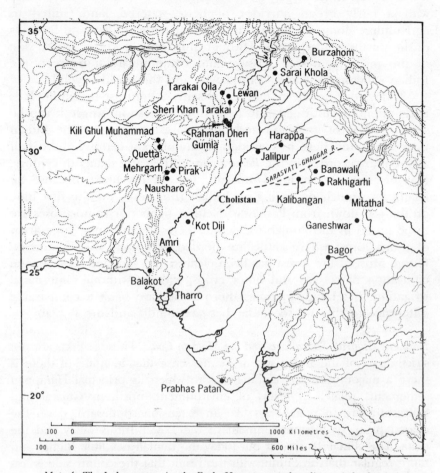

Map 4. The Indus system in the Early Harappan and earlier periods showing sites referred to in Chapter 7.

tinent, like the Southern Neolithic people of Karnataka, by land or sea.

Balakot on the old shoreline near Las Bela town, just west of the Sindh-Baluchistan border, is similar in some ways to the Gujarat sites, and also has a number of interesting features of its own which will be discussed in a later section. Sutkagen Dor, far to the west near the Baluchistan-Iran border, and a small number of other sites along the Makran coast, appear to be outlying trading posts or watering places for ships. Like the Gujarat sites they clearly have their own character, distinct from the more metropolitan settlements of the Indus system. But little is known about them so far, and there is clearly much to be discovered.

Chapter 7

FARMERS AND VILLAGE COMMUNITIES OF THE INDUS SYSTEM

This chapter covers two main topics: first, we shall review the early development of agriculture, particularly as it is represented by the excavations at Mehrgarh, and its subsequent spread throughout the Indus system; and second, we shall consider the developments which lead into the period of incipient urbanism, which we are calling Early Harappan. The extraordinary complex of sites on the Bolan river around Mehrgarh was discovered and examined by the French Archaeological Mission to Pakistan, under the direction of J-F Jarrige, in the early 1970s while excavating nearby at the later site of Pirak. Excavations on a regular basis soon followed, and have continued both at Mehrgarh and the neighbouring Nausharo from 1975 to the present (Jarrige & Lechevallier, 1979; Jarrige, 1981, 1984). As a result a more or less unbroken history of settlement in this area has been established, starting at Mehrgarh between c. 7000 BC and c. 2800 BC, and continuing at Nausharo from c. 2800-2000 BC. If Pirak is included in the series, the continuity extends for a further thousand years to c. 1000 BC.

THE BEGINNINGS OF AGRICULTURE AT MEHRGARH (c. 7000-4500 BC)

The Chronology of Mehrgarh. The absolute chronology of Mehrgarh rests mainly upon the available radiocarbon dates. Many of these were obtained before the complex stratification of the early periods had been fully understood, and give some widely divergent results. Unless further samples can be obtained the radiocarbon chronology must remain somewhat unsatisfactory and dependent upon wide extrapolation from any available sources. These problems are discussed frankly and wisely by Jarrige (1984), and more recently by Meadow (1993) and Possehl (1994a). The latter quote seventeen calibrated

126   *Origins of a Civilization*

dates giving a series from c. the 7th-5th millennia BC. These appear to offer an acceptable series even if they do not bear a systematic relationship to the stratigraphy of the excavations there. Table 1 follows the published work of J-F Jarrige and his colleagues, with slight variance of our own.

Table 1

Mehrgarh, the Beginnings of Agriculture
(Initial Agrarian Subsistence in Piedmont Zone))

BC	Mehrgarh Period	
7000	???	
6500	IA	Pre-ceramic Neolithic
6000		
5500	IB, C	Period of silt and floods
5000	IIA, B	Period of construction, chaff-
	IIC	tempered ware, granaries
4500		
4000	III	Painted pottery, female terracotta, figurines, granaries
3500	IV-V	
3000	VI	
2200	VII	

[after Jarrige (1984), Lechevallier (1984),
Lechevallier & Quivron (1985)]

The earliest settlements at Mehrgarh cover about two square kilometres in the northernmost part of the Kachi plain, on the bank of the Bolan river, a short distance below the point where it leaves the valley which connects it, via the Bolan pass, with Quetta, about 100 km to the north (*Plate 37*). After passing through a series of gorges the river water spreads out over the plain depositing its load of gravel and silt. The result is like an inland delta with extremely fertile soil, through which the river has cut new channels from time to time. The Kachi plain is still regarded as the 'bread basket' of

Baluchistan. The Bolan valley must have been one of the principal routes linking the mountain valleys of northern Baluchistan with the Indus plains; and it was probably used by animals such as deer and wild sheep moving down to the Indus plains to graze following the inundation. It seems clear that such a situation would appeal to early man, even before the beginnings of agriculture, because of the proximity of the river and the abundance of game, and in addition because of the presence of wild cereals. Thus, Mehrgarh was peculiarly suited to be a centre for the transformation from hunting and collecting to the domestication of animals and settled agriculture.

Before we consider more closely the evidence for the domestication of plants and animals found at Mehrgarh, something must be said about the nature of the excavations and the evidence they revealed, particularly that relating to the earliest periods. The first part of the site to attract attention was a small mound (MRI), where a sequence of occupation dating from the third and fourth millennia BC was discovered. Further exploration located a series of earlier stages of occupation to the north-east, between the first mound (MRI) and the river. At this point it was noticed that the river bank, which was here a silt cliff around 10 m in height, contained quantities of occupation debris. Examination of the bank, followed by excavation, disclosed that this was part of another mound, which had been completely engulfed in quantities of silt brought down by the river, so that it had become almost totally submerged (MR3). The buried mound with its many periods of rebuilding represented the oldest period of occupation in the whole complex, period IA. At a certain point there followed the period of silt deposition (IB, IC), which steadily rose with the level of the surrounding plain and interleaved with a scatter of occupation debris on the slopes of the buried mound. The cause of this repeated flooding and silt deposition is not clearly established, but it must relate to some major natural change higher up the valley (*Fig. 14 next page*). Thereafter, the flood deposits appear to have ceased and occupation of the site continued and developed on the new surface of the plain (periods IIA, B and III). These processes must have taken many centuries: the early settlement appears to date from c. 7000 BC; the period of flooding has been suggested to date to c. 5500-5000 BC, and the continuing occupation on the newly raised plain dates from c. 5000 BC onwards. There is no clear indication that at any time there was a complete break or hiatus in the occupation, although the excavators suggest that during the period of floods habitation at Mehrgarh may have been of a seasonal nature.

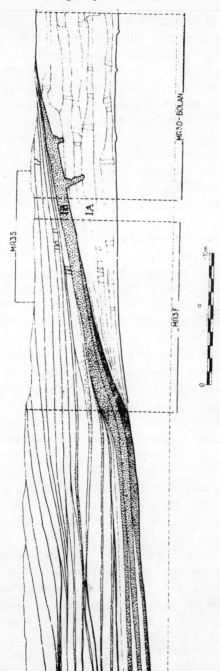

Fig. 14. Mehrgarh, section through river bank, showing original mound and subsequent flood deposits.

The early periods. Period I at Mehrgarh presents us with the earliest evidence so far discovered for the beginnings of agriculture and domestication in the Indus system. Throughout the ten or more building periods of the earliest mound there are structures made of handmade mud bricks of distinctive 'cigar-shaped' form. The structures take the form of small rectangular rooms, in groups of two or four, with associated fireplaces, assumed to be houses. From the start there is evidence of a number of crafts. There is a stone blade industry, using flint from selected river pebbles, and setting a pattern which continued through to the final occupation of the site several millennia later. By far the most numerous stone artefacts belong to period I, but the main 'type tools' recur throughout. The blades were used in various ways, but particularly interesting was the mounting of a number of blades in a bone or wooden haft with a bitumen mastic, so as to make a composite sickle (*Fig. 15*). Neolithic ground stone

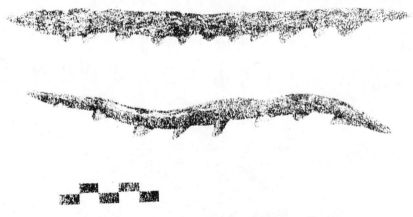

Fig. 15. Mehrgarh, sickles with stone blades set in bitumen.

axes occur rarely, and only in the second period. Various grinding stones or pestles indicate the grinding of grains and other substances. Bone tools, particularly in the form of needles and awls, are found from the beginning onwards. It is noteworthy that no pottery of any kind occurs in the early mound, and it is only in the slope deposits of the flood period (IB, C) that the first few shards of crude hand-made pottery are found. A single hand-modelled human figure of towards the end of period I, a few centimentres in length, has been found made in unburnt clay. Apparently, it is the ancestral prototype of the great number of terracotta female figurines found in subsequent periods at Mehrgarh.

Numerous burials were discovered in period I, the earliest being

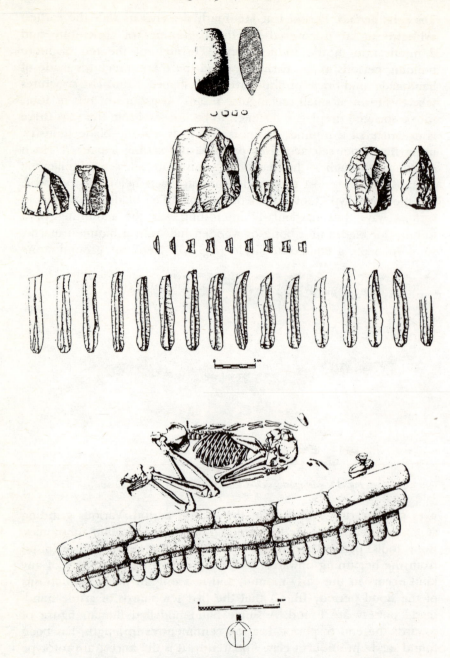

Fig. 16. Mehrgarh, Period I. Burial with stone blades, cores and a ground stone axe as grave goods.

Farmers and Village Communities of the Indus System   131

flexed bodies in simple oval pits, the bones frequently covered with
red ochre. In the later part of the period and the succeeding period
II, there were more elaborate burials where pits were dug and
a niche was cut into one wall, in which the body was deposited
(*Fig. 16*). A mud brick wall was then constructed to close the niche
before the pit was filled. In many of the graves, varieties of grave
goods were found, including bitumen-lined baskets; necklaces of
stone or shell beads, some of marine origin; stone and bone pendants
and anklets; and food offerings, including whole young goats. Many
of the items of adornment were found still in position on the
skeletons. Among the imported items from the graves were beads of
lapis lazuli, probably brought from a local source in the hills of north
Baluchistan; others of turquoise, almost certainly brought from either
eastern Iran or Central Asia. The marine shells too must indicate
long-distance trade. It is interesting to find such activities going on
at so early a date and before pottery had been introduced.

Periods II and III mark a major change at Mehrgarh, with the
spread of settlement upon the newly built-up plain. Structurally, one of
the most remarkable features was the creation of many compartmented
structures of mud brick, divided into smaller cell-like units, some in
double rows with a central passageway between them (*Fig. 17, p. 132*).
It is not clear from the published material to date what exactly these
were: probably some were houses, but the majority were almost certainly
storerooms or granaries, and it is tempting to see them as the remote
ancestors of the Great Granary at Harappa, excavated by Vats and
belonging to the Mature Indus civilization, dating between two and
three thousand years later. In terms of craft activities these periods saw
the proliferation of fine pottery; by period III, at least, much of it was
wheel-thrown and bore painted decorations in the distinctive styles
which have long been regarded as a hallmark of the ancient cultures of
Baluchistan. By that date there are many terracotta figurines, mainly of
women and some of animals. More significant must be the evidence of
the beginnings of metallurgy. A single bead of copper was found in a
burial of period I; but the first regular smelting of copper is attested to
in period IIB by the presence of a small ingot of that metal. Increasingly,
the evidence leads us to recognize that a spread of settlements was
taking place, bringing with it changes in social and economic relations
over a far wider arena. These are things to which we shall return in a
subsequent section.

Domestication of plants and animals. Before we leave Mehrgarh we
must consider the important evidence that it provides for

Fig. 17. Mehrgarh, mud brick compartmented building, period IIA.

transformation of the subsistence economy from one largely dependent on hunting, collecting and pastoralism to one centred around settled agriculture and the domestication of several species of animal. Figure 18 shows a comparative chart of the occurrence of animal remains in the different phases of periods I-III (Meadow, 1993). In the earliest levels of the Aceramic Neolithic over half of the animals represented are wild, the great majority of them being gazelle, along with smaller number of several other deer, nilgai, onager, wild pig, etc.; of the domesticated species goats predominate, followed by sheep and cattle in descending order of frequency. By the end of period I the situation has changed: gazelle have all but disappeared, other wild species constitute only a small percentage, sheep and goats together occupy over half of the domesticated species, with sheep being somewhat more numerous than goats. Cattle meanwhile have increased until they are the most numerous single domestic species, outstripping sheep and goats. The cattle can safely be assumed to be zebu *(Bos indicus)*, as not only is this already indicated by the actual bones recovered from period I, but also by the presence of terracotta models of humped cattle from period III. The

Farmers and Village Communities of the Indus System

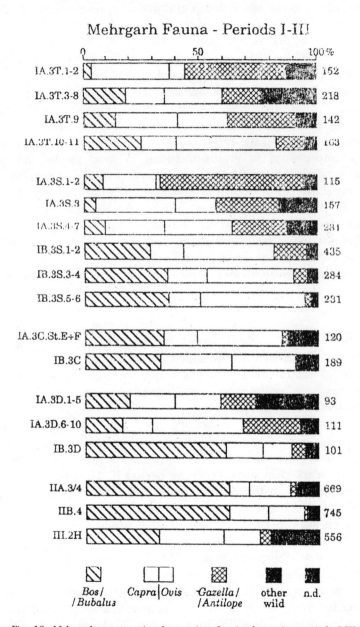

Fig. 18. *Mehrgarh, comparative frequencies of animal remains, periods I-III.*

same trends are even more marked in period II, sheep, goat and cattle between them occupy well over 90 per cent of the sample, and gazelle have all but disappeared. What is more, cattle now occupy 60

134 *Origins of a Civilization*

per cent of the total, while sheep and goats represent around 15 per cent each. These figures are evidently somewhat abnormal, because by the end of the occupation at Mehrgarh, in period VII, the proportions of the different species have returned to something closer to those of the end of period I.

Happily the excavators recognized the importance of recording not only the animal, but also the plant remains at Mehrgarh, particularly those of food grains, of which a large sample (nearly six thousand specimens) are reported. Many of the samples are in the form of impressions of grains included in mud bricks and other features made of earth; charred grains form a further category. They are highly significant: the two principal grains were barley and wheat. Costantini (upon whose report we rely) considers that there is clear evidence in periods I and II that wild barley is in course of development to its cultivated form; and the same can probably be said about wheat. Some grains of the wild types are found to continue alongside the cultivated ones, indicating that the wild plants, which had presumably originally attracted people to the locality, were still present there. He states that:

> The type of barley present at the site shows some characteristics that can be called 'local' . . . . The dominant type of naked barley had a short, compact spike with shortened internodes and small rounded seeds (Costantini, 1984: 30-33).

He suggests that in period I, these features can be ascribed to cultivated but by no means completely domesticated plants. They are particularly marked in the succeeding period II. Thus the occurrence of barley, so early in the development at Mehrgarh bears a striking resemblance to the early occurrences recorded at sites in south-west Asia at such sites as Ali Kosh and Beidha, which are attributable to comparably early dates. The Mehrgarh grains included a small percentage of wild, two-row barley *(Hordeum vulgare, spontaneum)*; also a small percentage of hulled six-row barley, and a much larger proportion of six-row naked barley. Costantini suggests that the naked barley from Mehrgarh has closer parallels to charred remains from archaeological deposits in southern Turkmenia and Central Asia than to those from south-west Asia. The small percentages of wild and distichum barleys remain more or less constant throughout the whole of the early occupation of the site, at least through to period VII.

Farmers and Village Communities of the Indus System

The cultivation of wheat appears from the very beginning of period I at Mehrgarh, and therefore runs parallel to that of barley. Several varieties are seen. According to Costantini (who once again is our authority for this section) naked wheat, together with typical hulled varieties, are present from the oldest deposits onwards. The hulled wheats *(Triticum monococcum)* and *(Triticum dicoccum)* are present throughout the whole occupation of the site, in small quantities; while the naked wheat, although representing less than 1 per cent of the specimens in period I, increases in frequency in period II and dramatically so in period III. This tendency continues through to period VII and coincides with a progressive decrease in the proportion of naked barley. The hulled wheat of period I, according to Costantini, had already undergone an intensive process of cultivation and domestication. The naked wheat, moreover, permits some reflections of remarkable interest. The naked wheat samples from period I can be referred to as *Triticum durum*; in period II, the morphology of the seeds, while being within the range of variation of the tetraploid *Triticum durum,* shows characteristics of small seed forms. In subsequent periods morphological and biometrical characteristics permit us to group the great majority of the wheat seeds with the hexaploid form *Triticum sphaerococcum.*

The plant remains from Mehrgarh also include a variety of jujube *(Zizyphus;* Hindi, *ber);* stones of the date palm in period I and II; and grape seeds in period V, all of which appear to be local.

There is not as yet any conclusive evidence regarding the actual methods of cultivation employed, nor as to whether or when any sort of irrigation was introduced in this period. In view of the fact that the rainfall was somewhat higher than today, it seems probably that grain production would initially have depended mainly upon the winter rains. We are inclined to think that in the very early stages minimal labour and effort would be used in the exploitation of natural resources, with limited recourse to labour-intensive work. In time this must have been augmented by other means, simple embankments of fields, and perhaps the construction of earth or stone embankments akin to the *gabar bandhs* found at later times in the region. These kinds of measures are still today employed by the local agriculturalists.

The Period of Agricultural Expansion (c. 4500-3500 BC)

We have dwelt upon Mehrgarh at some length because it offers the earliest and most comprehensive evidence to date of an early agricultural settlement on the edge of the Indus plains. It has been

136   *Origins of a Civilization*

carefully and systematically excavated and provides an extended sequence over some five millennia. At Kili Ghul Muhammad in the Quetta valley a small excavation revealed a comparable Aceramic Neolithic settlement, but dating from the end of that period only. There are reports that similar sites have been observed elsewhere in both northern and southern Baluchistan, but none has so far been satisfactorily excavated or adequately published. This does not mean that other such sites will not be found in the valleys of Baluchistan or along the piedmont zone of the Indus plains, but we must assume that at the time of the earliest occupation at Mehrgarh the human population was still relatively small and scattered, and that such sites may have been few and far between. At Mehrgarh itself the indications are that the production of grain, particularly wheat, and the construction of mud brick storehouses expanded steadily during the periods IIC to III. Along with these things the number of crafts and their products show a steady increase. The mass production of pottery with the introduction of the potter's wheel begins at this time, and increases steadily thereafter (periods III to V). So too does the variety and skill of painted decoration applied to the pottery, with geometric and animal designs, goats and birds.

Another special feature of Mehrgarh is that from period IV onwards a remarkable series of small female terracotta figurines occur. There is a general consensus that these represent deities. The presence of the new crafts, and particularly of the ubiquitous decorated pottery, points to the fact that Mehrgarh is now one agricultural settlement among many others. In the Kachi plain several large mounds provide evidence of settlements contemporary with the later periods of Mehrgarh. Related styles of pottery decoration begin to appear at sites in other parts of Baluchistan and beyond, and indications of trade and interaction increase.

We can only guess at what date agricultural settlements first began to appear on the Indus plains, and what changes in life-style this development entailed initially. As we have seen there is evidence that around 8000 BC there was a general increase in rainfall throughout the Indus system, and this must have created conditions favourable for an extension of agriculture (Singh, 1971; Misra, 1984). The Indus plains offer an environment very different from that of the piedmont zone. The bed of the Indus river appears often to have been unstable and liable to flooding and sudden shifts. Along the banks of the Indus were probably belts of gallery forest, such as we still see in places today, with abundant wild life, including gazelle, buck and deer, wild pig, with the addition of elephant and rhinoceros,

Farmers and Village Communities of the Indus System 137

now extinct in the region but represented on Indus seals. As the Indus plains were liable to annual floods and thereby received regular deposits of rich alluvium, many early (and for that matter later) settlements must have been buried. This has two implications: that buried sites are likely to remain unknown to archaeologists until suitable remote sensing techniques can be devised and employed to detect them; and that once reached they are likely to be in a better, or at any rate different state of preservation, to those which remained throughout on or near the surface of the plain. Whatever the reason, to date there are relatively few traces of early agricultural settlements on the plains, and those reported offer few radiocarbon dates. We should not forget that the spread of agriculture we are discussing is essentially the spread of the highly successful pattern of wheat and barley, cattle, sheep and goat, which we have seen emerge in the piedmont zone at Mehrgarh; and that this pattern appears to have been underlying the whole process of expansion, leading up to the emergence of the Mature Harappan civilization.

During the fourth millennium BC, population growth and the spread of agricultural settlements must have continued. This development seems to coincide with the successful translation of the agrarian system developed in the piedmont zone onto the plains of the Indus and its tributaries. Although we know of many sites, only a small number have been excavated and yet smaller number published, so the evidence on which our generalizations are based is still uneven and in many respects far from complete. For this reason some doubt must remain regarding the dates at which things happened and the significance we may attach to them. We can, however, recognize a marked change between this and the following stage, therefore it seems best to assign a somewhat arbitrary date for the conclusion of the stage of agricultural expansion and the beginning of the Early Harappan period somewhere between 3500 and 3000 BC. We shall refer to this as the period of expanding agriculture, and its successor as the period of Early Harappan urbanism. These two are treated by Shaffer (1992) as parts of a single Era of Regionalisation. We see important differences between the two parts: the former being a time when new settlements appear, some regionally distinct; while the second part, with its evidence of increasing interaction over a vast area, would appear to share important characteristics with its successor, the Mature Harappan period. For this reason we prefer to retain the already well-established terminology of Early and Mature Harappan.

It is probable that the first part of the process began at different

Origins of a Civilization

dates in different areas. In the South the process is clearly visible at Balakot, on the Makran coast in southern Baluchistan, and at Amri on the Lower Indus in Sindh. At the former site the occupation begins somewhere in the first half of the fourth millennium, with an agricultural settlement with barley, cattle, sheep and goats. At Amri the occupation goes back to c. 3500 BC. The pottery of the first period is still typical of Baluchistan, with some resemblances to that of Mehrgarh III, IV and V, and a repertoire of geometric painted designs. However, by the end of the period, c. 3000 BC, the first traces appear of new motifs, cattle and antelope, and the fish scale motif which will hereafter become a hallmark of both the Early and Mature Harappan periods. Like Mehrgarh the site is located on the *Kaccho* or older alluvium, but at Amri it is located within a few hundred metres of the active flood plain and in full view of the Indus itself.

Related sites begin to occur on the western edge of the Indus valley from Amri northwards. We have already discussed Mehrgarh on the Kachi plain. Farther north, in Dera Ismael Khan district, on the Gomal plain traversed by the Gomal, a tributary of the Indus, a whole cluster of sites has been reported and two, Gumla and Rahman Dheri, have been excavated. Radiocarbon dates suggest that at the latter the early settlement begins at c. 3300 BC, while at the former it begins somewhat earlier. In the earliest period at Gumla rough surfaced pottery is found, and thereafter a series of periods produce fine painted wares with geometric designs, cattle and fish. The geometric designs show remarkable parallels with the painted pottery of sites in Turkmenistan, such as Altin Tepe and Kara Tepe, north of the Elburz range. A similar relationship is to be found in the wide range of distinctive female terracottas. These again show surprising similarities to those of the same sites in Central Asia. It may be recalled that suggestions of trade and contact with Central Asia were already present very early in the history of Mehrgarh.

The continuing evidence seems to point to there being an enduring relationship and interaction between southern Central Asia and the western margins of the Indus system. Geographically, the two regions also share many common features. Another interesting detail is that large numbers of incised marks or graffiti occur in pottery from all periods at Rahman Dheri. These are certainly not a script as such, since the marks almost always occur singly, but they may well show the recognition of the need for identification of ownership, and as such be seen as a significant step towards the creation of a script.

Farmers and Village Communities of the Indus System 139

The most striking aspect of Rahman Dheri however is the evidence it offers of an overall planned form *(Plate 38)*. This was apparent from the first publication of an aerial photograph, showing the regular rectangular outline of the settlement, with what appeared to be a massive town wall and a regular grid of streets and houses constructed in mud brick. The latter, of course, is related to the final stage of occupation at the site and may therefore be contemporary with the Mature Harappan period, but the town wall appears to have been originally constructed by the time of the first occupation of the site, i.e. somewhere in the final centuries of the fourth millennium. We have confirmed this by examining the visible traces of the massive mud brick wall, both on the ground, and in relation to the section of the early occupation in one of the excavated trenches. This means that Rahman Dheri, with an enclosed area of c. 22 hectares, is possibly one of the earliest such town or city sites in South Asia and, in the light of the early radiocarbon date obtained there, can be seen to pre-date the Mature Harappan, and even marginally the Early Harappan periods.

Farther north, along the western piedmont zone, we come to Bannu district, which is effectively the basin of the Kurram river and its tributaries the Tochi and Gambila. Here again there is a cluster of sites, of which several have been excavated. The oldest so far is Sheri Khan Tarakai (Farid Khan et al 1991). Here a good series of radiocarbon dates indicates a long early occupation through the fourth millennium and probably going back to the mid-fifth. The painted pottery of the later occupation of this site is comparable with that of Mehrgarh III-IV. Other excavated sites include Lewan (see chapter 5), a large factory for making all kinds of stone tools. There are no radiocarbon dates, but traces of occupation which appear to belong to the beginning of the third millennium. The extensive Mesolithic blade industry and great range of heavy stone tools indicate that this site may in origins predate any of the agricultural settlements.

In the northern Punjab, on the edge of the piedmont zone, Sarai Khola (more correctly Sarai Kala) is another early settlement with a distinct character of its own. Here the earliest occupation has been called Neolithic. It is distinguished by a plain red or brown hand-made burnished pottery, some pots having spiral mat-impressed bases, and the presence of stone axes with ground edges, a few stone blades and numerous bone points. Radiocarbon dates suggest that the early period goes back to around the mid-fourth millennium BC. A related culture with many of the same elements is found in

140 *Origins of a Civilization*

Kashmir, at Burzahom, and in the northern valleys of Pakistan, notably in Swat.

Farther east, on the Punjab plains, a rather different picture is reported from Jalilpur, some 65 km south-west of Harappa and near the bank of the Ravi river. In the absence of any metal artifacts this has also been called Neolithic, but no radiocarbon dates are yet available. It has a distinctive pottery with a roughened or rusticated surface made by coating the pots with a slurry of wet clay, to which crushed burnt clay has been added, and numerous bone points. South of the Sutlej, in the Cholistan desert, Rafique Mughal (1990) discovered a large number of sites of comparable age in the internal basin of the dried-up Sarasvati-Hakra river. These he named as belonging to the Hakra phase. Although none has as yet been excavated or fully published, we shall see below that they represent an important nucleus of early settlement arising during the period of expansion of agriculture, and broadly datable to c. 3500-3000 BC. In the survey area covered, Mughal recorded no less than thirty-seven Hakra phase sites, of which over half were below five hectares in extent, and smaller numbers were in the 5-10, 10-20 and 20-30 hectares brackets. This desert-preserved complex offers a clear suggestion of the extent to which similar sites may be buried beneath the alluvium in other regions, and provides an important indication of the rapidity with which settlements and population spread and increased in the second half of the fourth millennium.

EARLY HARAPPAN INCIPIENT URBANISM (3500-2600 BC)

Extent. We have called this period Early Harappan, not because it can be compared with the full urbanism of the succeeding Mature Harappan period, but because we believe it represents a transitional or formative stage between the period of expanding agriculture, and the establishment of the Mature Harappan civilization. The Early Harappan period has been variously referred to as Kot Dijian, pre-Harappan (mainly in India), Early Indus and as pre-urban. We have commented above on the difficulty of assigning a hard and fast line to the junction between the end of the previous period and the beginning of this one: probably it is best to accept the uncertainty of the current evidence and suggest as a working hypothesis that the beginning of the Early Harappan may be placed somewhere between 3300 and 3000 BC, and extend up to the more firmly dated onset of the Mature Harappan around 2600-2500 BC. The process of development, or build-up towards urbanism, appears to

Farmers and Village Communities of the Indus System 141

gather momentum from around 3000 BC, so that one might also be justified in restricting the term Early Harappan to the centuries between 2900 and 2550 BC. We are dealing here with dynamic processes of change and expansion: the hard and fast lines suggested by the limited number of dates, and the archaeological terms we use, must be understood in this light.

We have chosen to use Possehl's (1993) summary conclusion of a detailed study of the dates available at that time, as it offers a simple, if somewhat over-generalised, view. Table 2 is derived from Possehl's endeavour to extract as clear a statement as possible from radiocarbon dates relating to the the Early Harappan period and its transformation to the Mature Harappan.

Table 2

Archaeological Phase	Average of Calibrated Dates
Pre-urban, Early Harappan	2867, 2808, 2772, 2723, 2699 cal. BC
Final Pre-urban phase	2651, 2649, 2607 cal. BC
Pre-urban/Urban transition	2574, 2533, 2508 cal. BC
Earliest Urban Harappan phase	2453, 2423, 2399 cal. BC

(after Possehl, 1993)

Because of the much greater number of excavated sites spread over so much greater an area, we may approach this period in a rather different way to its predecessors. We shall not attempt to describe all the sites or their features: rather we shall seek to delineate the area taken as a whole and the sub-areas or provinces within it in a more digested form, and consider what appear to be by and large the common and distinctive features of the communities who inhabited the Greater Indus system at this time. As in the previous section we will move in a clockwise fashion, starting at the mouth of the Indus and thence northwards to the valleys of the North West Frontier Province; then eastwards across the Punjab and the Pakistan border into East Punjab and Haryana. Finally, we shall turn our attention southwards through Rajasthan and Saurashtra.

Sindh Province. In Lower Sindh, Early Harappan sites are mainly located on firm ground, either on rock, as at Tharro, which has a stone fortification wall and was probably at that time still close to the

142   *Origins of a Civilization*

seashore, or on relatively hard ground at the edge of the Indus flood plain, as at Amri. Several related sites are found on the adjacent coastal strip to the west. Amri is archaeologically important because its excavation revealed a continuous sequence from the period of agricultural expansion through the Early Harappan into the Mature Harappan, and even into the post-urban period. It seems that the expansion of settlements was taking place from the hill valleys on the west down to the plains, and sites of the Amrian group are mainly found in the hinterland to the west of the Indus.

Only in exceptional circumstances are settlements of this period to be found east of the Indus, and then, like Kot Diji in the Rohri hills, they are also based on rock or other solid ground above the flood plain. Kot Diji is surrounded by a stone fortification wall, and has a well-documented culture sequence through the Early Harappan and into the Mature period. In the north-west of Sindh, the Mehrgarh sequence is taken up at nearby Nausharo. Only preliminary reports of the excavations at this important site have so far been published, but here too there is an excellent sequence through the Early Harappan period and into the Mature (Jarrige, 1993). Radiocarbon and other dates indicate that the Early Harappan period (I) began here at c. 2800 BC and passed through three recognizable phases before the beginning of the Mature Harappan around 2600-2500 BC. The sequence offers several exciting features, including compartmented copper seals in the second phase and numerous features which anticipate the Mature Harappan. A distinctive style of male terracotta figurines is characteristic of this period at Nausharo.

North-western Province. Following the Indus river northwards into the North West Frontier Province, Rahman Dheri shows a similar sequence, through from the period of Agricultural Expansion into the Early Harappan and (in a curiously muted fashion) into the Mature Harappan. Rahman Dheri apparently remained the same size and area as it had been in the previous period, and is the largest town reported in the region. A significant feature of the Early Harappan here is the presence of numerous stone seals, apparently anticipating the use of seals and script in the Mature Harappan period. For reasons which we shall explain below, the Rahman Dheri sequence is difficult to interpret, since chronologically the upper part appears to coincide with the Mature Harappan period, but without its characteristic artefacts. This suggests that it remained, for whatever reason, independent of the new style which had gained currency in much of the Indus system. In the Bannu Basin, a number

Farmers and Village Communities of the Indus System 143

of sites, such as Laklargai Dheri, Tarakai Qila and others, show a similar sequence. At the latter site stone seals occur, recalling those of Rahman Dheri. Many pots are marked with pre-firing signs. Here too the Mature Harappan is present, if at all, in a similarly muted form. In the western Punjab and northern valleys of the NWFP during the period of Agricultural Expansion as seen above, a distinctive culture arose. At Sarai Khola there is a clear-cut change to the second period when typical Early Harappan pottery makes its appearance around 2900 BC.

Punjab Province. To the south-east, in the Punjab plains at Jalilpur there is an equally clear break in the sequence, with the appearance of distinctly Early Harappan types of pottery. This site has so far not been dated. More important in every way must be Harappa on the bank of an old channel of the river Ravi. Here, the current American excavations have clearly demonstrated that an Early Harappan period settlement underlies the Mature Harappan city (Meadow, 1991). The Early Harappan at this site dates back to around 2900 BC, or perhaps a little earlier, and continues until the start of the Mature period, some four centuries later. The size of the early settlement has not yet been clearly delineated, but it was certainly considerable and, pending confirmation, may be estimated to be around 30 hectares. A significant discovery is a number of seals, and there are signs that the beginnings of writing may go back to the final stage of the Early Harappan. Already at this point it is becoming clear that the triangle formed by the Indus, Sutlej and the foothills of the Himalayas is an area which has so far produced little evidence of expansion or colonization during the Early Harappan period.

Eastern Province. South of the Sutlej, in the Cholistan desert, and east of the modern Indian border, we enter a different province, that of the dried-up Sarasvati river and the watershed between the rivers of the Indus system and those of the Ganges-Jamuna system. There are several important settlements in this area, a number of which are excavated. First is Kalibangan, on the banks of the now dry river; the radiocarbon dates are rather erratic, but they suggest a broad dating for the Early Harappan of c. 2900-2500 BC. The settlement appears to have been surrounded by a mud brick wall, and thus its precise area can be calculated at 4.5 hectares. Another interesting site is Banawali where a similar sequence is reported, but the early period is not radiocarbon dated. An important recent excavation is at Kunal, also in Haryana, where a clear sequence is reported from an early

144 *Origins of a Civilization*

Hakra period occupation, for which radiocarbon dates of c. 3000 BC are reported, through the Early Harappan stage, and on to Mature Harappan. Among important finds of this period are stone seals reminiscent of those recovered from comparably dated sites west of the Indus, such as Rahman Dheri. Still farther to the east are Rakhigarhi and Mitathal, both with an Early-Mature Harappan sequence but with ceramics that show a clear local character in the early phase, raising the question whether they should be classed as Early Harappan. In our view the many common features and forms justify their inclusion.

As mentioned earlier, the large group of sites in the Cholistan desert in Pakistan have been studied by Rafique Mughal (1990b): lying on the plain of the dried-up river, now part of the desert, many of them had been well-preserved and have enabled a whole settlement history for the region to be reconstructed. As we saw above, the oldest sites, those of the Hakra phase, belong to the same period as Jalilpur I and may be dated to the end of the period of Agricultural Expansion, i.e. c. 3500 BC. They are followed by the sites of the Early Harappan period of which around 40 have been recorded; and these in turn are followed by 174 Mature Harappan sites. Surprisingly, many of the sites of all periods are single period occupations, but a fair proportion were reoccupied in successive periods. The Early Harappan sites include two of between 20-30 hectares (Gamanwala, 27.3 hectares; Jalwali, 22.5 hectares), suggesting here, as at Rahman Dheri, that towns of no mean proportions grew up during the Early Harappan period. We must however regard these figures with some caution as it is not clear whether the areas were enclosed by town walls, and hence they may be rather generous. Curiously, the percentages of sites in the different ranges of size is more or less the same in this phase as it was in the previous Hakra phase.

Rajasthan. Some reference must be made to the position of Rajasthan, as it appears to have been a province in which indigenous cultural traditions flourished during Early Harappan times; and which even during the Mature Harappan urban period remained outside metropolitan influence, although there must have been trade and other contacts. There are many microlithic sites whose technology and choice of materials relates to the Mesolithic/Neolithic tradition of Central India, and which, as we have pointed out in an earlier chapter, probably represent both hunting and pastoral communities who must have had relations of various kinds with settled groups. From dated excavated sites it is apparent that the population included

Farmers and Village Communities of the Indus System 145

such communities, perhaps best represented at Bagor which, as we saw in an earlier chapter, begins life as a Mesolithic camp-site around 5000 BC., and by c. 3000 BC acquired, presumably through trade with neighbouring settlements, copper artefacts and pottery. The sources of their trade were probably in Rajasthan itself where, in the north, there is evidence, not as yet firmly dated, for an early settled population at the cluster of some fifty sites around Ganeshwar, which may date back to c. 3000 BC. These are situated near the Khetri copper deposits, where copper ore was extracted, and copious copper artefacts and evidence of copper smelting have been found. Similarly, in southern Rajasthan excavations at Ahar show another indigenous tradition, again with evidence of local copper smelting, which appears to have retained its own cultural character throughout both the Early and Mature Harappan periods.

Southern Province, Saurashtra and Gujarat. The position in Saurashtra and northern Gujarat is also not altogether clear. We are inclined to read it as showing that these areas too were more or less untouched by contact or colonization from the Indus valley prior to the beginning of the Mature Harappan, and that from c. 3000 BC onwards a local cultural tradition, rather than a broadly Early Harappan tradition, is manifested in such sites as early Prabhas Patan.

The Character of Early Harappan Incipient Urbanism

Our brief survey suggests that over a period of several centuries there was a steady expansion of settlements in the plains over almost every part of the Indus system. Exactly how this came about is not clear at present, but when we look at the full range of material remains of every kind—both from the sites we have referred to and many more—it becomes apparent that there are clear indications of increasing interaction and contact throughout the whole Indus system, and of the emergence of an inter-regional or Indus style. We shall now look briefly at some further aspects of this development and the evidence on which it is based.

Settlements and structures. The most substantial evidence of a settlement hierarchy comes from Mughal's Cholistan survey (referred to above). Here, in the preceding period of agricultural expansion, about half of all sites were temporary camp-sites, and only half were actual settlements. This presumably indicates that a substantial part of the

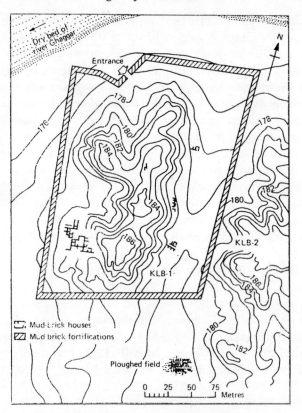

Fig. 19. Kalibangan, plan of Early Harappan town.

population were nomadic. In the Early Harappan period the picture changes: camp sites are only 7.5 per cent of the sample; 57 per cent of sites are simple settlements, while 35 per cent are classed as multifunctional sites, that is combining evidence of both settlement and craft or industrial specialization. Also striking is the evidence of the size of Early Harappan settlements: sixty per cent of sites are of less than 5 hectares; twenty-five per cent are between 5 and 10 hectares; and two sites are 22.5 and 27.3 hectares respectively. That Cholistan was not alone in having such a hierarchy is shown by the existence of comparably large sites elsewhere, even when the numbers of smaller sites are not known, being either buried or obliterated, or simply not found. We noted above that Rahman Dheri was around 22 hectares, Early Harappan Kalibangan at least 4.5 hectares, perhaps more, and Early Harappan Harappa at least 8.8 hectares.

Naturally, attention has been focussed on the larger settlements. Rahman Dheri suggests that the mud brick town walls were laid out

Farmers and Village Communities of the Indus System 147

on an oblong plan, with streets and houses on a regular grid pattern, and at least one major gate in the middle of the north and south walls (*Plate 38*). Several other Early Harappan settlements had town walls: at Kot Diji they were built of mud brick and stone; at Kalibangan of mud brick. The plan of Kalibangan is of a regular parallelogram on three sides, with an inset gateway on the north, toward the river (*Fig. 19*). There is much architectural detail available regarding houses, but this has still to be collated and critically compared. Mud brick appears to have been the general building material, and where stone was locally available this was also used. At Rahman Dheri and sites in the north-west region, courses of river pebbles were laid to form foundations for mud brick walls. So far there is no evidence of any other class of monumental structures, but there is ample evidence of kilns and of various craft activities within settlements.

Agriculture and subsistence. The range of distribution of settlements that we have been reviewing makes clear that there must have been many local variations of environment and hence of agricultural practice. However, there are common threads running through them all: for example, while the settlements are for the most part on firm ground, often on older alluvial deposits at a higher level than the modern flood plain and sometimes on rock, they are almost always close to active flood plains and therefore well-placed to exploit their agricultural and inundation or irrigational potential. It has been shown that there was a considerable increase in rainfall around 3000 BC (Singh 1971, Bryson & Swain 1981). This would have involved not only an increase in the summer monsoon rainfall, but more importantly of the winter rainfall, thus making the Lower Indus plains much more hospitable for agriculture and settlement. The probable nature of the agriculture was well-described by Lambrick (1964) who pointed out that two types of crop must have been grown, spring-harvested (*rabi*) and autumn-harvested (*kharif*). The first involved sowing seeds in the late summer or autumn on land which emerged after inundation by the river, or one of its tributaries or flood channels, and which would be ready to harvest by the following March or April. Such land often did not even require ploughing or irrigation, although growth would obviously be boosted if, as has been suggested above, there was more regular winter rainfall. This cropping pattern is well-adapted to producing wheat and barley. Autumn-harvested crops, such as cotton, sesamum (*til*) and pulses, would have required some irrigation. For this purpose, small field

148   *Origins of a Civilization*

embankments were probably raised, as they are today, before the annual flood, and water would flow into the enclosures and be impounded. There can be little reason to doubt that such methods of cultivation were developed and employed throughout the Indus system wherever they were applicable.

The archaeological evidence for Early Harappan plant economy is still somewhat unsatisfactory, as much research remains to be published. But the evidence of the earlier period at Mehrgarh on the one hand, and the much greater volume of evidence for the Mature Harappan period on the other, allow us to infer that many of the same crops and similar methods of cultivation persisted throughout. Wheat and barley in particular are the commonest basic crops; while legumes and pulses, sesamum and linseed, dates, grapes and jujube (*zizyphus*) are all reported. A discovery of great importance must have taken place during the Early Harappan period; this is the use of the plough. At Kalibangan a ploughed field was discovered which was covered by building debris of the early Mature Harappan period. This showed furrows crossing at right angles, the interval between those in one direction being about a fifth of that between those in the other. The excavator recognized this as a method of cropping two different plants on the same field, and which is still practised in the region today *(Plate 39)*. Evidence of ploughing is supported from another source; a number of terracotta models of ploughs have been found at Banawali and at Hakra sites along the old bed of the Sarasvati, on both sides of the modern Indo-Pakistan frontier. These however mainly belong to the subsequent Mature Harappan period.

Details of faunal remains from the Early Harappan period are also only partly published, and we can only repeat that the same predominance of cattle, sheep and goats is a constant feature wherever information is available. The current American excavations at Harappa indicate the wealth of material forthcoming from carefully conducted excavations and adequate specialist study of the results. As this material becomes available we expect that it will greatly enhance our knowledge of the Early Harappan period.

Crafts and technology. As with agriculture, many of the basic technological advances which had been made during the preceding periods were disseminated throughout the Indus system during the Early Harappan period. Again these crafts appear to represent an intermediate stage between the preceding periods and the Mature Harappan. Crafts include a stone-blade industry using high-quality flint brought from selected sources; the manufacture (or import

Farmers and Village Communities of the Indus System

from elsewhere) of heavier types of stone artefacts such as querns etc; the use of copper for making a range of small tools and weapons; a ceramic industry employing the potters' wheel and showing competence and skill in firing and decorative painting. Pottery now became an almost universal household possession; and a special feature was provided by the presence of sets of miniature pots, presumably toys, copying the forms of normal pots *(Plate 40)*. The manufacture of specialist items of adornment was also increasing, and included terracotta bangles and figurines. Terracotta models of bulls were particularly notable *(Plates 41 & 42)*. Several varieties of beads were made by specialized processes from semi-precious stones, ivory, bone and metal. Another highly specialized craft was that of making varieties of seals and or amulets out of stone, bone, ivory or clay.

There is no doubt that, when findings from the many excavated sites have been more fully published, there will be considerable information regarding actual craft centres and their activities, but until this happens and the results have been collated and studied, there is little more that can be said.

Trade and communications. During the Early Harappan period there appears to have been increasing contact and interaction between the several separate regional cultures of the previous period. We suggested that this was the result of growing trade and communication, and perhaps also indicated increasing political interaction and control. Earlier, we had referred to this process as one of 'cultural convergence', and this idea deserves further consideration. There is clear evidence that the potters over the whole Indus plains region began producing many standard forms of vessels and a limited repertoire of standard painted designs. Whether this standardization was achieved by trade or other means is still not clear, but the convergence is nonetheless a reality. In some marginal areas there is a remarkable change from a local or regional style in the previous period to the new inter-regional style; it is as though the latter had been introduced into that area at a certain point in time. But more generally there is a steady evolution from the earlier style into the new. We are inclined to interpret these developments as indications of the growing trade and interaction we spoke of. A similar inference may be drawn from a comparative study of other crafts and their products. Lahiri (1992) has made a systematic study of the available data and of the sources for the raw materials reported at published sites; one is left in no doubt of the range and extent of the trade and interaction which these things imply.

150   *Origins of a Civilization*

We know virtually nothing about the nature of the transport involved. It would probably be right to infer that longer distance trade would be by caravans of pack oxen or donkeys, as they certainly were in many parts of the subcontinent well into the nineteenth century. However, an innovation which was to have enormous ramifications throughout South Asia and which must have played a vital part in the development of both rural and urban life and trade, is in evidence from the Early Harappan period. This is the use of the wheel and the bullock-cart. The first evidence of the wheel comes from numerous terracotta models from sites such as Gumla, Rahman Dheri, Tarakai Qila, etc *(Plate 43)*. The models take the form of terracotta discs, modelled so as to reach their maximum thickness in the centre and then pierced with a circular hole to take an axle. Some are decorated with painted lines, suggesting the way in which solid wooden cart-wheels are still traditionally made in Sindh. At least by the beginning of the Mature Harappan period parts of terracotta models of timber cart-frames also appear at these sites. Both of these elements are well-known from the Harappan period, but the indications of their Early Harappan origins are particularly interesting. There is no positive evidence that the rivers were used, since no models or drawings of boats are known from this period, but it seems reasonable to expect that boats would have been employed.

Another interesting development in relation to trade is the appearance during the Early Harappan period of incised 'owners marks' upon pottery at many sites. It has been suggested that these are the predecessors of a script, as many of the marks coincide with later signs from the Mature Harappan script; even if this may not as yet be proven, at least they indicate that the need began to be felt for a means of communication through symbols. Even more significant in this context is the appearance of numerous stone seals during the Early Harappan period. As an example, significant evidence comes from Rahman Dheri, where the earliest seals are from the very beginning of the Early Harappan period, but larger numbers of seals are found from the later part of the period. Also important in this connection is the discovery at Lewan, in an Early Harappan context, of a lump of unburnt moulded clay with impressions of a cord and of fabric on the underside, and of two seal impressions on the upper. This suggests its use either for sealing a bale of merchandise, wrapped in a cotton fabric, or as a seal certifying the locking of a storeroom. One cannot but think of the modern Indian method of sewing up parcels and bales and sealing them with wax, as a descendant of such early examples.

All this evidence leads us to conclude that the term Early Harappan is used with good reason. Clearly, what is taking place in the centuries between 3000 and 2600 BC, alongside the continuing extension and spread of agricultural settlements over the Indus plains, is a build-up of human and technological resources and skills. The underlying continuity in almost every aspect of craft activity into the succeeding Mature Harappan period is everywhere in evidence. These things unquestionably form the foundation on which the subsequent Mature Harappan urban culture was established. In our discussion we have agreed closely with the conclusions reached by Mughal's detailed review of the evidence (1990a: 181-194). He recognizes that there are two phases of the Early Harappan period, the first beginning c. 3500-3400; and the second beginning c. five centuries later. He concludes that the 'core trends' of 'Urban Revolution' were already present before 3000 BC.

The evidence of internal trade, and perhaps already of some external trade, brings us to consider the ideas of Robert Adams (1974) regarding the 'homogenizing effects of trade—the way in which it leads to the forging of uniform regional and inter-regional styles' (cited by Possehl, 1986: 99-103). This summarizes precisely what we had in mind in our earlier reference to a process of cultural convergence. Another most significant instance of the same process is provided by the appearance of common symbols on painted pottery and other objects found in roughly contemporaneous contexts

Fig. 20. Kot Diji, Early Harappan 'horned deity' painted on pot.

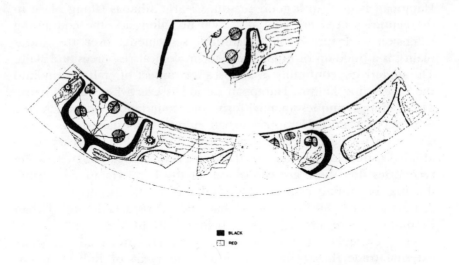

Fig. 21. Lewan, Early Harappan 'horned deities' painted on pot.

at widely separated sites over long distances. We previously cited (1982) the appearance of a buffalo-horned 'deity' on objects assignable to the Early Harappan period coming from sites as widely separated as Kot Diji *(Fig. 20)*, Gumla, Rahman Dheri, Lewan *(Fig. 21)*, Sarai Khola and Burzahom. These distinctive motifs deserve to be considered in relation to the appearance of a similar 'horned deity' in the iconographic repertoire of the Mature Harappan period. The suggestion is that not only did a common technology and life-style spread among widely separated settlements of the Early Harappan period, but that along with them went other less tangible elements of culture, including the establishment of a common fund of religious symbols and ideology.

Chapter 8

THE INDUS EMPIRE—SITES AND STRUCTURE

In this chapter we arrive at the culmination of a major part of this book. To some extent we may now change gear and treat the subject of the Mature Harappan civilization in a more holistic way than its predecessor. This is partly because over the years there have been so many publications offering descriptive accounts of the Indus civilization, so much detailed analysis of earlier excavations and fieldwork, so much recent research and synthesis, that it should now be possible to write at a more comprehensive level, not merely repeating what has been said before, but attempting to arrive at a clearer understanding of what the Indus civilization involved. There are other reasons for the subject's demanding fresh treatment. With the advance of knowledge over the past five decades it has become ever clearer that the Mature Indus civilization is not an isolated phenomenon; rather it must be regarded as an integral part of a process which began on the periphery of the Indus system with the beginning of agriculture, spread widely throughout the Indus system, and continued through the periods of Expansion of Agriculture and Early Harappan urbanism. When this model was first suggested some three decades back (Allchin and Allchin, 1968: 125; Mughal, 1971; Fairservis, 1971: 306), it was necessarily stated in a tentative way. Now the whole context is much clearer, and it follows that the pre-occupation of some earlier writers with seeking an outside source from which 'civilization' might have been introduced into the Indus world, and postulating migrations of already civilized peoples who might have brought either the 'idea' of civilization or an actual civilization with them (!), may be regarded as a chimera. As we see it the Indus civilization arose in the piedmont regions and plains of the Indus system, and was the creation of a long established population who were culturally, and perhaps also genetically, the direct precursors of that of the Mature Indus period. For all these reasons the term Early Harappan appears to us to be more appropriate than the term Pre-Harappan.

154 *Origins of a Civilization*

A CIVILIZATION IN THE MAKING

During the past decade the growing number of radiocarbon dates, and the refinement of their calibration, have made possible a clearer view of the time-scale of the emergence of the full urbanism of the Mature Harappan civilization. It may now be generally accepted that the century between 2600 and 2500 BC was a time of what Possehl (1990; 1994a: 106) has called 'paroxysmal change', as if the steadily increasing tempo of expansion and integration of the preceding three or four centuries had suddenly arrived at a point of 'melt down', so that within the space of one century a new social and political order emerged.

It must be admitted that the archaeological data from which to interpret this period of transformation have been, up till now, very limited. The existence of a 'transitional' period between the Early Harappan and the beginning of the Mature was first recognized by Casal at Amri (1964), but there are no radiocarbon datings directly relating to it. Other evidence for the period at Amri is slight. In the Kot Diji excavations (Khan 1965) there is a suggestion of a 'mixed' layer, which has been analyzed by Mughal (1990a), but which can scarcely be said to reveal a transitional period. Two more recent excavations at Nausharo (Jarrige 1993) and at Harappa (Meadow 1991) have both shown a clear progression from Early Harappan to Mature via an intermediate phase, but neither has been fully published to date, nor are there enough radiocarbon dates to establish their age or what exactly constitutes their transitional character.

Nevertheless, the nature of the developments witnessed by this remarkable century of change needs to be understood, and deserves consideration. There is a good discussion by Possehl (1990), where the need for an anthropological, as well as archaeological, perspective is recognized. Possehl draws attention to the manifest evidence of cultural continuity linking the Early and Mature Harappan stages, but remarks that there are also important elements of discontinuity which separate them. He admirably formulates the position:

> . . . it should be recalled that continuity, not discontinuity, is the dominant theme as we examine the emergence of the Indus civilization. . . . The intertwining themes of continuity and change must be understood, weighed and controlled; both dynamics are present and important.

It is not easy to identify with assurance what are the main changes

The Indus Empire 155

that constitute discontinuity with the previous period. This is because in almost every case both a continuity and change can be discerned, simultaneously at work. It is as though a steady process of quantitative change builds up to a point at which an abrupt qualitative change takes place. A pertinent example of the latter is the evidence related to the invention of writing, in the form of the Harappan script. Thanks to the current excavations at Harappa this can now be pinpointed at around 2600 BC. We shall discuss this topic more fully below. Another new element is the way in which at one site after another the settlements planned and constructed during the Early Harappan period are abandoned, and on top of them new, larger and more complex structural complexes are superimposed. In the course of this change the regular features associated with the Mature Harappan, such as drainage systems, wells, etc., appear. These too are touched upon below.

A third way in which changes occur is in the development of additional, more specialized urban industries and crafts. Looking back at the various industrial traditions of the previous periods in stone, metallurgy, pottery, etc. we can clearly perceive that they represent part of an old but steadily evolving tradition, and in some ways may be regarded as pre-urban rather than urban. But during the Mature period they are augmented by a variety of specialized urban crafts. For example, terracotta bangles fired with both red and grey colouring were a regular feature of Early Harappan sites, but now a more complex type of stoneware bangle, its manufacture involving firing the pieces while they were sealed in clay saggars, and often bearing scratched inscriptions suggestive of their luxury status, is found alongside them. A fourth new element is the imposition of a series of standardized weights and measures, pointing to some attempt to regularize such things as brick sizes, street widths, etc., and indicating their usefulness for purposes of trade and exchange.

One other aspect of the 'century of change' may be remarked on. Possehl (1990) points out that there is a considerable difference between the steady development of civilization in Mesopotamia, and the comparatively uneven pace of change witnessed in the Indus system during the Early and Mature Harappan periods. He refers to a marked contrast between the Early Harappan period, and the Uruk period in Mesopotamia (i.e. c. 3500-3000 BC) where we see signs of developments which began millennia earlier and flowered into full urban life during Jemdet Nasr and Early Dynastic times (i.e. c. 3000-2500 BC). This leads Possehl to suggest that trade with Mesopotamia may have played a significant role in the century of change in the

156 *Origins of a Civilization*

Indus culture. The role of trade will be discussed in greater detail below.

In the absence of firm evidence it is probably best to accept that we cannot clearly point to a single centre or area in which the Mature Harappan style first emerged, and from which it spread: rather it is more plausible to assume that it made its appearance more or less simultaneously over all those parts of the Indus system where its undiluted presence can be observed: this area we shall regard as the Indus heartland.

Extent. Stated in general terms the Mature Harappan culture occupies largely the same area as its predecessor, but with a number of significant differences. In reviewing them we shall therefore follow much the same route as in our review of the Early Harappan in the previous chapter. It seems logical to retain the same concept of provinces, using the term in a geographical rather than a political or administrative sense. For a further more detailed account the reader is referred to Mughal's comparative study of the extent of the Early and Mature Harappan (1992a), and to Kenoyer's synthetic study of the Indus valley tradition (1991).

Sindh province. The distribution of sites in Sindh province is largely dictated by the geographical confines of the Indus plains and and its delta, and as in the earlier period, scarcely extends westwards into the Baluchi hills, where indigenous cultural traditions continued, nor eastwards beyond the desert. A significant extension is, however, to be found along the coast to the west, where several sites which were evidently Harappan trading stations, colonies or outposts, have been found at intervals virtually up to the modern Iranian border. The only site so far studied systematically is Sutkagen-dor, on the Dasht river near the border with Iran, surrounded by a massive stone wall. Balakot, near Las Bela, is another coastal site which during Harappan times had a major shell industry. One has the impression that beyond these sites the Baluchi coastal strip too was otherwise outside the direct Harappan sphere of influence, and may rather have been in the hands of what Ratnagar (1994) refers to as client chiefdoms.

Sindh province has Mohenjo-daro, probably the largest Harappan city, now estimated to have covered some 100-200 hectares at the maximum, and which is certainly the most excavated. There are also several sites of the second grade (10-50 hectares), including Judeirjo-daro on the route between the Kacchi plain and the Indus; several of the third grade (5-10 hectares), including the industrial centre

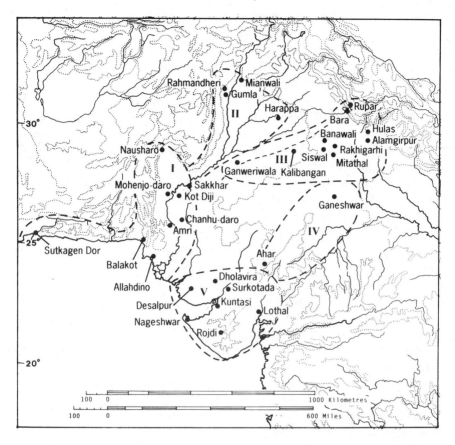

Map. 5. *The Indus Civilization, showing main regions and sites discussed in Chapters 8 and 9:—I. Sindh Province; II. Punjab and the North-west; III. Eastern Province; IV. Central and Southern Rajasthan; V. Southern Province.*

Chanhu-daro; and numbers of fourth grade (1-5 hectares) including Kot Diji on the edge of the Rohri hills. Although, there is no way of conclusively proving that Sindh, with Mohenjo-daro as its epicentre, was the core area in which the Mature Indus civilization first appeared, we are personally inclined to think that it was. But in another sense the heartland of the Mature culture was considerably wider and included also at least some part of the Punjab, the Ghaggar-Hakra valley, and even marginally part of the North West Frontier Province. As we shall see, there are clear indications of interaction with neighbouring chiefdoms or states, and even an outward expansion into a number of adjacent regions, in which settlements persisted which retained an Early Harappan style.

158   *Origins of a Civilization*

Punjab and North-western Province. In this period we have combined two provinces of the previous period, because in the Mature period a rather different situation seems to have prevailed. To the west of the Indus most of the sites known to us appear to remain part of a local tradition, rather than exhibiting a full Harappan style of culture. A good example of this is Rahman Dheri where radiocarbon dates indicate that the third major period is contemporary with the Mature Harappan although the material culture and particularly the pottery remains predominantly in the Early Harappan tradition, and offers few diagnostic signs of Mature Harappan contact. A comparable situation is found at Gumla, where period IV is patently contemporary with the Mature Harappan but sufficiently distinct from it to lead us to a similar conclusion. It is possible that the situation was like that which we shall see in the other provinces, where a number of settlements showing distinctive Mature Harappan features are found interspersed among sites continuing the Early Harappan tradition. On the basis of present information we believe that Mianwali on the Indus is the northernmost Harappan site in the west of the province. To the north-east Harappa stands alone as a first magnitude site being the same size as Mohenjo-daro. Its location has led several authors to conclude that it was a 'gateway city', on the edge of the Harappan domain and marking a meeting point for routes arriving from the Gomal and other passes leading into the Iranian plateau. A Harappan site is reported near Lahore, but in general it appears that in the northern part of the region and in the Potwar-Siwalik area the few early sites known continue in the Early Harappan tradition. Although the northern limits of the Mature civilization are still not precisely defined, some picture is emerging.

The south-eastern limits of this province broadly follow the southern edge of the Ghaggar-Hakra valley as they extend towards the north-east through the Cholistan desert. This is the area in which Mughal made his remarkable exploration and produced very important evidence relating to the changing pattern of settlement from period to period (cited in the previous chapter). In the Cholistan area he records that there is a marked shift of settlements during the Mature Harappan period from the north-east towards the south-west, and a marked increase in both the number of settlements (40 for the Early Harappan and 74 for the Mature), and of their size. For the Mature Harappan period one site, Ganweriwala, is of the first magnitude, being roughly the same size as Mohenjo-daro and Harappa; while 8 sites belong to the second grade (10-50 hectares); 20 to the third grade (5-10 hectares); and 44 to the fourth (1-5 hectares). A special feature is

The Indus Empire 159

the increase in the number of special purpose or industrial sites.

Eastern province. Lying to the east of the previous province, and substantially east of the modern Indo-Pakistan frontier is an intriguing and difficult region which includes the eastern parts of the Punjab, northern Rajasthan and Haryana. Here, we encounter two classes of sites, some continuing to show local Early Harappan features, while certain others, mainly larger, indicate the introduction of typically Mature Harappan elements (not only in common objects such as pottery, but also in seals and inscriptions). In the west, there are such major settlements as Kalibangan, where the Harappan town (a second grade site, some 12.5 hectares) is built over the remains of the Early Harappan; farther east along the course of the Ghaggar-Hakra is Banawali (a third grade-site of about 15.5 hectares), similarly built on an earlier settlement; while to the south-east lie Rakhigarhi, (probably a second grade-site of about 24 hectares), and Miṭathal. Although further detailed fieldwork, small-scale excavation and analysis of data is still needed before a clearer interpretation of the sites of this area is possible, the impression offered is of the penetration of urban Harappan elements into an already settled environment. The larger sites reveal an urban Harappan presence of a kind not as yet recorded in the smaller. Several interpretations suggest themselves. This seems to represent a culture contact situation, perhaps involving an outward thrust or 'colonial' expansion from the Harappan heartland; or at least the establishment of trade relations, perhaps involving interaction with local client chiefdoms or even nascent states in client roles.

Before we leave this area we must mention an intriguing report of a site-complex discovered by J.P. Joshi (1991). Broadly, lying along the bank of the Sarhind stream, a tributary of the now dry Ghaggar river, Joshi discovered a remarkable complex of major settlements, five of which had areas of between 225 and 100 hectares, ranking them as our first grade, while several other sites were of second grade. This site-complex appears to be something peculiar, and one may not be far wrong in accepting Joshi's concept of its having been an 'economic zone'. This discovery calls for urgent study, more accurate survey pilot excavation, and more precise definition of the exact age and period represented by these sites.

Central and southern Rajasthan. In Central and southern Rajasthan we find a similar state to that noticed in the Early Harappan period. Here, it seems that local cultures continued to flourish, linked in the

160   *Origins of a Civilization*

north to the important copper deposits around Khetri and including sites of the Ganeshwar group; and likewise, in the south, linked to further copper deposits and associated with sites of the Ahar culture. It seems certain that these two 'cultures' remained independent while they enjoyed trade relations with the urban Harappan culture, of which, for one reason or another they did not become a part. In the absence of clearer evidence and firmer dating one can only assume that these entities were able to resist the sort of expansionism we have suspected along the northern and north-eastern fringes of the Harappan culture area, and maintained a client or trade relationship, based in no small measure upon their copper production.

Southern province, Saurashtra and Gujarat. These areas are reasonably well-known, archaeologically, and hence a firmer picture emerges, which however is still complex and problematic. We have noted in the previous chapter that an Early Harappan culture pattern comparable to that of the Sindh heartland is not in evidence here, but that several local cultures arose at that time. During the Mature Harappan period a new element occurs in the pottery at many sites, which in consequence have been referred to as the 'Sorath Harappan'. We are inclined to refer to them as 'local Harappan', because it appears to be a local development taking place under the influence of the Mature Harappan culture, but demonstrably different to it in certain respects (Possehl & Raval, 1989; Sonawane & Ajithprasad, 1994).

In addition to the local or Sorath Harappan, there are certain sites where more typical Mature Harappan traits occur in association with a combination of local Harappan and/or purely local pottery. We are inclined to regard certain typical artifacts, particularly Harappan seals or inscriptions, as at Lothal, Surkotada, Desalpur, Dholavira or Rojdi, as hallmarks of a Mature Harappan presence, and as indications of the presence of a Harappan element in the population. This element we may expect to be represented by trading communities at ports such as Lothal, Nageshwar or Kuntasi, or actual colonies at, for example, Dholavira. Apart from actual ports the main area showing Mature Harappan elements is in the north of Saurashtra, in what is more properly called Kacch. This model may well require refinement once fuller publication of a number of the sites is available.

Among the Mature Harappan sites Dholavira, in northern Kacch, is the largest, having an enclosed area of c. 47 hectares (to be described below). It is interesting to enquire whether the presence of

The Indus Empire

sites identified as representing a Mature Harappan presence in the northern part of the area is a result of their being in close proximity with Sindh, because in Saurashtra proper, with the exception of Lothal and perhaps Rojdi, sites have been identified as either of local or of 'local Harappan' traditions.

Conclusion—the Harappan heartland. In terms of this rather cursory survey, it seems necessary to recognize some differentiation between the total area in which the Early Harappan culture flourished, or to which it spread during the course of the Early Harappan period, and the somewhat more restricted area which can be identified as Mature Harappan. This difference has been notably discussed by Mughal (1992a) who sees a major shift in cultural interaction with the greater Indus system from the northern to the southern parts of Baluchistan, with a spread along the coast towards both west and east; and more generally a shift of focus from the northern parts of the Indus system towards the southern. We are inclined to follow Mughal in seeing some connection between this shift and the rising interest in trade with Mesopotamia. This may well be the reason why the Mature Harappan heartland is centered on the coast and the Lower and Middle Indus valley.

CITIES AND SITES

The first cities of the Indus to be identified as such were Mohenjo-daro and Harappa, and the similarities of their basic layout were commented on by Wheeler (1947: 62) as being 'something more than coincidence'. It soon became clear that there was a broad parallel between both: to the west lay a high mound, approximately oriented on a north-south axis, and in both cases approximately twice as long as they were wide, while to the east was a more extensive area of occupation. It became common to refer to these two features as 'the Citadel' and the 'Lower Town' respectively. Another remarkable feature was that both the cities were approximately the same size. When the Archaeological Survey carried out its still largely unpublished excavations at Kalibangan, it was soon evident that its plan was also in many respects similar, although smaller than the other two cities. Like Harappa it stood on the southern bank of a river, with its orientation equally firmly north-south. The plan of the Kalibangan citadel was also clearly revealed, consisting of two almost equal rhomboids, divided from one

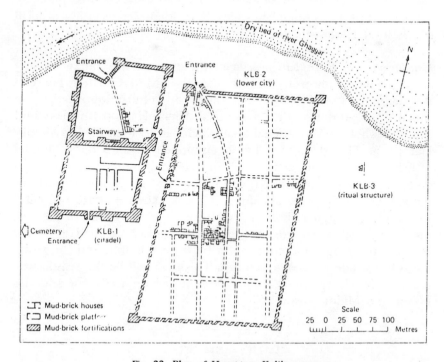

Fig. 22. Plan of Harappan Kalibangan.

another by a strong wall *(Fig 22)*. Of these two the northern half was found to contain regular housing; while the southern half, approached through a major gate from the south, contained a series of mysterious brick platforms, probably having some religious significance, perhaps as scenes of sacrifice. The lower town also had a regular grid of streets, recalling those of Mohenjo-daro. Another surprising similarity was that in all three cases there appeared to be regular ratios of size between different elements of the urban plan: at Kalibangan the citadel being approximately 120 x 240 m. and the lower town 200 x 400 m. At Mohenjo-daro the equivalent figures were approximately 200 x 400 m. and 400 x 800 m.; suggesting that the two larger cities were literally four times the area of the smaller. The subsequent discovery and excavation of Surkotada showed a still smaller variant form consisting of two near square fortified areas, aligned more or less on an east-west axis, and measuring c. 60 x 120m *(Fig 23)*. Several other major sites have been reported to share a plan involving a

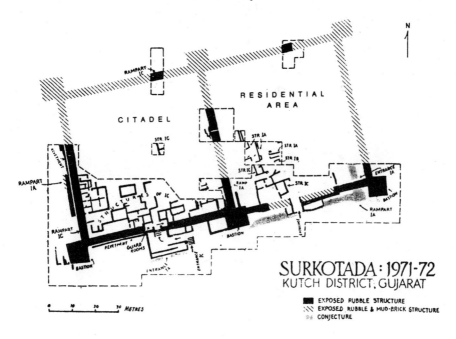

Fig. 23. Plan of Harappan Surkotada.

citadel and lower town, but have not been excavated or published. It is worth commenting that the citadel mounds appeared in each case to have been artificially raised by the construction of massive mud brick platforms, at Kalibangan and Harappa, actually above occupation of the Early Harappan period.

More recently two further Harappan sites have been excavated which serve to dispel something of the picture of apparent uniformity of the planning of settlements. At Banawali the town is surrounded by a brick-walled enclosure of somewhat irregular form, suggesting that originally its plan was a rhomboid of c. 240 x 300 m. (Bisht 1982; IAR 1983-84). However, the south-east corner, close to the bank of the Ghaggar river, is somewhat strange and may have been an indented area, reminiscent of that found at Kalibangan, designed to catch the breeze from the flood plain of the river. There is no clear citadel at Banawali, but one quadrant of the enclosed area was divided off from the remainder, representing approximately half of the total area, by a massive brick wall. This area includes some high ground where structures were built over the earlier occupation and, whatever its function may have been, this feature is regarded by its excavator as an 'Acropolis'.

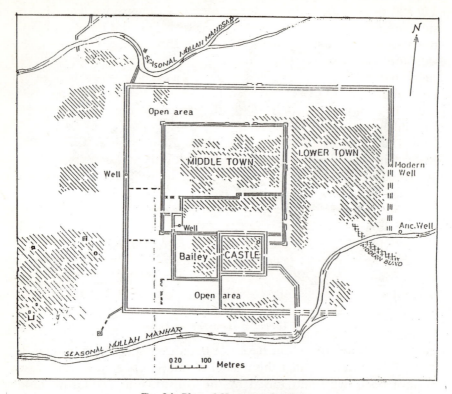

Fig. 24. Plan of Harappan Dholavira.

The other important site is Dholavira in Kacch (*Fig. 24*). Although excavations have been going on for several seasons, little has so far been published regarding whole aspects of the work and nature of the settlement (Bisht 1989; 1991). The site is on a desolate island in the northern part of the Rann. It appears that an earlier occupation existed on the site, but whether this should be classified as Early Harappan or as a local culture, is not yet clear. The main site is rectangular, surrounded by a wall of stone rubble and mud brick, some 700 m. east to west and 600 m. north to south. Within this enclosed area there are several major features. In the eastern sector is a main area which the excavator names 'the Lower Town', but which is otherwise not clearly described. To its west lies a square area of around 300 m., also surrounded by a wall and referred to as 'the Middle Town'; and adjoining it to the south are two smaller square-walled areas, the 'Castle' and the 'Bailey'. The former is described as standing majestically to a maximum height of 16 metres, surrounded

The Indus Empire

by stone-faced ramparts with mud-brick filling, measuring around 140-120 m. The Bailey is of nearly identical dimensions, and is also surrounded by a wall. The excavator tells us that the main walls are remarkably strongly constructed, having three parallel stone walls with infilling of mud brick between them. We are not sure that the suggested defensive nature of the Castle and Bailey is correct; it may be that if and when these features are more extensively excavated they will be found to be closer to the Citadel complex at Kalibangan, for which a religious function is generally accepted. Structural finds from Dholavira include some fine ashlar masonry slabs, stone pillar bases and stairs, of a quality hitherto not recorded at any other Harappan site. There are also reports of impressive water supply and drainage structures.

Among the finds recorded from Dholavira are quantities of copper objects including a bronze animal figurine, and much evidence of copper working; there are also bead-working shops, and evidence of other craft activities. Finds include numbers of typical Harappan seals, some inscribed. Another extraordinary find is a Harappan inscription with nine letters each c. 37 cm. in height, composed of inland cut pieces of a milk-white material. Evidently, the inscription had originally been mounted on some kind of board above a gateway and, after falling face downwards on to the ground, had been left to lie undisturbed. All in all Dholavira appears to be one of the most exciting discoveries of the past half century!

Architecture and monumental types. There is extensive evidence relating to the main features of the architecture and building techniques of both common houses and larger monuments. The general features of the domestic architecture have been frequently described in earlier publications and we shall not repeat them here. We should however also point to the volume of recent research carried out by Michael Jansen and his colleagues relating to the drainage and water supply at Mohenjo-daro (Jansen, 1987, 1993, etc.). This aspect is one which has attracted less attention at other cities, but nonetheless deserves it. One of the common features that has emerged with the increasing number of excavated cities is the presence of massive surrounding walls; these may be built of mud brick, burnt brick or stone, where locally available, and are in most instances interspersed by square bastions or towers at the corners. There are also reports of square towers at some major gateways. Among the monuments are the Great Bath, the so-called granary and the pillared hall at Mohenjo-daro; the Great Granary excavated at Harappa (looking very much

166 *Origins of a Civilization*

like the descendant of the compartmented granaries of Mehrgarh, several millennia earlier); and the citadel of Kalibangan. Most of these were already well-described in the prime reports, and have been further discussed by many scholars since. For this reason we shall not repeat this descriptive material, and comment only briefly on some matters.

The function of the 'citadels' and the monuments that have been discovered on them, becomes more complex with each new discovery. At Mohenjo-daro they include the Great Bath, whose architecture has been reassessed with meticulous detail by Jansen (1993). There has been general agreement that the bath must have had a religious function. A recent publication has drawn attention to the existence of rather similar baths, apparently used ritually in contemporary Elam (Gropp, 1992). The adjacent 'Great Granary', a term which in our view is almost certainly a misnomer, we believe to have had some civic function, probably linked to religious ritual. It consists of a number of brick platforms with finely laid brickwork paths between them, and recalls the brick platforms in the southern sector of the Kalibangan citadel, where there is evidence of associated animal sacrifice and ritual hearths. A third major monument on the Mohenjo-daro Citadel is the pillared hall, whose brick floor and pillar bases was discovered by Marshall.

Special purpose sites and areas. Apart from major settlements or cities there are a number of special purpose sites, although few have been excavated or published. As we saw above there appear to have been a number of ports or trading posts: some situated on the coastline within territories apparently comprising parts of the Harappan domain; and others outside the domain. The best known of these sites is Lothal, on the Gulf of Cambay, which has been both extensively excavated and fully published (Rao, 1979, 1985). Here, a small oblong settlement surrounded by a sturdy mud-brick wall stood near a tributary of the Sabarmati river *(Fig 25)*. Whether some parts of the site stood on a brick platform, and if so how much, is not altogether clear, but certainly in the south-east corner an extensive area of such brickwork was found, and described by the excavator as an 'Acropolis'. In this sector a group of twelve brick platforms is reasonably identified as a storehouse, as many clay sealings were discovered in it, some with the impressions of the cords and materials used for wrapping bales visible on their undersides. Along the east side of the site ran a brick platform, described as a wharf, and beside it was a remarkable burnt brick basin of around 219 x 13 m. in size, which the excavator

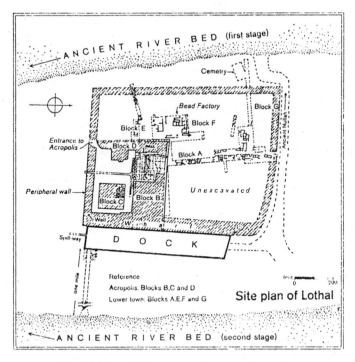

Fig. 25. Plan of Harappan trading station at Lothal.

described as a dockyard. Plausible as this seems, we must point to the difficulty it raises, in that the sill of the main entrance to the dock is at a level which would make it seem that ships of even modest draft could only enter when the surrounding water level was so high as virtually to inundate the whole settlement. An interesting complex in the excavation revealed a whole bead factory, with ample raw material and waste from which to identify its function and deduce the techniques of manufacture.

Another site identified as a port comes from western Saurashtra, where excavations at Kuntasi on the Phulki river have revealed a small Mature Harappan settlement, which Dhavalikar (1993, 1995) identifies as a craft centre. Here, typical Harappan seals, some with inscriptions, were found. The evidence for craft activity included bead-making, among them long-barrel carnelian beads, beads of faience and steatite, of lapis lazuli, bangles of shank and ivory, and perhaps also copper smelting are in evidence. Also, numerous furnaces and storage areas were found. Yet another such site was at Nageshwar where a shell-working industry was discovered.

168 *Origins of a Civilization*

We have noted above that Sutkagen-dor, near the Iranian frontier, appears to have been another riverside trading post. Dales (1962) has given a good description of the remains, but it has not been excavated; nor have other probable ports along the Makran coast. Balakot near Las Bela, excavated by Dales (1979) revealed evidence of a large-scale industry in Harappan times, manufacturing bangles and other items from varieties of shell.

We must also mention, however briefly, the discovery of a Harappan outpost at Shortughai in north-eastern Afghanistan (Frankfort, 1989). This site was evidently located near to Badakshan so as to benefit by and perhaps control the mining of lapis lazuli and other precious materials from this area. The typical ceramics and metal objects found there suggest that craftsmen from the Indus must have accompanied the traders to this remote spot.

Other special purpose sites or areas deserve mention. Chanhu-daro produced evidence of a variety of industrial activities: a bead-making factory was excavated by Mackay (1937); at another spot extensive evidence of the in situ manufacture of bangles and other items of conch shell were discovered. At Harappa one may mention the industrial area lying to the north of the Citadel mound, with its evidence of copper working, and also the nearby granaries or warehouses excavated by Vats, and built upon a series of raised brick platforms. We recall the concentration of sites on the Sarhind stream in Haryana, discovered by J. P. Joshi (1991), who identified them as an industrial complex; and finally we may mention the many industrial sites reported by Mughal in Cholistan. It is not clear from publication to date what industries these represent. Another site, close to Rahman Dheri, was evidently devoted to the manufacture of the distinctive Harappan terracotta 'cakes'.

Agriculture and Other Subsistence Strategies

The evidence suggests that there was a further, considerable increase in rainfall around 3000 BC and that the favourable regime continued until c. 1800 BC (Singh 1971). This provided a natural boost to agricultural production, particularly as it involved both an increase in monsoon precipitation and more importantly in winter rainfall. There is more evidence of Mature Harappan agriculture from a larger number of sites than for any previous period. Studies are available of both wheat and barley from several sites (principally Mohenjo-daro, Harappa, Chanhu-daro,

The Indus Empire 169

Kalibangan and Nausharo): three principal varieties of wheat occur *(Triticum aestivum, Triticum compactum,* and *Triticum sphaerococcum),* and three of barley *(Hordeum vulgare, Hordeum nudum vulgare,* and *Hordeum sphaerococcum).* Various legumes have been found including lentils *(Lens culinaris)* from Nausharo; chickpea *(Cicer arietinum)* from Kalibangan; and field pea *(Pisum arvense)* from Harappa. Stones of date, grape and jujube also occur. Among oilseeds, mustard *(Brassica juncea),* linseed *(Linum usitatissimum)* and sesamum *(Sesamum indicum)* have been found. Finally, cotton *(Gossypium sp.)* has been reported at Mohenjo-daro. Another discovery of great significance is of a number of millets: *Eleusine Coracana,* finger millet, *ragi,* from the lowest levels of Rojdi; *bajra, (Pennisetum typhoideum),* from Babar Kot in Saurashtra and, at a slightly later date, sorghum, *jawar, (Sorghum bicolor)* probably all present as introductions from Africa, and due to assume a significant role in areas of low rainfall throughout South Asia during subsequent, post-Harappan times (Possehl, in press). It seems likely that these African introductions were a by-product of the rise of sea trade between India and the ports of Mesopotamia and the Gulf. It may be remarked that rice is not strictly present in any Mature Harappan site, so its occurrence at Rangpur in Gujarat may more safely be assigned to the post-urban period.

We have already mentioned the discovery of a ploughed field surface at Kalibangan dating from the period of interface of the Early and Mature Harappan periods, and to the not infrequent finds of terracotta model ploughs, datable to the Mature Harappan period, in the Punjab and Ghaggar valleys. The introduction of the plough, and the development of complex field regimens, involving in some cases furrows crossing in both directions, one series closer together and the other wider, suggests considerable agricultural sophistication. That the ploughs were simple wooden 'ards', without ploughshares for turning the soil, was not of great importance in the fine alluvial silts of the Indus plains, where to this day the same forms of plough as we can see in the terracotta models are still to be seen in use in the fields *(Figs. 26 and Plate 44).* What was important was that with the growing availability of plough cultivation an agricultural revolution capable of great increases in crop production was achieved. All told, one has the impression that some aspects of Harappan agriculture followed very closely on the pattern which we infer to have spread during the period of agricultural expansion. If there was change it seems to have been in the marshalling of productive forces, choosing the most suitable areas for various crops, exploiting the several types of flood irrigation, where relevant, and rainfall, well and perhaps

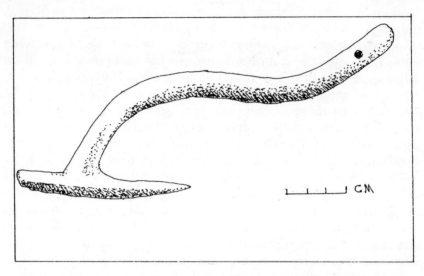

Fig. 26. Banawali, drawing of terracotta model of a wooden plough, Harappan period.

canal irrigation where feasible. Inevitably, the growing size of cities must have necessitated employment of transport of food products from agricultural to urban areas, and the construction of larger storage facilities within cities.

The animal husbandry which accompanied the agriculture seems still to have been based upon the keeping of cattle, particularly *Bos indicus*, sheep and goats. Bones of pig are also regularly found, suggesting that pigs were kept within the orbit of settlements, probably much as today, that is to say running wild and acting as scavengers. Jungle fowl also appears to have been domesticated. Bones of buffalo are found rarely and seem to indicate that the buffalo was at this period not yet regarded as a domesticated species. Bones of elephant and camel also occur rarely and it is not clear whether either species was as yet fully domesticated.

The total picture of Harappan subsistence probably was complex, involving also specialist groups of pastoralists breeding and herding cattle, sheep and goats, and selling their products to the settled population. These people may have been either settled on the periphery of regular settlements, or semi-nomadic, living for periods of the year in forests or grazing lands. It is also possible that some groups engaged in the organization of transport of goods and thus provided a service for traders. As part of this complex society there must still have been many tribal groups of hunters and collectors,

The Indus Empire 171

similarly related to settled populations. These people may have been responsible for the numbers of wild animal bones recovered, thus supplying the city population with various types of game. The evidence of the consumption of fish at most riverine sites is certain proof that fish was also a regular item of diet, leading one to suspect that there were specialist groups who were responsible for catching fish.

Crafts, Industries, Factories and Workshops

We noticed above that much of the basic technology and craft skills inherited by the Mature Harappan civilization was the direct legacy of an already ancient tradition within the Greater Indus system. These crafts have for the most part been described in a general manner and some have been studied more completely. But it is only in the past few years that serious attention has been given to their study. Two main lines of research can now be recognized: the first is to study the technologies involved in the different industries and crafts with the aid of proper scientific analysis; the other is to attempt to rediscover details of the organization of craft production, the degrees of specialization, social stratification, and localization involved, etc. An excellent survey of recent work has been published by Bhan, Vidale and Kenoyer (1994), with a helpful bibliography.

During the Mature Harappan period new products of technically complex crafts appear, some of which are explicitly urban. Some of these have also received detailed attention and are well-described. The range of crafts is quite extensive. They include metallurgy, the smelting and alloying of copper and bronze, working in gold, electrum, silver and lead; working in stone, making stone blades, and larger objects, such as querns; bead-making from semi-precious stones, particularly carnelian, metals, paste, shell and ivory; ivory carving; production of pottery, terracotta figurines and bangles; a special craft was the production of stoneware bangles; faience was made, both of the more common silica type and of a ground steatite paste; steatite was also used for various products, such as beads, inlays and particularly for the manufacture of the distinctive Harappan seals which are one of the hallmarks of the whole civilization; and last but not the least, stone-carving, producing the small but interesting repertoire of sculptures known from the major cities. There must also have been a number of crafts of which few if any recognizable traces survive, among them the manufacture of textiles, and particularly cotton, is probably the most important. The existence of

172 *Origins of a Civilization*

cotton is known from one small fragment of textile which had been preserved by chemical reaction, and by large numbers of cloth impressions inside small faience vessels which had been formed around cotton bags filled with sand.

In the light of all this material our present aim is to consider aspects of some of the industries which have been studied and which throw some light on the organization of production and related matters.

We saw in a previous chapter that the Indus valley, with its strictly limited sources of workable stone was, since very early times, remarkable for the way in which certain places, where good supplies of suitable materials were available, had been exploited through the ages. One example of this is the Rohri hills where from Lower Palaeolithic times onwards people had come to make stone tools, and where stone procurement and working continued throughout the Mature Indus civilization. When we made a brief survey of some of the hills in the seventies we were astonished to find spots where actual workplaces were still clearly visible. The hills are all flat-topped, and many have a deep layer of large nodules of fine grey or buff flint, weathered on the outside to a dark blackish brown. Everywhere we went, the uppermost nodules had been used as a source of flint for tool-making in earlier times and the ground was strewn with broken and unfinished artefacts and debris from their manufacture. Selected areas on some of the hills had been cleared by the Indus workmen, and all the earlier debris tipped down the hillside to expose the unused nodules beneath. Further groups of small areas, each large enough for a man to sit on cross-legged, had then been cleared completely (*Plate 45*). In front of each were piles of broken blade cores and blades of the distinctive Indus kind, debris from various stages of their manufacture and hammer stones still as the workmen must have left them. Indus blades and blade cores can be distinguished from those of earlier periods by their greater length and regularity, which is considered to have been achieved by the use of a copper punch, possibly set into the ground, for removing blades. Although quantities of selected raw materials, debris and broken stone blades were scattered around, unfortunately we could see no other tools such as metal points or hammers of bone or other materials that might have given more precise indications of how the blades were produced. This was clearly a major industrial area and source of supply for settlements in the plains.

What probably distinguishes the Indus period from those of previous users of the flint resources is the clear indication that the blades were transported to the nearby river bank where they were

The Indus Empire

173

loaded onto boats and transported to Mohenjo-daro. In the river nearby a dense mass of finished stone artefacts was discovered, probably indicating an embarkation point, or perhaps the place where some laden vessel sank. It is evident that material from this place was dispatched to Mohenjo-daro, where a study of the stone-blade industry found in the excavations revealed an almost identical range of tools and tool sizes made of this material. We do not know to how many other sites the worked stones from Sakkhar may have been transported. It is highly ironical and says little for the research that went into a major and extremely expensive piece of work that when the recent UNESCO project to preserve Mohenjo-daro was in progress, vast masses of limestone were brought from the Rohri hills to construct flood spurs, probably destroying great areas of this unique and priceless heritage.

Another specialist craft of the Harappan period was the manufacture of beads from semi-precious stones, particularly agate and carnelian. This craft too was already an ancient one and there is plentiful evidence of it from the earliest times at Mehrgarh, and at Mesolithic and early Neolithic sites in the western borderlands and Ganges valley. It is closely related to the much older tradition of making microliths from the same range of semi-precious stones, which was practised around the Indus region, but apparently never within it. Heating the stone to improve its colour and workability is common to both traditions. During the Harappan period it became notably more organized and industrialized. There are limited sources for good quality carnelian and it is likely that the major source for the Harappan cities was from Ratnapura near Broach on the Narbada. Here one may assume that the raw materials were mined, as they still are today, from shallow pits, roughly prepared for manufacture, heated until the desired colour was achieved, and then shipped from local ports to urban centres.

The discovery of a number of Harappan carnelian bead factories is obviously of considerable interest. The process of manufacture was first discussed by Mackay when he excavated a factory in Chanhu-daro (Mackay 1937), and has since been researched by other scholars (Allchin, 1979); (Kenoyer, 1994). Another factory was excavated at Lothal. The great numbers of beads found at all the main Indus sites clearly show that they were much sought after and that craftsmen were working at many centres. The importance of the craft is highlighted by the fact that Harappan beads, particularly the long barrel-shaped varieties, were among the major objects of export to the cities of Mesopotamia at this time. Another specialized variety of decorated carnelian bead was obtained by etching with an alkali

174   *Origins of a Civilization*

paste which was then fired to produce white decoration; alternately, black decoration was achieved by painting with a metallic oxide before firing. It is not clear where this sophisticated technology was first developed, nor where it was practised, but our expectation is that it was probably limited to a number of urban centres.

Among other bead-making stones lapis lazuli appears to have been always a rarity. The Harappan trading post at Shortughai in Badakshan, northern Afghanistan, near to the place where lapis lazuli was, and still is mined, must indicate the Harappan interest in obtaining, and perhaps seeking to control the dissemination of such rare materials; and one may assume that they were carried overland to the Indus valley, for local consumption and perhaps for onward shipment. The discovery of a small cache of lapiz beads at Kuntasi in western Saurashtra led Dhavalikar to suggest that they were destined for export to the cities of Mesopotamia rather than for the home market.

Another specialized craft whose products are found in quantities in the cities is shell-working, to make bangles, beads, inlays and other items. The conch shell was one of several marine species favoured for this. We saw in the previous chapter how marine shells were brought to Mehrgarh even in the sixth millennium BC, and it is probable that there was an unbroken tradition of long distance trade in this commodity from then on. In Harappan times we find a number of outlying places where shells were obtained and also worked. Excavations at coastal sites including Balakot, Lothal, Nageshwar and Kuntasi, have revealed that they were all probably what may be called 'resource centres', obtaining shells and other raw materials, either locally or from further afield, and having local workshops to produce bangles and other items of adornment. There is evidence that raw materials were carried to inland sites and to workshops or localities in the major cities. Chanhu-daro in particular appears to have been a centre for this as well as many other crafts, with much evidence of the waste products from sawing up conch shells and manufacturing bangles.

The manufacture of stoneware bangles is an interesting example of a distinctly urban craft, since examples of the bangles and evidence regarding their manufacture seems almost wholly restricted to Mohenjo-daro and Harappa (Vidale, 1989). The technique of manufacture was highly sophisticated: suitable clays were selected and specially prepared; the firing techniques were also unique, employing clay saggars in which the unburnt articles for firing were stacked *(Fig. 27)*. The saggars consisted of terracotta jars coated with an additional layer of wet clay, and sealed with a lid and more clay. A typical unicorn bull seal impression was found on the neck of one such saggar. It is clear that

The Indus Empire

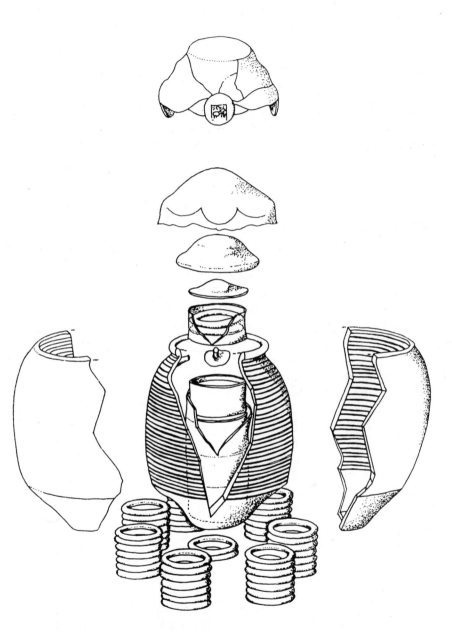

Fig. 27. Reconstruction of the several elements employed in the manufacture of stoneware bangles.

176   *Origins of a Civilization*

the bangles were luxury items, designed for a special clientele, and in numerous cases they had short inscriptions scratched on them. Altogether, the rediscovery of the techniques of manufacture is an exciting piece of work, made by the Italian team who worked at Mohenjo-daro in the early eighties.

The multiplicity of crafts and the demand for their products must have led to consideration of how and from where to obtain requisite raw materials. Dhavalikar (1995: 210-11) has gone so far as to characterize the Harappans as 'the most enterprising people in Indian history' and to liken them in this respect to the British who 'came to India with the sole objective of exploiting the rich natural resources'. We shall consider his view further in the next section.

Trade and Transport

The picture that is emerging, of Harappan concern with obtaining access to all sorts of raw materials and other goods, leads us to consider two main questions: the means of transport employed in these activities; and the different levels and types of trade they involved. Transport must have been of several different kinds, by sea, river and land.

Means of transport. It has become increasingly clear from the evidence available at the western end of the routes that both land and sea transport played a role in the contact between the Indus valley and the cities of Mesopotamia.

Our knowledge of land transport has to be partly based upon inference. The common importance of bullock-carts is an oft-cited aspect of the Harappan civilization, based first upon the appearance of terracotta wheels and frames for model carts, along with terracotta models of the beasts themselves, and supported by evidence of actual wheeltracks discovered in urban contexts. We infer that such carts would have been used primarily on the Indus plains, to carry grains and other foodstuffs from the rural area to the cities *(Plate 46)*. Probably, they were also used for carrying other commodities to and from riverside points of disembarkation; and possibly also from one city to another. It is strange that no certain evidence of the domestication of the camel has been found, nor of its employment for transport and travel, although small numbers of camel bones have been found in the excavations at Mohenjo-daro, Harappa and Kalibangan. One would expect camels to have been used, particularly

The Indus Empire

in desert places. Equally, the evidence suggests that horses were extremely rare in Harappan contexts. As such they are likely to have been kept for elite usage or for ceremonial purposes, rather than for common transport or communication. For whatever reason neither the camel nor the horse is depicted on seals, nor are they found in the form of terracotta models. It is probably correct to conclude that in Harappan times long-distance travel in areas where the terrain was unsuitable for using carts would have been mainly done by pack animals. This is the pattern which persisted into this century in many parts of South Asia. Our guess is that, for long-distance transport in general, caravans of pack animals, particularly bullocks, but also donkeys and perhaps domesticated onagers, would have been employed.

The concrete evidence for sea transport is not as firm as one might wish, but its indications are quite unequivocal. There are remarkably few representations or models of either river or ocean-going ships from the Indus sites, but this is also true of Mesopotamia *(Plates 47 & 48)*. However, considerable quantities of trade goods of apparently Indus origin have been found in Mesopotamia, and there are also many inscriptional references to Meluhha, ships of Meluhha, men of Meluhha, and to some of the classes of objects known from archaeology; and finally there is the growing evidence linking ports on the Arabian coast of the Gulf, Failaka (Kuwait), Bahrain (ancient Dilmun), and Oman (ancient Magan), with maritime trade between Mesopotamia and Meluhha. That Meluhha was located near the mouth of the Indus, or elsewhere in coastal India or Pakistan has now been generally accepted (Ratnagar, 1981: 68-71). We still cannot say what proportion of the trade was carried by Indian ships and what by Mesopotamian or those of intermediate centres. It may be reasonable to assume that as in historical times the trade was shared between carriers from several rival countries.

There must also have been sea connections between the various Indus ports we have mentioned, and with the ports controlled by client chieftains along the Baluchistan coast. How far coastal trade extended southward down the west coast of India is another interesting question. As we saw in an earlier chapter, it seems probable that the rather sudden appearance and expansion of the Southern Neolithic cattle-keeping and agricultural communities at the beginning of the third millennium BC may coincide with the export of gold from ancient sources in Karnataka, and also possibly the export of cattle which were kept in large numbers and were perhaps being captured from the wild and domesticated.

178   *Origins of a Civilization*

A second type of water transport would have been by river, including ferries for simple river-crossings and larger boats for carrying goods from production points to cities. This trade must have been complemented by sea trade and perhaps overlapped with it. There is much evidence from the observations of travellers, from the time of Alexander onwards, and particularly in more recent centuries, for the importance of river transport throughout South Asia including the Indus system. The Indus and other major rivers must have provided major lines of communication and trade, linking the major cities with each other. Once again, archaeological evidence is on the whole lacking. There are a few representations of what are patently river craft from Harappan sources, and the evidence we cited above of the movement of stone artefacts between Sakkhar and Mohenjo-daro is a good example of the role of river transport.

The evidence of trade. When we consider the variety of crafts we have reviewed and the growth of specialist craftsmen who practised them, we are led to conclude that several varieties of trade must have been involved in their manufacture, exchange and distribution. As we earlier suggested (1982) there must have been three distinct levels at which trade was carried on: first, as internal trade within the confines of the Harappan 'state' or domain; second, with chiefdoms or regions adjacent to the Indus domain, which for the most part had not yet reached the stage of city or state formation, and these we believe would have been largely within South Asia and Iran; and third, with more distant states who had achieved such a status, such as Sumeria, the Gulf region, and parts of Central Asia.

Trade within the Indus domain. Several kinds of internal trade may be posited, the first and probably by far the commonest being local. By this we mean the distribution of local agricultural produce and craft products of daily and domestic utility, such as pottery or stone tools. We suggested in the previous chapter that this level of trade had already developed during the Early Harappan period. Much of it may have been conducted on a basis of barter or exchange; perhaps, as in Mesopotamia, some commodities such as grain or other basic foodstuffs served as a form of exchange currency. Next, must have been trade at the provincial or city level. Here we envisage the existence of different specialist craft centres in towns or cities, many of them requiring the importation of raw materials, copper and other metals, stones, semi-precious stones such as carnelian, ivory, shell, etc. Not only does this imply the long-distance transport of such materials, for example of shells from littoral sites such as Balakot, Kuntasi or other coastal sites, to major production points in cities or industrial towns, such as Chanhu-daro; but it also must have involved a further stage of distribution, when the manufactured products from specialist workshops were in turn exported to other cities or markets. This trade we would expect to have involved greater distances and therefore to have been called upon to have more specialized transport, either by boat, where this was possible, or by cart or pack animals. An example of such trade has already been cited in the transport of stone blades and other artifacts of general utility, from the quarries and factory sites at Sakkhar by river to Mohenjo-daro, and probably to many other places throughout the domain. Already, at this level, a more specialized type of exchange would have been called for, and it seems likely that the unification of the system of weights and measures, and the employment of seals to mark packages, and even the use of script, would have been brought into play. Further, it seems reasonable to expect that distribution of this kind would have been in the hands of specialist merchants and perhaps caravan leaders.

Trade with neighbouring regions or chiefdoms. The second type of trade which we envisage is that which was carried on with areas outside the Harappan domain. As we have seen above, it is difficult to determine which if any of the neighbouring regions were independent 'chiefdoms' or even 'states', and which may have been at times absorbed into the greater Indus 'state' or 'empire'. These changes would have affected the hills and valleys to the west of the Indus, and even some parts of the Indus plains in the north-west, the problematic areas of the east Punjab, Haryana, perhaps too the Ganges-Jamuna Doab, Rajasthan, Saurashtra, Gujarat; and at a further remove, the Deccan, including both Maharashtra and Karnataka, and the middle to lower Ganges valley. Where we find settlements which display the full marks of the Mature Harappan style, including the presence of seals, weights, and the Indus script, we may assume that the area was at any rate at some time regarded as part of the Harappan domains. Where these things are not in evidence, trade may have involved either some kind of organized Indus expeditions, in search of sources of raw materials, etc., or perhaps actual colonization, with the establishment of trading stations or factories. Presumably, this must also have involved creating suitable relations with the local population, to establish a basis of trade. An extreme example of this type of activity is probably to be sought in the trade settlement or

180 *Origins of a Civilization*

colony at Shortughai in north-eastern Afghanistan, mentioned above. Lothal, too, may have been a Harappan trading station or colony established in a locality which was not part of the central Harappan domain. In more remote cases the situation is hardly in doubt: for instance, if the Karnataka region were a source for the Harappans to obtain gold, such trade must have involved not only long-distance travel, overland through diverse regions, but possibly also a sea voyage from a Harappan harbour to a seaport from which an inland source could be reached. Evidence of this kind of trade may be found in the fine disc beads, probably of steatite paste, from the Neolithic period at Piklihal, as indications of their having been exported from the Indus system, perhaps in exchange for gold. Equally problematic is the nature of the trade contacts between the Indus valley and Central Asia, as exemplified by finds from Altyn Depe or Dashli. As we saw in the previous chapter, the beginnings of these contacts went back to much earlier times, and one is tempted to see them as involving more than simple trade, perhaps with longstanding ties, even of kinship, between merchants or elites at the two ends of the trade routes.

Indus Trade with Mesopotamia. Almost as soon as Marshall's excavations at Mohenjo-daro began to appear in print, in the 1920s and 1930s, it was recognized that Indus seals and other Indian objects had been discovered at a number of sites in Mesopotamia. Studies of trade texts in cuneiform followed, many mentioning the role of intermediate trading states such as Dilmun and Magan; and it was noted that the materials stated to have come from Meluhha included some categories which coincided with imports which must have come from either the Indus valley, or elsewhere in South Asia. A recent important study is Ratnagar's *Encounters* (1981) which offers a constructive synthesis of archaeological and historical data, including a survey of the Mesopotamian evidence. Chakrabarti's *External Trade of the Indus Civilization* (1990) offers another systematic review of all aspects of the subject. A short, helpful summary of current thinking on Harappan trade, with references to many recent publications, is in Kenoyer (1991). Ratnagar suggests that Mesopotamian area contacts with the Gulf ports began long before the Sargonid period, perhaps as early as 4000 BC, and she points to 'Mesopotamian initiative—initiative from a land of neither islanders nor coastal dwellers, a land lacking good wood and ships—which opens the story of external trade around the end of the fourth millennium (1994: 117-118).' If this is correct Mesopotamian sea trade with the Indus world would have

The Indus Empire

begun during the Early Harappan period, or at least by the critical period of transition c. 2600-2500 BC. One would expect the initial steps would have come from the Western termini, and the involvement of Indus ships would have followed.

By comparison with the reasonably direct sea route to Mesopotamia the overland routes raised quite different problems, as they must have passed through inhospitable, mountainous territories controlled by a series of separate powers, progressing from city to city until the goal was finally reached. Chakrabarti (1990) stressed the role of nomadic groups such as the Powindahs in the actual transport of such land trade, but noted that the initiation and control of the trade must have been in the hands of a professional merchant class. We agree with this; people whose own life-style involved long yearly migrations from the mountains to the plains, or from the Gujarat coast to the interior of Central India, as pastoral people do today, had experience of travelling and could supply pack animals; while the purchase and sale or exchange of quantities of goods, dealing with government officials and the security of a caravan would require the ability to keep records, experience of the outside world and contacts at the right level all along the route. In the early stages trade, by whatever route it came, must have been comparatively restricted, but it burgeoned towards the end of the third millennium, as is indicated by the nature and frequency of textual references and actual finds. Ratnagar suggests that state-sponsored expeditions to obtain goods or materials are in keeping with the evidence of Indus-Mesopotamian relations, but this does not mean that it was the only way of trading.

It is generally agreed that the earliest finds in Sumeria indicative of Indus trade date from the Early Dynastic III period (2600-2370 BC), that they continue through the Akkad period (2370-2100 BC), and on to the Isin Larsa period (2000-1763 BC) (Ratnagar 1981: 200-07). Not the least significant aspect of this time-scale is that the trade begins almost at the point when the century of change was giving birth to the Mature Harappan civilization. As we saw in the previous chapter the Early period already provides evidence of a process of what we have called 'cultural convergence' (Allchin, 1980:153), which is taken to be associated with growing internal trade between the widely scattered parts of the Early Harappan culture region. With the rise of the Mature civilization this internal trade must have rapidly increased, and been augmented by growing external trade with both Central Asia and Mesopotamia.

There has been some divergence of emphasis and interpretation

180 *Origins of a Civilization*

as to the extent of the trade with Mesopotamia and its significance. At one extreme Shaffer (1982a; 1982b [1993]) has argued that external trade was 'neither extensive, intensive, direct or of any particular importance to the development of the Harappan culture'. At the other extreme Possehl (1986, 1990) has argued that 'Trade, broadly defined, focussing to some degree on the Mesopotamian contact with ancient India . . . may have played a significant role in the century of paroxysmal change that seems to have led to the development of Indus urbanism'; Mughal (1992) has drawn our attention to the shift in orientation from the northern Indus valley southward to the sea as constituting 'the most significant change in the life of the Harappan civilization'; and Ratnagar (1994) has posed the question, 'Is it then too far-fetched to suggest that the emergence of the Harappan civilization, in curious parallel with the Mesopotamian, coincided with intensification of resource procurement, manifested by the expansion of the geographic horizons of two contemporary and neighbouring societies?' We shall return to this subject in the following chapter.

As we saw in an earlier chapter, Mesopotamia was in a geographical position to develop trade with major metropolitan trading partners in several directions: the Indus empire on the other hand had fewer alternatives, as at this stage there was effectively no eastern outlet to turn to if trade with the west became difficult. This came later with the opening up of the Ganges valley and the outlet to the Bay of Bengal, following the urbanization of the region, in course of the second urbanization.

Chapter 9

THE INDUS EMPIRE—PEOPLE AND CULTURE

PEOPLES OF THE HARAPPAN DOMAIN

Earlier studies of the relatively small number of human skeletal remains found in excavations at Mohenjo-daro and Harappa tended to become enmeshed in attempts to assign them to arbitrarily defined 'racial types'. Some of the results can only be described as grotesque. In recent decades more material has been discovered, and attempts have been made to refine its interpretation. Early signs of this change are to be found in D. K. Sen's paper on 'Ancient Races of India and Pakistan' (Sen, 1964 & 1965), where a plea was made for a more scientifically and statistically oriented approach to the study of human remains. Since that time relatively few scholars have been working in the field: among them K. A. R. Kennedy and a group of his colleagues and students, occupy a major position. When fully published, the results of their continuing studies, particularly in so far as they relate to the Indus civilization and its population, are likely to make a major contribution. Sen concluded that the population of Harappa, Mohenjo-daro and Lothal were broadly speaking homogenous, at least with regard to shape of the head and nose and to stature. He also concluded that at that time it was safer to assume that 'they originated in the local soil' rather than to 'bring them from thousands of miles away'. More recently Hemphill, Lukacs and Kennedy (1991), with a considerably larger database to work from, have come to rather different conclusions, based on a rigorous multivariate study. A major factor of this approach is that it represents relations between individual examples and groups in terms of distance or proximity rather than in unquantifiable identities or differences. The outcome differs from Sen's in that the new analysis leads one to conclude that there is, as might be expected, a considerable element of heterogeneity between the populations of the main Harappan

184   *Origins of a Civilization*

sites. This is particularly noticeable between those from Mohenjo-daro on the one hand and the rest of the main sites on the other. Like Sen they see no reason to look elsewhere than in the area of the Indus river system for any part of the population at that time. One of their most interesting conclusions is that there is a biological break between the population of Mehrgarh in the very early period (c. 6000 BC) and that from c. 4500 BC onwards. They also find that, once the newer population was established, there was little difference between it and the population of the Harappan period. As they see it the Harappan population has closer affinities with that of the Iranian plateau and the Near East than with that of India, east and south of the Indus. There is however a second break in the biological continuity at some point after the Harappan period, the significance of which we shall touch on in the next chapter.

The Harappan language or languages. Unless or until a generally agreed reading of the Harappan inscriptions is achieved, or a satisfactory bilingual inscription is discovered, there is no way in which we can be certain in what language they were written. In other words, speculation regarding the language or languages of the Harappan domain is likely to remain at the level of speculation or hypothesis until one or both of these requirements is met. This situation has not however discouraged the dozens of aspirants who have attempted to read the script. The ever-growing number of different readings, and the variety of languages they are alleged to reveal, are testimony to the fallibility of the great majority, if not all.

Reason suggests that for so large an area, in contact with so many outlying regions, several, if not many, languages would have been spoken in the Harappan domain. It seems probable however that only one central language would have been used in the inscriptions. This would presumably have been the language of the ruling elite, whoever they were. An exception to this is indicated by a small group of round seals found in Mesopotamia which, while they appear to employ the Harappan script, do so in a way which is unique. Hunter (1934) who first commented on these seals inferred that their texts must represent a language different to that of the remaining Harappan inscriptions. We can rule out the most preposterous of the suggested candidates for this central language (such as the script, and presumably language, of the Easter Island inscriptions). We can also rule out, with some confidence, suggested West Asian languages, such as Sumerian or Elamite, since it seems reasonable to assume that had any one of these been introduced to the Indus they would have

People and Culture   185

brought with them their own already existing scripts. We can leave aside postulation of an unknown language, since there is no reason to believe that so major a language would have disappeared without trace. We are left with two main contenders, either a Proto-Indoaryan or other Indo-European language; or a Dravidian language. Parpola has given a detailed and systematic discussion of the evidence relating to both these candidates, and we recommend interested readers to refer to his work (Parpola 1994, chapters 8 and 9).

There are several reasons to question the hypothesis that the language of the inscriptions was Indo-Aryan or Indo-European. First, however, it may be remarked that in view of the ancient and long standing links between the Indo-Iranian borderlands and southern Central Asia, it is very probable that Proto-Indoaryan speaking peoples were among those who participated in these contacts during the Mature Harappan period; thus their language or languages were almost certainly already among those spoken in the Indus domain. But this does not mean that Proto-Indoaryan had already by that time become, as it surely did later during Post-urban or Late Harappan times, dominant in the Indus region or in the Indo-Gangetic divide. A second argument, which appears to us to be a telling one, rests on the rarity of horse remains at Harappan sites (small numbers of samples are reported from Surkotada, Kalibangan and Dholavira), or of representations of the horse in any Mature Harappan context. Both early Indo-Iranian and Indo-Aryan speakers are, almost wherever they are identified, associated with horses and related cultural traits, such as horse furniture, horse-drawn chariots and horse burials. The virtual absence of any evidence of these things in the Indus civilization makes it most unlikely that the language of the Harappan inscriptions can have been a form of Proto-Indoaryan.

We agree in most respects with Parpola's conclusions on this subject, and we believe particularly that the most likely contendent as the language of the Harappan inscriptions is an ancestral language of the Dravidian family. This has been the most frequently and strongly supported hypothesis since its adoption by Marshall (1931) and Hunter (1934). The arguments for it are several; first, a careful analysis has shown 'beyond any reasonable doubt' that Elamite and the Dravidian language family are 'truly cognate' (McAlpin 1981). This would suggest that at some time in the past they were in closer geographical proximity than the modern distribution of Dravidian indicates. Next, in spite of doubts regarding its significance, the fact remains that a Dravidian language, Brahui, is still spoken by nomadic pastoralists in the Baluchi hills, west of the Indus: it is in no way

186 *Origins of a Civilization*

improbable that Brahui is a surviving remnant of an earlier more extensive spread of Dravidian speech, and this would therefore lend support to a Dravidian candidature for the predominant language of the Indus civilization. But this does not necessarily mean that Brahui is directly descended from that language.

Social complexity. From what we have seen of the Harappan civilization it certainly seems that in both its city and its non-urban population there was a considerable degree of social complexity and stratification. There is reason to infer that in many areas within and around the Indus system tribal populations including hunting, fishing and collecting groups continued to flourish, just as they did and do in many parts of South Asia into the present century. It is probable that with the growth of cities many of these groups would have found markets for the sale of their produce, such as honey, fish, wild fruits or firewood to neighbouring city populations; and fishing people would probably also have supplied boats for river travel and ferrying. There must also have been pastoral groups who specialized in keeping and breeding sheep and goats or cattle, who formed separate communities within the main structure of society. By analogy with later Indian society, one may expect some of the latter to have developed into long-distance carriers, taking village produce to cities, and offering their services to the urban population, and playing a role in longer-distance trade, as suggested above. Then, there must have been a rural population who included agriculturalists and probably specialists in village craft, engaged in the manufacture of agricultural and domestic equipment. The cities introduced a wider range of specialized groups. Among these one may infer a much more varied range of specialist craft groups, potters, stone workers, metal workers in copper, bronze, silver and gold, jewellers, seal cutters, bangle-makers, bead-makers, sculptors, and many more. Another specialized activity of both the rural world and the city must have been the construction of carts and wheels. There must also have been specialized boat-builders, and sailors who were available to take their share of the trade. As we have pointed out, there must have been groups of merchants who specialized in city, inter-city and inter-state trade, including that with Sumeria. The emergence of a specialized merchant class implies that they may have served a role in the manipulation of exchange and credit, somewhat akin to the bankers of later times. The cities too must have produced many other specialist groups. For example, exponents of the art of writing; exponents of the art of measuring, surveying and urban planning;

People and Culture 187

and not least, religious and ritual specialists. Finally, the widespread presence of urban drainage systems reminds us that there must have been a class of menials who cleaned and maintained them. With increasing social complexity, we are inevitably led to enquire how the system worked, what if any was the central cohesive factor that held things together. Can we speak of a Harappan 'state'—a term which so far we have used very sparingly? This we shall now consider.

A state or not a state? In the past two or three decades there has been a growing interest in elucidating the nature of the socio-political cohesion of the Harappan domain; this has led to a debate as to whether there was a Harappan state, and if so what form it took. We cannot discuss this interesting topic with the detail it deserves, but shall restrict ourselves to suggesting further reading for those who wish to follow the debate, while indicating what we see as some salient points, and finally putting forward some ideas of our own.

A helpful discussion of the question is in Jacobson (1986: 137-173, with extensive bibliography); Ratnagar (1991) offers another thoughtful and systematic consideration of the whole problem, with comparisons drawn from a number of relevant examples of early states. This work is particularly valuable because of its author's knowledge of the Mesopotamian evidence. Another useful source is Kenoyer (1991), which provides a succinct, clear and balanced account. An attempt to break down some of the earlier stereotyped views has been made by Shaffer (1982).

Broadly speaking, the main drift of the argument leads most scholars to a positive conclusion that there must have been some sort of centralized state power and thus that it is reasonable to speak of a Harappan state. It has been pointed out by Ratnagar that the Harappan state, in common with other examples, must be thought of as 'early', in that it shares with them a number of characteristic features. These include vestigial tribal structures, relatively simple technologies, non-monetary economies and unspecialized administrative structures. There is no doubt that in several important respects the Harappan state differs from those of either Mesopotamia or Egypt. An outstanding difference appears to be in respect of the role of the king. The relative invisibility of royalty, with all its claptrap and accoutrements, in the Harappan state, stands in marked contrast to the prominence of these features in Egypt or Mesopotamia. The reason for this contrast is not altogether apparent; clearly the availability of numerous written records adds to the visibility of royalty in these cases, but is absent for the Indus; some have seen in

Origins of a Civilization

188

this contrast a reflection of a profound difference in values, but this may be to overstate the case. One may also cite the comparably low profile of the king in Early Historic India, and the general absence of royal tombs or palaces in the archaeological record of all early periods in South Asia. It may also be that the Harappan state was somehow less developed than the other two, and perhaps retained more of an earlier character as a chiefdom. Several writers have pointed towards the 'uniqueness' or 'Indianness' of the Harappan system, and this aspect needs to be further explored.

A different hypothesis of what the Harappan state may have involved is offered by Kenoyer (1991) who sees it as composed of several competing classes of elites who maintained different levels of control over the vast regions of the Indus and Ghaggar-Hakra valleys. Instead of one social group with absolute control, he envisages the rulers or dominant members in the various cities as including merchants, ritual specialists, and individuals who controlled resources such as land, livestock and raw materials. These groups may have had different means of control, but they shared a common ideology and economic system. This view points to something rather similar to Ratnagar's unspecialized administrative structures.

Our own reading of the situation is as follows. We have seen how the amelioration of climate during the fourth and third millennia BC led to a steady expansion of agriculture and hence of the population throughout the whole Indus system. During the Early Harappan period this produced a growing number of small chiefdoms, both throughout the Indus system and in adjacent regions, and among these there is evidence of increasing and widespread trade and of a 'convergence' of craft production and even of religious symbolism. The suggestion is that there was a progressive movement towards the formation of small city-states, and that ultimately this led to the appearance of a centralized state, and to some sort of state control over the many smaller chiefdoms and/or city-states. There may have been additional influences at work in this process. It seems inevitable that the main towns of some of the chiefdoms would grow in size and importance, as a result of growing population and economic power: this would lead to an almost natural process of transformation from towns to cities. But the evidence which has been suggested of a 'great leap forward' during the century of 'paroxysmal change' still needs to be further elucidated, as this appears to hold the key to the completion of the process. Because of the obvious parallels between the Indus and Mesopotamia, it may be helpful to consider the Mesopotamian situation in this context.

People and Culture 189

In Mesopotamia, there was a period of several centuries between the first appearance of cities with their own city-states, and the achievement of a united kingdom. During this interval (the Early Dynastic period, c. 3000-2500 BC) the city-states remained largely independent but were involved in repeated internecine battles. History suggests that this ultimately gave rise to the achievement of a united state of Akkad under Sargon (c. 2370-2316 BC). Lacking textual support, the Indus situation must necessarily be less easy to analyze, but there are both comparisons and contrasts that suggest themselves. Several things which may be regarded as hallmarks of the early cities and city-states in West Asia, the development of a script, monumental architecture, etc., are, as far as we know, absent, or at best present only in embryonic form, during the Early Harappan period. Nonetheless, as we understand it, other hallmarks of change, which can equally be regarded as precursors of the emergence of cities, are present in the Early Harappan. What we called 'cultural convergence' may from this point of view be seen as evidence of the homogenizing effect of trade on craft products; similarly the widespread distribution of certain religious symbols, such as the horned deity, seem to argue for increasing cultural integration over considerable distances and areas. These things lead us to expect that a parallel movement towards political integration was taking place in the Early Harappan world, even if it was not as far advanced as in contemporary Mesopotamia.

At a certain date, during the 'century of change' (c. 2600-2500 BC) a new, far-reaching development took place in the Indus region: this included the creation of a script; the introduction of new concepts of planning and monumental architecture, along with the creation of a number of new or replanned cities, starting with Mohenjo-daro and Harappa; and the imposition of a uniform 'new' style upon craft manufactures, including the production of a number of expressly urban crafts. Moreover, it is important to remember that at no time, either during the Early or the Mature Harappan periods, did Indus society exist in a vacuum. On the contrary there was a many-sided development of trade, first between the towns and emergent cities of the Indus system itself; then with neighbouring regions on all sides; and finally with more distant regions, including Central Asia and Mesopotamia. The external trade probably first developed via overland routes to both the north and west, and thereafter was augmented by sea trade in the case of the latter. As we understand it each one of these stages of development would have produced powerful economic stimuli for the Indus region. The

190 *Origins of a Civilization*

introduction and rapid spread of the cultivation of millet in South Asia, with the possibility of extending the agricultural productivity of even the environmentally least favoured areas, is a good example of the sort of stimulus we have in mind. Our expectation therefore would be that the sea trade with Mesopotamia and perhaps also Egypt began during the century of change, and this, the evidence indicates, is what it did.

This leads us to advance an hypothesis regarding the emergence of the Mature Indus civilization. If the initial introduction of sea trade with Mesopotamia came as a result of trading expeditions from Mesopotamia arriving in the Indus, it may be expected to have produced a rapid local response. It is not inconceivable that between 2600-2500 BC some forgotten Indian leader, of the calibre of a Sargon or one of his predecessors, heard from travellers returning from Sumeria of the wonders of those lands and sought to gain local control of the trade. Towards this end our hypothetical leader set about unifying the area we referred to as the Indus heartland, causing his architects to design new styles of city plan and structures and his priests or merchants to perfect and establish a script for use in mercantile operations, etc. How the unification was achieved remains obscure. It may well be that it involved some use of *force majeure*, but a major stimulus must have been derived from capturing for the Harappan state its share of the trade with Mesopotamia and the Gulf states.

If the sea trade was indeed a stimulus to this development, the likelihood is that the epicentre of the movement would have been in a city well placed to receive it: what city can we conceive of within the Harappan culture region better fitted for such a role than Mohenjo-daro? In the same way it is interesting to recall that several scholars have identified Harappa as a 'gateway city', well placed to command the major land routes which traversed the Iranian plateau and which led to Central Asia. We saw in the previous chapter that the major function of the Harappan seals appears to have been mercantile, in one way or another. Although, it is obvious that the excavations at Mohenjo-daro and Harappa in the 1920s and '30s were on a larger scale than any more recent work, the relative volume of inscribed seals found at those sites is disproportionately large, some 68 per cent of the total coming from Mohenjo-daro and 19 per cent from Harappa, leaving a mere 13 per cent for the seals found at all other sites, including those in West Asia! (Mahadevan, 1977:7). This figure seems to point towards the dominant position of Mohenjo-daro in the Indus response to Mesopotamian trade.

We must repeat that in this discussion we are not thinking of

People and Culture 191

one-sided trade, but of a full exchange between the states at either terminus. Human institutions do not flourish in isolation, but in open situations of cultural interaction. We suggest that this hypothesis may help to explain how the Harappans, as comparatively late starters in the urban enterprise, were able so rapidly to catch up and even in some respects surpass their western trading partners.

In this context it is interesting to recall Possehl's (1986: 100-103) important discussion of the effects of trade on culture change. In the passage we quote he discusses a number of historical and ethnographic examples of these effects. He writes:

> One of the most interesting observations to be made on the case under consideration is that generally little evidence exists for the diffusion of social or cultural forms. Trade clearly plays an important role in the promotion of change; however it seems to act as an 'energizer' of this process not as a modeler for specific actions or institutions . . . .

> Turning to the Harappan case once again, I would be reluctant to presume it to have been a 'secondary' phenomenon . . . . Any notion that Indus urbanization is likely to have been the result of dependency on Mesopotamia or Mesopotamian institutions is thus based on a misunderstanding of theory.

To conclude, we repeat our view that the long period of evolution of settled agriculture in the Indus system was the basis on which the Early Harappan and Mature Harappan stages of urbanization took place. Nothing that we see leads us to believe that the changes that took place or the institutions which they gave rise to were imported from outside, or that they were mere copies of any exotic system. Our conclusion, therefore, is that the Harappan state was a thoroughly indigenous growth, and that just as in the agricultural system, the manifold arts and crafts, and other aspects of life, it had an already distinctly 'Indian' (or should we say 'Indus'?) style of its own.

Writing

Among the first published finds from the Indus civilization was a seal from Harappa containing an inscription of six characters which Cunningham (1875) described as 'quite unknown'. Since that time

192 *Origins of a Civilization*

some 3000 inscriptions have been discovered: the majority are on stone seals, but others are impressions of seals on clay or pottery, on copper tablets and other copper artefacts; inscriptions on bone or ivory; and graffiti scratched on pottery, stoneware, etc. Nearly ninety per cent of all these inscriptions derive from the excavations at Mohenjo-daro and Harappa.

In the interval since that discovery much time has been spent in attempts to read the script. In a recent study Possehl (1996) has briefly reviewed no less than thirty-five different attempts at decipherment, and there are no doubt several more. He comes to some critical conclusions, both in respect of the research methods that have been adopted and the results achieved. He cites the absence of critical cross-reference to previous work and the failure of so much time and research to lay a foundation of established data. To date there is no consensus regarding the methodology of research. The conclusion is somewhat depressing. Apart from the concordances of Mahadevan (1977) and Koskeniemi and Parpola (1979, 1980 and 1982), today we are no nearer deciphering it than was G. R. Hunter in 1929!

In some ways this is to overstate the case, since many related advances have been made. The quantity of new data relating to all aspects of the civilization collected in the past fifty years has been considerable: many new sites have been discovered and further sites excavated; many additional inscriptions have been added to the corpus. In addition to the two concordances, Parpola has published two splendidly illustrated volumes of *The Corpus of Indus Seals* and Inscriptions (1987, vol. 1 *Collections in India*; 1991, vol. 2 *Collections in Pakistan*) and a third volume is awaited. The same author's major study *Deciphering the Indus Script*, (1994) offers a scholarly review of almost all aspects of research bearing on the script and its contents. Likewise, Possehl's recent work, *Indus Age: The Writing System* (1996), makes a useful contribution to the methodology of research. All this holds out the hope that a solution to the problem will sooner or later be achieved.

We hold the view that a reading of the script is more likely to be achieved as a result of the access of new data, than through isolated attempts at producing 'magical' readings. An example of what we have in mind can be found in the emerging results of the Pakistan-American team's current excavations at Harappa. Here, a well-conducted excavation, with proper planning, observation and recording, and systematic use of radiocarbon dating, has demonstrated how, during the final stage of the Early Harappan period, numbers of scratched graffiti begin to occur on pottery (Meadow & Kenoyer,

People and Culture　　　　　　　　　　193

1995). Comparable graffiti have been known at many other sites in the Indo-Iranian borderlands. Those from Rahman Dheri are good examples (*Plate 49*), but their stratigraphic positions, dating and sequence development have not hitherto been clearly established. Another important aspect of the work at Harappa is that the first of many actual inscriptions in the Harappan script occurs in a context objectively dated to c. 2600 BC. Hopes are raised by such new data that a greater understanding of matters relating to the script will result from this project, perhaps even its long awaited decipherment.

Our own views on the script remain much as we have stated them on earlier occasions. Having considered the available evidence, we have a clear impression that the Indus script was a local invention; that it was used for personal or corporate identification, and in particular for mercantile purposes though its employment on seals used to seal storerooms or bundles of merchandise, or stamped on the necks of jars (*Plates 50 & 51, No. 1*). It was also used to inscribe such luxury articles as stoneware bangles (*Plate 51, No. 2*). We are inclined to regard the find-spots of Harappan seals as indicating the presence of Harappan merchants, if not in some cases of actual 'administrators'; and we can now note that the inlaid inscription found at Dholavira represents what was probably a 'civic' use of script. One must remember that all the inscriptions found to date are short, and there are no longer inscriptions comparable to the clay cuneiform tablets of Mesopotamia. This certainly leads us to think that the seal inscriptions are essentially short 'addresses', probably giving no more than a name, perhaps a title, and perhaps a place. In spite of this limitation, the importance of obtaining an agreed solution to the problem remains. It seems likely that an agreed reading will involve a substantial advance in our knowledge of the language of the texts.

Science and Technology

From the excavations of Harappan sites large numbers of stone weights have been discovered: these were analyzed by Hemmy (1931) and found to show remarkable accuracy and regularity. Together they formed a series with ratios of 1, 2, 3, 4, 8, 16, 32, 64, 160, 200, 320, 640, 1600, 3200, 8000, 12800. One of the most common weights was that with a value of 16, weighing around 13.5 to 13.7 gm. More recently, Mainkar (1984) has made a fresh study of these materials and of further examples from the Lothal excavations. As a result he

194 *Origins of a Civilization*

proposed a new structure, dividing the weights into two series, and thereby producing a striking new symmetrical progression. The first series advances from .05, .1, .2, .5, 1, 2, 5, 10, 20, 50, 100, 200 to 500. The most frequently occurring weight of Hemmy's analysis now appears with the value 0.5 in this series, or in terms of later Indian metrology with a value of 120 *rattis*. Ratnagar (1981) has noted the occurrence of 'Indus' weights at a number of Gulf and Mesopotamian sites, and remarked upon the presence of examples of the same common weight of c. 13.5 gm. These finds certainly indicate that such weights played a regular part in mercantile practice. Mainkar's second series has a sequence of ratios similar to the first, but with a different base, the unit weight of the first series being 50 per cent higher than that of the second series. The significance of these two series is not as yet fully explained.

Attention has also been drawn to a number of carefully constructed scales which offer indications of Harappan systems of linear measurement, although sadly all are truncated and incomplete. These too have been studied by Mainkar and they also show remarkable precision in their manufacture: there are three specimens—from Mohenjo-daro, Lothal and Harappa. The first is made of shell, with regular graduations with an average size of 6.7056 mm., with a hollow circle carved on one graduation and a solid dot on the fifth of the series. Mainkar suggests that this represents a unit which when complete would have been either 67.056 or 670.56 mm. in length. The Lothal scale is calculated to be 25.56 mm., and the Harappa scale at 93.4 mm.

A major contribution to our insight into Harappan science and technology has been offered by the late D. P. Chattopadhyaya (1986). With characteristic enthusiasm he took up the reported regularity of different ratios of brick size, suggesting that brick technology might be investigated as an avenue of approach towards Harappan mathematics. Following a lead from Mainkar, he suggested that the regular sizes and proportions of bricks might provide a bridge from the small, exact scales to a brick-based technology, perhaps rather metrology, and that this might be developed as a means of studying other, larger, elements of Harappan metrology. We have noted above the suggestions of excavators regarding the apparent relationships of street widths, houses, rooms and courts, and even of two walls; and we believe that this subject deserves to be treated with greater attention and detail and with a more integrated approach than it has hitherto been accorded. It is to be expected that there was some relationship between the precise small-scale measurements and those

People and Culture 195

of larger scale. At one end these may lead us towards the beginnings of Harappan exact sciences, mathematics, geometry, astronomy, etc., and at the other towards practical applications such as town-planning and wider uses in technology.

The study of the science and technology of the Indus civilization is clearly an exciting one which is likely to progress as new data, particularly from properly conducted excavations and from subsequent scientific analysis, become available. Studies of such industries as the stoneware bangles of Mohenjo-daro (Halim & Vidale, 1984), the conch shell industry (Bhan & Kenoyer, 1980-81), the carnelian industry (Mackay, 1937; Kenoyer et al., 1994), the frit micro-bead industry (Hegde et al., 1982), show how much can be gleaned from such an approach.

Harappan Art

We saw in the previous chapter that the custom of making simple figurines of clay and later of terracotta began at Mehrgarh during the Early Agricultural period, i.e. in the 6th or even 7th millennium BC. The practice continued both at this and many other sites from that time forward, through all periods. It is therefore not surprising to find that terracotta figurines which in some respects may be regarded as lineal descendants of the earlier examples are found at almost all Harappan sites. Of the subjects portayed some are human, some are animal, besides others. The human figurines are predominantly female, generally single figures, but also sometimes holding a baby. They are often shown wearing heavy ornaments and jewellery, and with elaborate headgear. In one case a woman kneels before some activity, perhaps making dough (*Plates 52 & 53*). Male figures are less common, but occur occasionally, some with small goatee beards; generally they appear to be nude. Animals are mainly humped Indian cattle, but there are also some fine portayals of heavy Indian bison (*gaur*) (*Plate 54*), buffalo, sheep, goats, Indian rhinoceros, elephant, boar, hares, monkeys and birds. A number of small terracotta masks of humans, some with horns and small beards, and a lion mask have also been found. There is also a small class of grotesques, sometimes human and sometimes animal. Among inanimate objects the most common are terracotta models of bullock-carts indicating that their prototypes were constructed in several different patterns, and terracotta models of ploughs, which show a striking similarity to their modern counterparts in Sindh.

196 *Origins of a Civilization*

It has generally been accepted that this terracotta art served more than one role, in some cases as children's toys and in others as domestic religious icons. Indicative of the former function are the climbing monkeys with holes pierced for a string to be inserted in them (*Plate 55*); cattle, with movable heads pivoted on a stick; and models of carts and ploughs. In the second, religious, role the female figures in particular have been thought to represent mother goddesses; while a number of grotesque figures are suggestive of malevolent spirits. The female figurines offer a clear indication of the cultural continuity which links the popular art of the Indus cities to that of the preceding periods. However, the whole range of the Harappan terracottas displays a distinctive style and character which distinguishes them as the products of their age.

Art of a quite different, distinctly urban, character is represented by the small repertoire of stone and bronze sculptures. Of the examples known to date, the great majority come from Mohenjo-daro, and a smaller number from Harappa. Bearing in mind the scarcity of suitable stone for carving and the distances which its acquisition probably involved, it can well be appreciated that stone would always be an expensive material, and that its use would be reserved for special purposes. The most important series are all carved in either a fine-grained metamorphosed limestone, or a metamorphosed talc schist. One series shows bearded male figures: the best-known is the much discussed but incomplete 'priest king', with his hair tied in a bun and held in place by a fillet, wearing a figured garment with a trefoil pattern. From other, also incomplete, examples of the same series it may be inferred that the figure was seated. It is impossible to decide whether this enigmatic figure represents a deity, priest or king. A second series consists of recumbent animals, either rams, bison or composite beasts. An outstanding example comes from the Citadel mound and shows a recumbent animal carved as seated on a solid block of stone. It is generally believed that this beast is a composite animal, having the horns and (now missing) head of a ram, the body of a bull, and the trunk of an elephant. The other outstanding example has only recently been published; and although the find-spot and circumstances attendant on the find are unknown, it can safely be inferred that it too comes from Mohenjo-daro (Allchin, 1992). This is without doubt the finest piece of Harappan stone carving to date. It depicts a simple recumbent ram: some of its features may clarify those of the former example (*Plate 56*). For instance, the hooves, tail and cape-like frill over the shoulders and upper body appear to be those of a ram rather than a bull. Four other, mostly fragmentary examples of the same type,

People and Culture 197

are known from Mohenjo-daro, and one other specimen, also from an unknown source, is in the Metropolitan Museum, New York. There can, we believe, be no reason to doubt that both these series were primarily intended as religious icons. Two other striking stone sculptures come from Harappa. One is a small, red sandstone figure of a naked man with a pendulous belly, the other a small fragmentary dancing figure, apparently also male, though this has been disputed, with the broken left leg raised in a posture reminiscent of later representations of Siva Nataraja.

The repertoire of bronze sculptures too is very small. It includes two little bronze 'dancing girls', both fragmentary; a number of bronze figures of animals, buffalo and rams, and some models of carts or *ikkas*. The whole series has been made by the lost wax method, and show remarkable technical sophistication. Finally, there is a small group of mainly tiny sculptures made in faience depicting with great charm tiny monkeys, squirrels (*Plate 57*), and a parrot.

Seals. A far larger body of artwork is represented by the Harappan glyptic art, in the shape of carved steatite seals, together with related sealings, amulets or other objects. The seals seem to have served an essentially practical function, being used to mark clay sealings on bales of merchandise or on storeroom doors; these seals, at least, were undoubtedly associated with merchants and their work. Others, one may suppose, were used for institutional purposes, perhaps by officers of civic government, priests or temple officials. The seals in general contain several distinct elements: many carry a short inscription; the vast majority have a carved field, depicting an animal or one of a variety of scenes. A third element, usually found in connection with certain of the animals, is an unidentified object or symbol.

By far the commonest subjects at all the main seal-producing sites, are a bovine with a single forward-pointing horn (*Plate 58*). This beast is usually described as a unicorn. The body is that of a humpless animal, without dewlap, but in all other ways characteristically bovine. Unlike nearly all the other creatures on the seals, this animal is evidently not conceived as an actual species, and in our view must have been intended to be a symbolic or mythological creature. Nearly all the unicorn seals have a curious object, frequently described as a standard, in front of the animal. This cannot as yet be definitely identified: various ideas of its significance have been put forward. Mahadevan has suggested that it represents a device for filtering Soma.

198 *Origins of a Civilization*

The second most common animal on the seals is the Indian bison or gaur. These are shown with great natural fidelity, heavily built, with short, curving horns. The head is invariably half-inclined towards the ground; and under it stands a shallow dish or bowl, from which it appears to be about to drink. In several instances its head is actually shown as bending into the dish. A third beast, less common than the others, but carved with great care so as to give a clear picture of the actual variety of the beast, is the zebu or Indian humped cattle. These are shown as large, heavy specimens, and as objects of admiration. The buffalo is the least commonly depicted of the bovines, and like the gaur, tiger and rhinoceros, is sometimes shown with a shallow dish beneath its head. Equally rare are the sheep and the goat. Of these, the representations are scarcely sufficient to determine which species or variety is intended: occasionally a beard and short, raised curved tail suggest a goat, while the form of the horns in some cases indicates the markhor goat, the wild goat, the urial or the ibex. One example of a goat is accorded a 'standard'. The one-horned Indian rhinoceros and the elephant are both well-drawn and clearly identifiable. The rhino in almost every case stands over a shallow bowl (in one instance it, too, is accorded a standard) (*Plate 59*); while the elephant, like the zebu, is invariably shown without any bowl or standard, suggesting that the rhino was regarded as wild (along with the gaur and the buffalo). The tiger is also usually depicted by a regular schema so that it is clearly identifiable. The presence of a shallow trough or bowl is probably intended to show that it, too, is a wild species.

There are also a number of composite animals, or parts of animals, depicted on the seals. A particularly fine example is a creature which has sometimes a human face shown in profile (sometimes the head of an elephant), with the horns of a zebu, the tusks and trunk of an elephant, the mane of a lion, and the body of a bull; with the forelegs and hooves of a bull (and occasionally also hump of a zebu), the hind-quarters, hind-legs and claws of a tiger, and a stubby erect tail like that of a goat (or sometimes long erect curving tail of a baboon) (*Plate 60*). Other bovines have the body and head of a gaur, with a second or sometimes a third head, or heads, of a unicorn and another bovine emerging from the region of the neck. An extraordinary round seal, unfortunately incomplete, shows the heads and necks of six animals, unicorn, gaur, zebu, a tiger, and two other unrecognizable beasts, meeting in a kidney-shaped central object. Another composite animal is a tiger with bovine horns.

One group of seals is of peculiar interest in that it shows scenes representing mythological or socio-religious themes. Several of these

People and Culture   199

iconographic types recur a number of times at a site, and often occur at more than one site. Perhaps the most famous is the figure of a horned deity, possibly ithyphallic, seated in yogic fashion on a low throne, surrounded by wild animals, including an elephant, buffalo, tiger, rhino and goat (*Plate 61*). Another type shows a figure seated in a tree with a tiger standing beneath, looking over its shoulder at the tree. A third shows a composite creature with the hind-parts of a tiger and the fore-parts of human form, with a long hair lock, the horns of a ram, and a plant sprout crowning its head. Another important piece shows a man wrestling with two tigers, recalling the hero fighting lions in the Gilgamesh epic of Mesopotamia. The horned tiger is shown on one seal, apparently being menaced by a female spirit who combines a human form with the horns and tail of a bovine, probably a buffalo. A peculiarly interesting and unique seal was found at Chanhu-daro and has unfortunately been subsequently lost. It appears to show a recumbent figure with female genitalia exposed and a sprout emerging from the head; over this prone figure stands a rearing gaur. The beast is shown (uniquely among Harappan seals) as ithyphallic and is evidently about to copulate with the recumbent female. We shall discuss the interpretation of this scene below. Finally, there is a complex scene which depicts a pipal tree with a horned deity standing in it (*Plate 62*). Another horned figure kneels in a position of supplication or adoration before the tree, and behind it stands a ram with wavy horns and a human face. Below this scene stands a row of seven figures of indeterminate sex. An indistinct object beside the foot of the tree has been interpreted (convincingly) by Parpola as a severed human head set on a small throne (or altar). The interpretation of this scene has been discussed in detail by Parpola (1994, section 14.3) and we shall not discuss it further here. Throughout all these scenes there is a clearly defined set of schema used to represent the different elements. The sex of many of the figures is not clearly indicated; the genital organs or other determining features are often absent or invisible. We are inclined to believe that most if not all anthropomorphic figures with plant sprouts emerging from their heads are intended to be females.

Harappan Religion and Tradition

The study of Harappan religion is still at an early stage. This subject has, perhaps more than most, been confused by attempts to interpret evidence according to preconceived concepts. Already, by 1931, Marshall offered a lengthy discussion of the evidence from the excavations to date, and drew the striking conclusion that 'all the material of a religious nature recovered from Mohenjo-daro and Harappa appears to be characteristically Indian'. His views were based upon comparisons of what he had found in the excavations at Mohenjo-daro with evidence from much later times. In a way his approach can be regarded as a pioneering venture in ethno-archaeology. But it should, nonetheless, be noted that Marshall was not altogether critical in his use of such material, and sometimes read into his data whatever he wished to find. Nevertheless, his views on Harappan religion have remained largely unchallenged. With the added data which are now available, and with the new perspective they provide, it should be possible to carry the study much further. Since Marshall's time it has become clear that for several millennia *before* the beginning of the Mature Indus civilization its human and cultural foundations were being put in place within the Indus system. With this new perspective Harappan religion could be looked at as an integral stage in the development of Indian religion. Moreover, it would suggest that it is not necessary to go beyond the frontiers of the Indus system to seek its origins.

During the past five decades there have been major changes in the understanding of archaeological data and a realization of the need for a systematic theoretical basis for its interpretation. The resulting discussion has tended to become entangled in a whole series of new terms and ideas: 'New' archaeology, 'processual' and 'post-processual' archaeology, etc. To some extent these controversies have obscured the underlying demand: that archaeologists should never forget that the objects they discover are the products of intelligent human beings, living in societies. This calls for a systematic study which views artefacts as parts of industrial or craft traditions, rather than as isolated phenomena, and views evidence for religious practices or beliefs as attributes of man and of the social groups in which he lives. Thus, their interpretation must be as parts of societies functioning as integrated entities. We believe that this type of systematic approach needs to be applied to the study of Harappan religion. A bold beginning has been made along these lines by Subhangana Atre in her study of *The Archetypal Mother* (1987), and there is obviously great scope for extending this sort of enquiry.

Materials for study. The empirical data available for the study of the Indus religion is not inconsiderable, and we shall briefly point to some examples:

1. The first category must be the study of excavated sites, particularly when these appear to have had some special or religious

People and Culture 201

connotation. It is a matter of history that many of the earlier excavations were not conducted with the technical care and thought they deserved, and that thus much of the data they produced was of limited value. In spite of this, much information has been obtained; and, as Ardeleanu, Franke and Jansen (1983) have ably demonstrated, much more data can still be obtained by systematic sifting of the records of some of the earlier excavations. In the example cited, the structural history of the Great Bath can be clearly traced, while the study of all the major objects discovered in its vicinity clearly shows them to be predominantly of ritual or elite importance. When we look around we are surprised to find how much potential there is for this type of systematic study, and how much material there is. The Citadel at Mohenjo-daro yielded, in addition to the Great Bath, the adjoining area of brick platforms referred to by Wheeler as a Great Granary. We have long doubted this identification, and believe that a similar study would throw light on the history and functions of this mysterious complex. Perhaps, it represented something quite different, akin to the brick platforms found on the citadel at Kalibangan. A third complex on the Mohenjo-daro Citadel is at its southern end, where a large brick assembly hall was unearthed. In a nearby room pieces of the very rare stone sculptures were discovered, suggesting that this may have also been a temple area. Here, too, similar systematic study is called for. At least two structures in the lower city have been identified as probable temples, both are in the HR area: the one identified by Wheeler as a temple was the find-spot of another rare stone sculpture which was almost certainly a religious icon; and the other identified by Dhavalikar and Atre (1989) is suggested to have been some sort of fire temple. These buildings too deserve to be subjected to similar intensive study. At Kalibangan three types of structures have been seen as possibly having had religious function: the first is the enclosed area in the centre of the Citadel mound. This contained a series of brick platforms separated from each other by narrow passages. On the surface of this area were discovered a line of distinctive hearths which it has been suggested were ritual fire altars, and a brick-lined pit containing ashes and animal bones. A second interesting structure at Kalibangan was a small square enclosure, east of the lower town. This contained a series of ritual hearths and pits containing ashes and animal bones. The third category of religious structure reported from Kalibangan is in the form of small 'fire rooms' containing similar ritual hearths, within the confines of ordinary houses. The Kalibangan report, containing the fruits of many seasons of costly excavation still awaits publication!

2. A second body of archaeological data consists of the examples of stone sculpture discovered at Mohenjo-daro and at Harappa.

202 *Origins of a Civilization*

These have already been reviewed above (on p. 198-99). Several series occur: the first is of recumbent rams; a second is a composite animal, being a ram with what is possibly an elephant's trunk; and the third is a small group of seated male figures who may be either deities or 'priest-kings'. It is strange that these rams, which depict urial sheep in a most naturalistic manner, are very rarely seen in the range of animals shown on the seals. Similarly, the style of the seated 'priest-kings' does not find immediate echoes in the seal repertoire. Whether the bearded males are intended to represent royal or priestly portraits, or actual deities, is not clear. With Mesopotamian models in mind we are inclined to regard them as royal figures whose portraits were set up in the temple before the deity.

3. We have reviewed the body of relevant data contained in the seals, sealings and amulets from most of the excavated sites in a previous section (p. 199-201). We saw that there were a number of themes, some apparently related to others, some independent, which occur more than once. For instance, some themes occur on several seals and amulets, etc.; and in such cases it is interesting to notice the way in which, perhaps constrained by size of the item, the artist has been selective and attempted to include enough essential detail to convey to the viewer the underlying theme or story. A comprehensive study of the full distribution of such themes, in both space and time, would be very informative. Atre has suggested that some scenes are parts of sequences from some mythological episode. The same theme may occur in both early and later contexts at Mohenjo-daro, suggesting that it was of lasting significance. Some themes occur at several different sites: for example, the tree spirit and tiger theme is found at Mohenjo-daro, Harappa and Kalibangan. While the prime function of the seals may have been practical, probably mercantile, the employment of recognizable mythological or religious themes must also tell us something regarding their currency and extent, and certainly suggests that they were commonly recognized among the seal-using elite. One of the most problematic aspects of the seals is when they appear to contain concepts or ideas which are later found in the Rig Veda. Thus, the strange theme of the bison copulating with the recumbent female with a plant sprouting from her head, referred to above and coming from Chanhu-daro, may be compared with the Vedic theme of the union of heaven and earth (*dyavaprithivi*), the latter represented as the Earth Mother (*mata bhumi*) and the former by the bull of heaven (*dyaur me pita*). Thus, a Harappan theme may find echoes in the Rig Vedic hymns to

View of Lewan factory site, Bannu Basin, NWFP, Pakistan.

A hut similar in plan, floor and other features to that from the Lewan excavation (Fig 13), being constructed near Attock, Pakistan, in 1980 by Afghan refugees from Jalalabad. The frame was afterwards thatched with straw.

The Indus in the Karakoram.

The Indus in flood near Bilot, at the north-western edge of the plain on the NWFP - Punjab border.

The Indus near Mohenjo-daro (winter 1992), showing the wide shallow bed and low bank. Flood water may overspill the bank at any point, tending to do so upstream from Mohenjo-daro, and inundates different parts of the plain.

The Lower Indus plains from the north-west side of the valley opposite Hyderabad.

The Indus in Lower Sindh from the north-west side of the valley, showing some of the remaining gallery forest on the river's edge.

Mehrgarh, view of site, with entrance to the Bolan Pass in the distance.

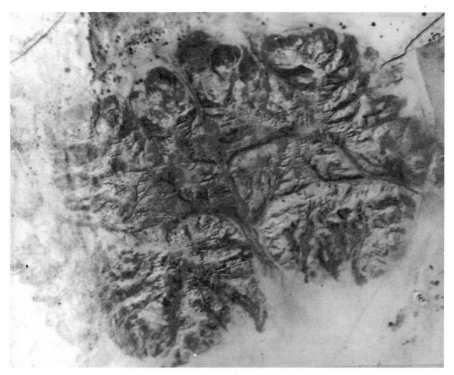

Rahman Dheri, aerial photograph of mound. The outline of the massive brick defences is clearly visible on the east and west sides.

Kalibangan, ploughed field surface, junction of Early and Mature Harappan, c. 2600 BC.

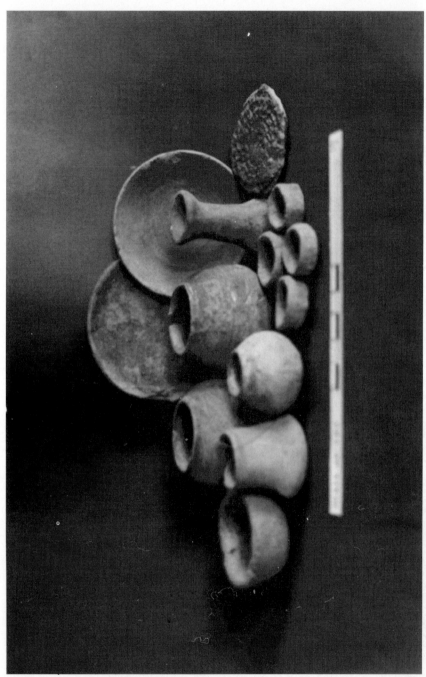

Tarakai Qila, group of miniature pots of Early Harappan period.

Tarakai Qila : terracota model of ox of Early Harappan period.

Tarakai Qila : terracotta models of oxen of Early Harappan period.

Tarakai Qila, terracotta model cart-wheels, some with painted designs.

Modern wooden plough photographed in fields near Mohenjo-daro.

Harappan stone-working floor exposed on hilltop near Sakkhar. At the time of the photograph (1976), and since, the area has been in imminent danger of destruction by modern industrial quarrying.

- Chanhu-daro, terracotta model of a bullock-cart.

Indus river transport, photographed near Sakkhar.

- Carved stone representation of a river boat from Mohenjo-daro.

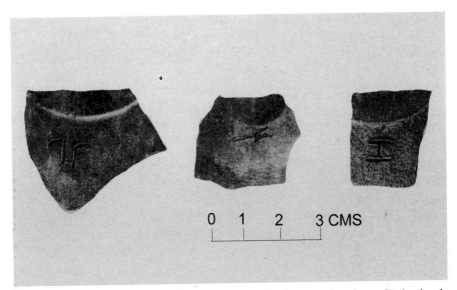

Rahman Dheri, potshards with pre-firing graffiti on exterior face. Such shards belong to the Early Harappan period or its regional equivalent.

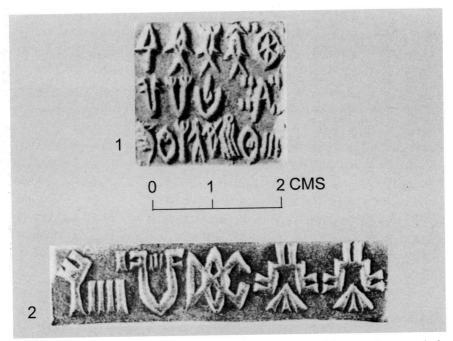

Mohenjo-daro : 1 stone seal with inscription, but without other symbols (M-314); oblong seal with inscription only. (M-1262).

Mohenjo-daro: 1 inscribed seal impression on neck of jar (M-1372); 2. inscribed stoneware bangle (M-1629).

Mohenjo-daro: terracotta seated figure of woman, perhaps making dough.

Standing female terracotta figure with heavy ornaments.

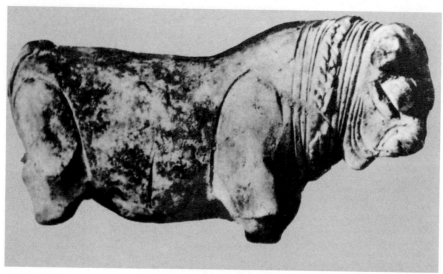

Mohenjo-daro, terracotta figurine of a bison (*bos gaurus*).

Mohenjo-daro: terracotta monkey with pierced hole for inserting climbing string, height c 3.5 cm.

Mohenjo-daro: stone ram of uncertain provenance, maximum length 49 cms and height 27 cms. This is probably the largest and best preserved item in the whole repertoire of Harappan sculpture.

Mohenjo-daro: tiny figure of a seated squirrel in faience, height 2.3 cm.

Mohenjo-daro, steatite seal of unicorn standing in front of characteristic ritual stand (M-8).

Mohenjo-daro, steatite seal of Indian rhinoceros (M-1134).

Mohenjo-daro steatite seal depicting composite beast (M-300).

Mohenjo-daro, steatite seal of seated figure with horned headdress, surrounded by wild beasts (M-304).

Mohenjo-daro, steatite seal with complex mythological content (M-1186).

View of the modern town of Sehwan from top of the high mound (of archaeologically undetermined age), with the Indus in far left distance. The tall flagpole to the left in the middle distance marks the site of the shrine containing the grave of the celebrated Saint Lal Shanbag Kalandar.

View of the dried-up flood plain of the river Sarasvati (Ghaggar), from the site of the Harappan town at Kalibangan. The former flood plain is clearly recognizable in the areas under crops. The far edge of the plain may be recognized in the line of trees in the far distance towards the right of the picture.

Kausambi, brick facing of rampart.

Mahasthangarh, view of moat from ramparts. Although the moat is now almost filled with alluvial deposit, it is still clearly visible on the ground.

Aerial photographs of Sisupalgarh.

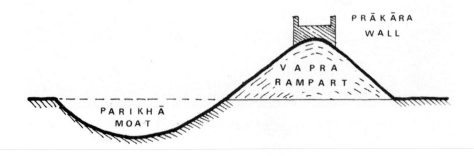

Diagrammatic section through a moat and rampart.

Part of stone city walls of Rajagriha.

Shards of Rouletted ware from Arikamedu.

1

2

3

4

Anuradhapura, inscribed shards from periods J and I.. 1 and 2 from period J5 (calibrated dates c 340-370 BC); 3 from period I2 (Calibrated date c 300 BC); and 4 from period G5 (Calibrated date c. 1st century AD).

Sarnath, Lion capital of the time of Ashoka.

People and Culture 203

Parjanya (RV V. 83), where Parjanya is likened to a thundering bull sprinkling Earth with his semen and fecundating her, thereby causing plants to grow.

We must now conclude by expressing the hope that more systematic study of the problems raised in interpreting the Harappan religion will be undertaken and with a view to solving some of the outstanding questions. For instance, more attention needs to be given to some significant seals from Mesopotamia, such as the 'Indus style' cylinder in the Louvre (Collection De Clercq 1.26), with a view to explaining the source of this 'thoroughly Indian' iconographic material. Another area where systematic study is called for is in determining the conventions employed by the Harappan artists to indicate the sex of many of the figures. Following Marshall, the famous 'Proto-Siva' seal, for example, has been generally regarded as male, even ithyphallic, and yet Sullivan (1964) and Atre (1987) have argued that it is a female. Our own position on this problem is one of neutrality, since some analyses seem to favour the one view, some another. But now that we are armed with much better illustrative materials than formerly, in the clear photographs supplied by Parpola's *Corpus of Indus Seals and Inscriptions*, a systematic study becomes possible and may well produce results. Probably, Marshall was broadly correct in speaking of Harappan religion as 'thoroughly Indian', but so many questions remain to be answered, and there is a need for more dedicated study.

The Place of the Indus Civilization

In the ancient world. In spite of the differences, it cannot escape notice that, once radiocarbon dating supplies India with a chronology, there is a broad parallelism between developments in Egypt, Mesopotamia and the Indus during the millennium from c. 3000-2000 BC. In Egypt, the former date witnesses the beginning of the use of writing, the union of Upper and Lower Egypt into a single kingdom, and the commencement of the Early Dynastic period; this is followed around 2575 BC by the Old Kingdom with the extraordinary burst of pyramid building, and the exaggeration of the royal cult. Around the middle of the third millennium we hear of Egyptian expansion into Nubia and growing evidence of foreign trade and contact with Syria, the Levant, Asia Minor and even the mysterious land of Punt—sometimes believed to refer to peninsular India. In Mesopotamia, writing emerges during the last centuries of the fourth millennium and in the cities of Sumeria, Uruk, Eridu, al-Ubaid and Ur there is a great period of royal temple building, stone sculpture and cylinder seals which contribute to the city culture. At the same time there begins evidence of external trade and even of colonial expansion along the Arabian shores of the Gulf. This development reaches a climax in the reign of Sargon and the uniting of the kingdom of Akkad (c. 2370 BC). As we have seen above, there is reason to link this broad parallelism with the increase of long-distance trade between all three of the civilizations, and to think of this trade as playing a positive role in the advancement of each one in its own tradition.

At first sight the Indus sequence is notably different in that the Early Harappan period provides no evidence of writing, although there certainly are occasional seals; it provides evidence of a growing proliferation of agricultural settlements, among which some appear as the heads of local settlement hierarchies, such as Rahman Dheri or Kalibangan, there is certainly some indication of regular planning and layout of town or city walls and streets, and there is evidence of external trade and contact, especially with Central Asia. For the Indus the century of change comes from 2600-2500 BC, and leads directly into the uniting of the Indus heartland, the burgeoning of cities of hitherto undreamt-of size, Mohenjo-daro, Harappa, etc., the emergence of full city life with its concomitants, external trade with the west on an unprecedented scale. Gordon Childe (1952: 183-84) already read the evidence correctly when he wrote:

> India confronts Egypt and Babylonia by the third millennium with a thoroughly individual and independent civilization of her own, technically the peer of the rest. And plainly it is deeply rooted in Indian soil. The Indus civilization represents a very perfect adjustment of human life to a specific environment, that can only have resulted from years of patient effort.

If one needs further confirmation of the profound and lasting character of the Indus civilization, and of its being the antecedent of the later civilization which sprang up during the Iron Age and Early Historic period, one cannot do better than to visit the modern towns and villages of Sindh and the Punjab. Standing on the top of the high mound at Sehwan, on a winter's dawn, looking through the smokey haze that hangs over the town, it is not difficult to envisage the centuries slipping back some four and a half millennia

People and Culture 205

and to picture this as a Harappan rather than twentieth-century town (*Plate 63*).

In conclusion we must remark that the Indus civilization, as it is currently known to us, is only a part of what it once was. Thinking of the enormous wealth of arts and crafts which have distinguished the region during historical periods, we may not be wrong to conclude that many of the more ephemeral crafts of later times must have had their origins in the earlier period. We are thinking particularly of such things as decorative designs of textiles, wall painting, decoration of woodwork, etc. Sadly, many of these things may be altogether lost; although future excavations may still reveal something of these vanished aspects of life.

In relation to the rest of South Asia. In chapters 5-8, we have focussed on the greater Indus river system to the exclusion of other areas. We have traced the development of settled agricultural communities from the first beginnings on the western margins of the system around 7000 BC, through the period of spreading agriculture to almost all parts of the area, into the formative period of early urbanism which we have called the Early Harappan period, and into the full urbanism of the Mature Harappan period. We have seen how already between 7000-5000 BC, a subsistence economy based on the cultivation of wheat and barley and the keeping of cattle, sheep and goats, had achieved a stable norm. This norm was so well-suited to the environment of the Indus plains and their piedmont zones, that it remained the subsistence base upon which the Indus civilization itself was established. In the following chapters we shall shift our viewpoint, and focus upon developments east and south of the Indus system, and upon the foundations for the 'second' urbanization, first of the Ganges valley and then of South Asia as a whole.

Chapter 10

CHANGING SCENES: INDUS TO GANGES

In chapter 5 we saw how, by around 6000-5000 BC, some parts of South Asia had witnessed the emergence both of a predominantly pastoralist life-style involving the keeping of cattle, sheep and/or goats, and of settled agricultural communities, commonly referred to as Neolithic. We noticed how each of the main Neolithic groupings: those of the Ganges Vindhya region, Kashmir, the southern Deccan, and the Indo-Iranian borderlands, had tended to base their agriculture on certain staple food crops: rice, apparently from early times in the Ganges-Vindhya region; millet in the Deccan; and wheat and barley in the Indus system. In chapters 6 to 8 we made a detailed survey of the Indus life-style and saw how the Indo-Iranian borderlands very early developed a stable balance of subsistence between cattle, sheep and goats, and an agriculture based upon the cultivation of wheat and barley. This pattern subsequently spread, with certain local and regional modifications, throughout the whole Indus system; and has remained the basis of life there ever since. We selected it as particularly significant because, we argued, it provided the subsistence base and indeed life-style which directly underlay South Asia's first urban society, the Indus civilization. Now, and in the following chapter, we shall see how in the aftermath of the Indus civilization new agricultural regimes came into being in which these three main cereal types were combined in different ways and proportions so as to provide a more stable agricultural base under differing climatic and environmental conditions.

Before we approach our next major theme, the developments leading to the second urbanization, a process which began in the Ganges valley and spread to cover South Asia, we shall touch on a number of relevant but subsidiary topics. First, we shall consider more specifically the circumstances attending the end of the Harappan civilization, including the complex role of environmental changes.

Changing Scenes 207

Next, we shall consider the subsequent period in regions to the north-east and south-east of the Indus system. This period has been quite often referred to as a 'Dark Age' or even a 'prehistoric night'; but looking at it afresh we may find that this view altogether misses its true significance. Whatever it may have been called by earlier writers, we shall be arguing that it can now be seen as both the final act of the story of the first, Indus, urbanization; and as the starting point for the second, Gangetic, stage of urbanization during the succeeding centuries. Finally, we shall briefly look at the way in which protohistoric archaeology and tradition confront each other in the north-eastern extremities of the Indus system.

THE END OF THE INDUS CIVILIZATION

The past five decades have produced major changes in thinking on many aspects of the Indus civilization, including the underlying causes of its decline. During this time a new understanding of Plate Tectonics has emerged; and this, as we discussed in chapter 2, is basic to understanding the continuing uplift of the Himalayas and the consequent changes in the courses of rivers which flowed from them. A second major advance has come from a growing understanding of climatic change, particularly rainfall, and its role in relation to the environment and consequently to human culture. Two examples of such climatic change are particularly relevant; Gurdip Singh's (1971) analysis of pollen profiles from lakes in Rajasthan, to which we have referred several times, led to his suggestion that increases in rainfall directly contributed to the rise of the Indus civilization, and likewise that a decrease in rainfall contributed to its end. Commenting on this thesis, Bryson and Swain (1981) showed that Singh's conclusions were consistent with independent climatic data, from both South Asia and beyond, on the dynamics of the monsoon. They also pointed out that such changes were important for understanding the agriculture of the Indus civilization; as not only would an increase of this magnitude result in doubling summer rainfall, but would also imply a considerable increase and extension of winter rains. The second example is the work of the Cambridge-Baroda project in the Thar desert during the seventies which showed how a pattern of climatic fluctuation led to the periodic extension and contraction of the desert through time, and thereby affected the prehistoric settlement pattern both within the desert and in surrounding areas. A major change has also

208   *Origins of a Civilization*

occurred in archaeological thinking, broadening its scope away from intensive studies of single sites and excavations, towards an extensive geographical approach to settlement patterns and many other aspects of human culture which were formerly neglected. We may recall Mughal's study of settlement patterns in the Cholistan area to which we have referred several times and the complementary explorations of the Archaeological Survey of India in Eastern Punjab, Rajasthan and Haryana (Joshi et al. 1984), referred to below. A powerful addition to all these developments will come from more extensive use of satellite imagery. Such new trends hold out great hopes for the future and for the solution of many problems which were virtually insoluble by earlier, more traditional archaeological methods. Therefore, it seems useful to take a fresh look at the end of the Harappan urban phase with these points in mind.

Misra (1984), in a long and thought-provoking discussion of the natural factors affecting the Indus civilization, accepted the widespread evidence of river change and tectonic disturbance as influential, but concluded that Singh's hypothesis that rainfall variations contributed to both the rise and decline of the civilization was not acceptable. We cannot altogether agree with this conclusion. We have been struck by the concurrence of the rainfall changes observed by Singh and confirmed by Bryson and Swain, with the archaeological dating of developments in the Indus system. Thus, the earliest agriculture on the Indo-Iranian borderlands (c. 7000-5000 BC) coincides with Singh's phases II and III (c. 6000-5500 BC) with increased precipitation and increase of carbonized vegetable remains in lake deposits; and the Early and Mature Harappan phases coincide with Singh's Phase IVa (c. 3000-1800 BC), with its considerable increase in rainfall. It is therefore interesting to find that Singh's Phase IVb (c. 1800-1500 BC) discloses the beginning of a fresh period of aridity which corresponds with the end of the Mature Urban culture and the early part of the Post-urban period. We shall return to this below.

The causes of the end of the Indus civilization are still some of the most puzzling aspects of the whole story. This is not the place to discuss this problem in greater detail, and we shall mainly confine ourselves to considering the main causes which we see as contributing not only to the breakdown of the Indus urban culture, but also to the main thrust of this chapter, the prelude to the second urbanization. There have been several recent discussions of the Post-urban period which can be referred to. They include Misra, 1984; Jarrige, 1985, 1994; Kenoyer, 1991; Mughal, 1990b, 1992a, 1992b; Possehl, 1994a; Allchin, 1995, chapters 3-4; Sonwane & Ajithprasad,

Changing Scenes 209

1994. There is considerable variation in the terminology used by different authors in describing the period which follows the end of the Harappan. Shaffer (1992) employed the term 'Localization Era' referring to what he perceived to have been the breakdown of the centralized authority of the Harappan period into a series of local, regional groupings. For the most part the term Late Harappan, or occasionally post-Harappan, is that most commonly used, but we have followed Possehl in calling the period 'Post-urban'; and have proposed to divide it into three sub-divisions, Early, Middle and Late. In the final analysis, the terms employed are not as important as the data and concepts involved, and we do not believe that these various loosely related and largely overlapping terms need cause much confusion.

The growing number of radiocarbon dates from excavated Harappan sites indicate that the civilization continued down to around c. 2000 BC; a smaller number of dates suggest that, in some areas and at some sites at least, it survived until c. 1850 BC. There are still regrettably few dates for the Post-urban period in many provinces, particularly from key sites. For example, in Sindh there are as yet no radiocarbon dates for the Post-urban period at Jhukar or Chanhu-daro. Nor are there, in the Punjab at Harappa (as far as we are aware), any radiocarbon dates for the Post-urban period which is characterized by pottery of the Cemetery H type. However, there are dates from other related sites. For example, we may accept the four dates from Sanghol, between 1900 and 1600 BC, as broadly defining the period in the Punjab. We believe that it is helpful to divide the Post-urban period into the sub-divisions mentioned above because each of them has a rather different character and, as we shall see, represents a different stage in the unfolding drama. The Early Post-urban period, which we may expect to date from c. 2000-1700 BC, covers a time when the Harappan civilization was either still flourishing in some parts of the domain, or at any rate was still very much present in people's memories. By contrast the Middle period, which we believe dates from c. 1700-1300 BC, represents a time of greater regionalization of cultures and the growing emergence of a distinctly post-Harappan style. Finally, the Late Post-urban period, which we may date from c. 1300-1000 BC, witnesses an increasing pace of development towards new cultural groupings. This is particularly the case in the north-east province, including modern West and East Punjab, Haryana and parts of Uttar Pradesh; and to a lesser extent in Saurashtra and Gujarat.

Sindh. In Sindh, the indications are that some sites were abandoned around 2000 BC or in the following centuries, and we believe that we may not be far wrong in suggesting that the core of the Indus

Map 6. *Northern India-Pakistan in the late second and early first millennia BC, showing sites mentioned in chapters 10 & 11.*

civilization begins to break up around that time, coming to an end shortly after. The Early Post-urban period may be said to extend from that date to c. 1700 BC. Not all sites suffer the same fate: Mohenjo-daro peters out; while at nearby Jhukar and Lohamjo-daro somewhat smaller settlements of the Post-urban Jhukar period (c. 1900-1600 BC) continue, built upon the remains of the Harappan. A similar picture is found at Chanhu-daro and Amri. The Jhukar culture contains a number of intrusive objects, such as round button seals, which find their closest analogues to the finds from the Bactrian archaeological complex. Thus, we may expect the Jhukar phase in Sindh to straddle the Early and Middle Post-urban periods. There appears to have been a further deterioration of climate in

Sindh in the Late Post-urban period, towards the end of the second millennium, when at Chanhu-daro and elsewhere there were no more than small camp sites of probably nomadic people, and no major settlement of that time has as yet been identified. It looks as though this period is till now largely lacking in evidence of settlements.

As we saw in chapter 6 there are several factors that probably contributed to the abandonment of the urban sites. These include economic factors, particularly the decline of Mesopotamian trade which had been flourishing up to c. 2000 BC. The reasons for this are unimportant to our discussion, but its decline must have been serious for the Indus cities as, unlike the merchants of Egypt and Mesopotamia, they had no alternative major trading partner to turn to. It would appear that they must have had considerable trade within their own region and its hinterland to fall back on, but this too seems to have been undermined by other causes. In Sindh particularly, and perhaps in other regions to a lesser extent, there was clearly a steady deterioration in the climate and environment. Uplift of the Himalayas due to Plate Tectonics is probably the principal underlying cause of changes in the course of the rivers of the Indus system, as we have outlined in earlier chapters. Flam (1993) has shown that there was a major shift of up to twenty miles in the course of the Indus, c. 2000 BC, which brought it into immediate proximity with Mohenjo-daro. Part of the cause of this must have been tectonic disturbance in the Himalayas and the northern Punjab plains. Around this time the course of the Sutlej was away from the Hakra channel and into the Indus. The volume of the Hakra's flow would thereby have been reduced; while that of the Indus would be correspondingly increased. As a result the Indus floods would have become greater in volume and more erratic. It is also possible that some decline in rainfall, due to causes indicated in the previous chapter, had already begun prior to 1800 BC. A decline in rainfall would mean a reduction in vegetation in much of the Indus system, and a corresponding increase in erosion and in the gravels and silts carried by the rivers in times of flood and deposited in the plains. This in turn would have led to the Indus in particular building up its bed and probably also the level of its flood plain. Previously, with some rainfall throughout the year and a more regular flow, the Indus channel must have been somewhat more deeply incised into the plain than it is today, with a flood plain of considerable width, itself cut into and to some extent contained by older alluvium. This is what we see in regions of slightly higher

212   *Origins of a Civilization*

rainfall today, and is the pattern of, for example, the Narbada in its lower course across the plain of Gujarat. Cities such as Mohenjo-daro, Amri and Kot Diji would have been sited on hard ground at the valley edge or on the older alluvium at a higher level than the flood plain, as are cities in most river valleys in the subcontinent today. A reduction in rainfall in the plains of Sindh and the immediate hinterland could well have been an added cause for the abandonment of Mohenjo-daro and other urban sites, as it would seriously have reduced their agricultural base and their ability to support the city population.

Another part of the complex picture of events in Sindh is supplied by the evidence of sites on the Kachi plain; at Nausharo the final period IV of Harappan occupation is dated to c. 2200-2000 BC. This probably more or less coincides with the clear evidence from neighbouring Mehrgarh VII and Sibri of new influences showing 'too many intrusive elements . . . and similarities with the Bactria-Margiana archaeological complex to be seen as a purely local assemblage' (Jarrige, 1995: 305-311). Thus, these sites suggest that the final stage of the Harappan urban tradition in this region came into contact with new elements having Bactrian-Central Asian affiliations. The next point in the sequence is supplied by the occupation of the neighbouring site of Pirak (c. 1800-1700 BC) where a very different set-up and style of pottery is accompanied by terracotta models of horses and Bactrian camels. This new trend shows a marked break with the Harappan style and may indicate a major folk movement from the north, from Bactria-Margiana (Jarrige, 1994). The Pirak settlement continues right through the second millennium and into the first, and witnesses before the end of the millennium the first introduction of iron. Another significant introduction is of sorghum millet. It has been pointed out that this was part of a general re-orientation of agriculture, involving exploitation of both summer and winter harvests, so as to adapt to the arid climatic conditions which prevailed during the second millennium (Jarrige, 1985).

Cholistan. Returning to the plains we find a major change in the settlement pattern of the Cholistan region (Mughal, 1990b). As we have seen in chapters 7 and 8 a small cluster of sites developed in the area around the modern Derawar Fort in the Hakra valley during the period of Early Agricultural Expansion; during the Early Harappan period settlements spread out along the valley eastwards as far as the neighbourhood of Fort Abbas. The persisting clustering of sites suggests that at that time there must have been a ready availability of

Changing Scenes

water in this area, in what may well have been an internal drainage system, suggesting the substantial demands of agriculture upon the Hakra river's already probably limited flow. During the Mature Harappan period the number of settlements multiplied and spread both eastwards and westwards. In the Post-urban period there is a dramatic fall in the number of settlements and a tendency for them to follow closely along river channels. In other words there must have been a considerable reduction of the volume of water flowing down the Hakra river. In the Late Post-urban period through to the early first millennium BC there is no more than a slender string of small settlements, in the eastern part of the area, strung out along its now dried-up course.

Once again we must enquire whether this changing settlement pattern can as yet be related to natural events; and once again there is a clear coincidence. The history of the several tributary streams which flowed from the Himalayas into the now dry river course known variously as Ghaggar, Hakra and Sarasvati is of crucial importance and considerable complexity (see chapter 6). We shall not discuss here questions regarding its lower course through Sindh and to the sea, as little can be said on this regarding the Post-urban period. It is generally accepted that at one time the river received the water of the Jhelum and that this was subsequently captured by the Indus; similarly it is generally accepted that the original Sarasvati and perhaps other streams lost their headwaters when they were captured by the Jamuna. Finally, the residual flow of the Sarasvati dried up altogether. Established settlement patterns from the late fourth millennium BC clearly indicate that the river was flowing at that time; their continuing expansion during Early and Mature Harappan times likewise indicates that it continued to flow down to c. 2000 BC. The major reduction of sites in the Early Post-urban period (c. 2000-1700 BC) and their concentration along certain of the river channels strongly suggests that a major part of the river's water supply was lost around that time; while the final settlement pattern of the Late Post-urban period indicates that the river was by then dry (i.e. by c. 1300-1000 BC).

North-Western (Punjab) Province. The rough triangle formed by the Indus, Sutlej and foothills of the Himalayas is an area in which almost no Mature Harappan sites are known, and very few which can be assigned to the Early or Middle Post-urban period. The reason for this situation is not clear, and we shall not dwell on it here, except to remark upon the marked contrast with the region east of the Jhelum.

214 *Origins of a Civilization*

Saurashtra and Gujarat. In chapter 7 we saw how in Rajasthan, Saurashtra and Gujarat there appeared to be a somewhat different situation to that in the Indus system proper, in that in each of these areas local cultures arose during the Early Harappan and continued to thrive during the Mature Harappan period. It was only at coastal sites in Gujarat-Saurashtra, and in northern Kacch that sites which might be regarded as Mature Harappan colonies appeared. Again, with the end of the Mature Harappan period these distinctive sites disappeared, while local cultures continued to flourish. A substantial number of such sites are known, and some, such as Rojdi, actually increased in size at this time. Thus, whatever precise combination of factors may have been the cause of the depopulation of Sindh, their effects were evidently not felt so acutely in Saurashtra and Gujarat. Indeed, it may be that there was some marginal movement of population into these areas from Sindh, seeking to escape the effects of the deteriorating climate there, but we cannot be sure that any such movement took place. As we see it, the evidence for contacts between Sindh and Saurashtra is much more in the context of the Mature Harappan period itself, and particularly in the securing of sources of raw material and control of the Mesopotamian sea trade. These interesting questions deserve further research.

The Post-urban Period in the Sarasvati-Drishadvati Valleys

The area lying to the south and east of the Sutlej river presents a remarkable contrast to its more northerly neighbour. This region has been the subject of extensive explorations over the years by the Archaeological Survey of India, and a summary and analysis of this work is to be found in Joshi et al., 1984, and Dikshit, 1984, on which the following discussion is primarily based. The area involved is roughly bounded by the Sutlej river on the west, by the Himalayas on the north, and by the Ganges on the east. Today, it includes parts of Punjab, northern Rajasthan and Haryana. Through it a whole series of rivers and streams flow, or flowed out across the plains to join either the Ganges or the Indus system. Among these the Sarasvati, later captured by the Jamuna, and the Drishadvati are particularly important. It is also significant that much of the area today enjoys a rainfall notably higher than that of any part of Sindh. In addition, as we have seen earlier, both the winter and summer rainfall can be expected to have increased correspondingly during the Early and Mature Harappan periods. It must, however, be remembered that the rainfall remains highly variable,

Changing Scenes 215

and the riverine water resources must have at all times played a major role in life and agriculture.

As we have seen in earlier chapters, parts of this area were already extensively settled during Early Harappan times. Joshi lists an aggregate of 127 sites of that period. We would expect there to have been a correspondingly larger number of sites of the Mature Harappan period, but the report lists only 79. These figures have possibly been distorted. A likely cause of confusion is that, as we saw in chapter 7, many of the smaller sites of the Mature Harappan period in Haryana continue to show typical Early Harappan pottery, while a smaller number of (mainly larger) sites show an element of typical Mature Harappan features. Our expectation is that some of the sites listed as Early Harappan should more properly be assigned to the Mature period: thus the total number of sites attributed to the Early Harappan period is likely to be a little too large, while that for the Mature Harappan may be correspondingly too small. Even so, with the addition of an eastern group of sites around Saharanpur, the aggregate figure is 110; and we believe that if we compensate for the possible distortion a truer figure for Mature Harappan sites would be around 160. Whatever the correct figures may be for these two periods, it is the Post-urban or Late Harappan distribution which is most surprising, in that it offers an aggregate of some 149 sites in Haryana and Punjab, plus a further 130 sites in Uttar Pradesh. To this situation we must now turn our attention.

It is interesting to consider what the causes were of this great expansion in the number of sites and presumably also of population. If we are right in suspecting that the drying up of the Sarasvati was a contributory factor, perhaps a major cause of the depopulation which we believe occurred in Sindh, then it seems likely that the considerable population base which formerly existed in what is now the Cholistan desert was progressively forced back by the dying river, and would have moved up the river course towards the north-east, so long as its depleted waters continued to flow. This factor is one which we must bear in mind when we go on to consider the linking of archaeological and traditional evidence for this area. It is also possible that some reduction of rainfall may have actually rendered this area more attractive for clearance and habitation.

It is apparent from the distribution maps that sites of the Early Harappan period are particularly found along the courses of the Ghaggar (or Sarasvati) and Chautang (or Drishadvati) rivers and their tributaries; and that the same distribution underlies the Mature Harappan sites, with an additional extension of sites to the east of

216 *Origins of a Civilization*

the Jamuna in the vicinity of Saharanpur. The contrast of this earlier pattern with the sites of the Post-urban period is very striking. The major change is the great increase in the number of settlements spreading out across the plains in the eastern part of the area, in a belt between 100-200 km in width, running from north-west to south-east, following the edge of the Himalayan foothills. Here the great majority of the Post-urban settlements occur. Also, there are now considerably more sites to the east of the Jamuna, clustering at the northern end of the Doab, and extending southwards.

A number of interesting sites have been excavated in the region: some like Banawali were built over the remains of a Mature Harappan town, with its considerable structures; but others, such as Bara, Hulas and Sanghol, appear to be new foundations of the post-urban period. At Banawali, the brick structures of the Mature Harappan were replaced by house walls made of pressed earth. There is still much work to be done to establish more accurately the relative size of settlements and the nature of the settlement hierarchy, before we can determine whether any of them deserve to be called cities, but the general impression is that there were no cities during this period. Radiocarbon dates are few and far between and suggest that the period lasts from c.1800 BC to c. 1300 BC. One of the more consistent series of dates comes from Sanghol in Ludhiana district. Among the excavated sites Bhagwanpura in Kurukshetra district is important because it has been fully published (Joshi et al. 1993). At both Sanghol and Bhagwanpura there is reported to be no break between the earlier and later phases of the Post-urban period. It appears that the characteristic red ware of Harappan tradition which dominates the earlier phase (IA) is, at a certain point, augmented with the distinctive Painted Grey Ware and a coarser grey ware in the later phase (IB). There appears to have been a continous occupation through much if not all of the Post-urban period. A somewhat unsatisfactory series of thermoluminescent dates suggests two main stages of occupation, the first (IA) dating from the Middle Post-urban, and the second (IB) dating from the Late Post-urban; the excavator concludes that the dates of these two are from c. 1750-1300 BC for the former and c. 1400-1000 BC for the latter.

Bhagwanpura is important for a number of reasons. A small settlement on the banks of the Sarasvati river, for the earlier phase of occupation the structures revealed are simple round houses with light timber frames. In the second phase much more substantial houses with many oblong rooms of mud brick were being built; and in the late stage of the occupation burnt brick was used. Horse bones were found in the phase IB but not in IA; so too were small terracotta female figurines recalling those associated with Taxila (Hathial) and other sites of the Gandhara grave culture. Numbers of copper objects Were found in IB, but none in IA; and no objects of iron were found in either phase. The fact that the typical Post-urban Harappan tradition of the early phase is augmented by characteristic Painted Grey Ware in the second, and the growing number of settlements of this Late Post-urban phase suggests that there was a substantial increase in population during these centuries.

The excavations at Hulas, in Saharanpur district, are still not fully published and the radiocarbon dates are scarcely enough to provide a firm chronology for what has proved to be an unusually interesting site. The early dates suggest that the site was founded in the late stage of the Mature Harappan period and, like Bhagwanpura, continued through the Post-urban period and into the Painted Grey Ware period. The published descriptions suggest that the latter period is clearly differentiated from the earlier by occupying a separate though contiguous area.

Some of the most significant finds of the Post-urban stage in this region are not narrowly archaeological, but rather botanical. An outstanding example is a study of the plant remains from the Late Harappan period obtained from the excavations at Hulas, in Saharanpur district. These have been studied by K. S. Saraswat of the Birbal Sahni Institute in Lucknow (Saraswat, 1993). The cereal grains include evidence of rice (*Oryza Sativa*); two types of wheat (*Triticum sphaerococcum* and *Triticum aestivum*); one type of barley (*Hordeum vulgare*); oats (*Avena sativa*); two types of millet, *jawar (Sorghum bicolor)* and *ragi (Eleusine coracana)*, lentils (*Lens culinaris*), horse gram (*Dolichos biflorus*), green gram *(mung dal) (Vigna radiata)*, several other leguminous plants, including field peas, chickpeas, etc. A single seed of cotton (*Gossypium arboreum*) is also reported to have been found. Such a wide range of foodgrains is quite remarkable and far removed from any of the typical assemblages of the Mature Harappan period.

We have seen in earlier chapters how the Harappan economy was based primarily upon wheat and barley. We have indicated that the decline in rainfall during the second millennium probably forced many farmers in drier regions to adopt new strategies to feed themselves, and particularly how millets, probably introduced from Africa, found a place in this new scheme. Similarly, we have seen that in the Ganges Neolithic times there is evidence of the exploitation of rice from the final stages of the Mesolithic; and that there is evidence from Chirand, Khairadih, etc., that rice was a major crop in Neolithic

218 *Origins of a Civilization*

and Chalcolithic times. It is evident that a new pattern of mixed agriculture became established in this region, and that it embraced all three of the major cereal groups, wheat/barley, rice and millets. This new pattern established in the Indo-Gangetic divide during the second millennium was to become the basic pattern for the succeeding millennia, and indeed for the rise and spread of population and settlements during the period of the second urbanization. It is also noteworthy that the basic cropping pattern of the East Punjab, Haryana and Ganges-Jamuna Doab, down to modern times, follows the same lines.

PROTOHISTORIC ARCHAEOLOGY AND TRADITION

In this book, up to this point, we have aimed to utilize the empirical data supplied by archaeology, along with geography, geology, environmental studies of various kinds, and have so far made little or no attempt to relate such data to historical tradition. There are, however, several small exceptions to this: for example, in our discussion of the languages spoken in the Harappan empire, or of the possible interpretation of Harappan seals in terms of later, Vedic texts. The time has now arrived when we must modify this position.

At the outset it must be pointed out that the area we are now considering is one of peculiar significance in Brahmanical tradition. Thus, Manu (II. 17-22), probably in the late centuries BC, in his discussion of the sources of the law and of established right practice, refers to four successive areas as worthy of emulation. The four appear to represent chronological sequent statements, each one naming a wider area than its predecessor. The first (and probably oldest statement) names the land between the divine rivers Sarasvati and Drishadvati as a 'god-delineated land' known as *Brahmavarta*, and states that the practice of that land is called right practice (*sadacara*). The subsequent verse restates the case and says that *Brahmarsidesa* is another name for that area, and that it includes Kurukshetra, and the area occupied by the Matsyas, Pancalas and Surasenas. This restatement of the geographical area is noticeably wider and includes land to the east of the Jamuna. The two succeeding statements we shall refer to later (*p. 232, 260*).

We may ask when the sanctity of this area was first recognized or arose, and whether it goes back to the burgeoning settlements of the Post-urban period. In this context it would seem worthwhile considering whether either Vedic or late Vedic literature provides us

Changing Scenes 219

with any clues. A prime source must be the *Samhitas* of the Vedas, and particularly the Rig Veda. The Rig Veda is in no way a unitary or homogeneous text: the bringing together of the hymns into *Samhita* form may have involved more than one stage, and one can recognize probable earlier and later hymns, and even *Mandalas*. Many of the hymns may already have been ancient when they were first gathered into the *Samhita*. The hymns of *Mandalas* 2-7 have been seen as constituting the core of the collecting process, while those of parts of *Mandalas* 1 and 10, which contain many important metaphysical speculations, are evidently of later date. There is really no way in which the text, or any part of it can be dated, but there is a general consensus among scholars that the compilation of the hymns into a single collection (*Samhita*) took place around 1500 BC. There has also been wide agreement that the whole work, including its latest parts, was complete before the beginning of the Late Vedic period, i.e. probably by 1000 BC.

The 'geography' of the Rig Veda centres around rivers: the term *Sapta-Sindhava* (seven Sindhu rivers), is generally taken to include the Sindhu (Indus) itself, the five rivers of the Punjab, the Sutudri (modern Sutlej), Vipas (Beas), Parushni (Ravi), Asikni (Chenab), and Vitasta (Jhelum), and the Sarasvati (probably including courses of the modern Sarsuti and Ghaggar-Hakra). A number of other tributaries of the Indus are mentioned, among them the Kubha (Kabul), Krumu (Kurram), Gomati (Gomal) and Suvastu (Swat), all being western tributaries, and the Drishadvati (probably modern Chautang) and Apaya, being eastern tributaries. The references to the Sarasvati are particularly numerous and interesting. The Sarasvati river is described as the seventh (*saptathi*) of the Sindhu rivers and as *Sindhu-mata*, perhaps Mother of the Indus (RV VIII. 36.6). Again, she is referred to as 'great among the great, and mightiest of rivers' (RV VI. 61.13); and as following from the mountains to the ocean (RV VII. 95.2), with various kings ruling on her banks (VII.21.18). She is also delightfully described as *ambitame, naditame,* and *devitame*, 'most motherly', 'most riverly' and 'most goddessly' (RV II.41.16). There are however other references to Sarasvati which seem to regard her as already more of a goddess than a river (see for example RV I.164.49). But this is not the case in the majority of Rig Vedic references. Indeed, no other river in the Rig Veda is accorded so many references, nor such respect.

The hymns certainly recognize divine interventions in relation to nature in, for example, the role of the serpent Vritra penning up the waters in a mountain cave from which Indra released them, allowing

220 *Origins of a Civilization*

them to flow again, thereby letting flow the seven Sindhu rivers (RV I.31, II.12). Or, Indra's intervention on behalf of the king Sudasa when he temporarily made the deep river Parusni fordable and later returned its waters to their normal channel (RV VII.18.5-9). Such references incline one to think that the authors of the Rig Veda were at that time aware of the effects of tectonic upheavals in the mountains and of occasional diversions of river courses and exceptional floods. In this respect, they may bear some relationship with the archaeological observations we have outlined regarding the drying up of the Sarasvati, after the capture of its waters by the Jamuna, etc. For us, it was a most moving experience to stand on the mound at Kalibangan, and to see still preserved in the modern cropping the area of the flood plain of the Sarasvati still clearly visible (*Plate 64*). This could be seen, even before the access of modern canal irrigation to the area.

We are entitled to ask who were the Indo-Aryan speaking authors of the hymns, and what relation did they have with the long-established population of the region, whose presence is well-attested to by the archaeological record. The latter must be borne in mind and considered alongside that provided by tradition and literature, to see whether the two categories offer one another support, or not. One may certainly enquire what, if any, is the archaeological evidence which may relate to the arrival of new elements of the populations, with a distinctive culture, or which might be interpreted in terms of an intrusive elite who established power over an existing population. It is upon this kind of comparative evidence that we may reach a realistic view of such matters.

In a recent publication one of us proposed an hypothesis for the arrival of Proto-Indoaryan speaking tribes in the Indo-Iranian frontier regions around 2000 BC (Allchin, 1995). These tribes evidently formed part of a southern extension of the culture complex which arose in Bactria and Margiana around that time. Parpola (1994, 148:159) offers a helpful discussion of the linguistic and archaeological evidence. He suggests that these incomers may be identified with the Dasas (Old Persian, *daha*), and constituted an earlier Indo-Aryan speaking wave closely related to the later Rig Vedic Indo-Aryans. These people were warlike and equipped with horses and chariots, and they were hungry to conquer the militarily less equipped local agricultural communities. According to our hypothesis, a process of conquest and interaction between these people and the rulers of the Indus civilization began at that time, and continued for several centuries. The process involved several elements. Perhaps the most

Changing Scenes

important was the growing tendency for language replacement which led to an even greater proportion of the indigenous population of the Indus area abandoning their original speech and adopting Indo-Aryan dialects. Equally significant was the emergence of a culturally plural society, in which those who regarded themselves as direct descendants of 'Aryan' families claimed higher status and precedence, while those whose occupations, colour or antecedents left no doubt that they were of indigenous extraction found themselves relegated to a much lower position, as Sudras are clearly regarded in RV X.90.13. Between these two extremes must have been a large number of people of less clearly determinable origins who would have sought to raise their status in the hierarchy by adopting Aryan ways and language. These ideas are not new: D.D. Kosambi, (1952, 1956) has already explored facets of the process. But one needs to know more about the processes of acculturation, and, for instance, regarding the relationship of 'Aryan' groups with the ruling elite of the Harappan civilization, or its successor states. Kosambi discusses references in the Rig Veda to non-Aryan Brahmins, the sons of Dasa women, and sees 'good reason to believe that the first Brahmins were the result of interaction between the Aryan priesthood and the ritually superior priesthood of the Indus culture' (Kosambi, 1956: 96-101).

The process we have envisaged probably did not happen all at once, but is more likely to have developed over centuries. For example, Parpola identifies the Rig Vedic Aryans with a second 'wave' of Indo-Aryan speakers who emanated from the same regions of Central Asia as their predecessors and were probably closely related to them in language and culture. This 'wave' he suggests followed the same tracks as the earlier, but arriving after some centuries, around 1500 BC. Like their predecessors they too were warlike and out for conquest, fighting not only the older population of the Indus plains but also with their predecessors, the Dasas, who by this time were probably already culturally and ethnically involved with each other; and he interprets the Rig Vedic references to their battles with the Dasas in this light. In our earlier work, we expressed doubt whether it was yet possible to determine if this second 'wave' originated in the Bactrian region or simply derived from the already partly acculturated earlier settlers as they moved eastwards into the Indus valley and beyond. Either alternative, or both, are possible, and although we prefer our own reading, Parpola's thesis has much to recommend it. Whatever may have been the case, the important thing from our point of view is that groups of Vedic Aryans moved eastwards and settled in the valleys of the Punjab and the Sarasvati.

222 *Origins of a Civilization*

Here, they must not only have fought with rival groups and among themselves, but also established relations of various kinds with the already settled population. Their presence should therefore be in evidence archaeologically in the sites assignable to the Middle and Late Post-urban periods (which as we have seen may be dated to c. 1700-1300 and c.1300-1000 BC respectively). But as yet it is scarcely attested in the archaeological record, presumably because their material culture and life-style were already virtually indistinguishable from those of the existing population. There has been widespread acceptance that the pottery called 'Painted Grey ware' should belong to the Rig Vedic Indo-Aryan speakers. We cannot accept this view: such items of material culture are very rarely the private monopoly of any one ethnic, racial, let alone linguistic group, but are the products of craftsmen, working within traditions, and serving whole communities. Therefore, while the 'PGW' may be, either wholly or partly, contemporary with the events we are discussing, it cannot be identified as either the product or property of any one section of this already culturally and ethnically plural society. In contrast, the literary production of what is likely to have been one segment of that society may be recognized in the hymns of the Rig Veda. It was in the interaction of these several groups within the Indus system, and particularly in its north-eastern parts, that, by the Late Post-urban period, a new concept of 'Aryan' ethnicity was well and truly established. We should like to stress our view that the process was predominantly one of cultural interaction and adaptation, leading to the emergence of ethnic self-consciousness. The society this gave rise to was in essence culturally plural, involving elements from the culture of the existing population as well as from the newcomers. We believe that there is no reason to hunt vainly for archaeological traces of the presence of groups of 'invading' Aryans; nor could the arrival of relatively small numbers of Indo-Aryan speaking groups possibly lead to the emergence of an 'Aryan race'. What the process almost certainly did produce was a society in which power and social prestige were enjoyed by those who claimed to be the descendants of such immigrants.

Chapter 11

THE SECOND URBANIZATION

THE COLONIZATION OF THE GANGES VALLEY

In the previous chapter we have seen how, during the second millennium BC, there was a dramatic reduction in the size and number of settlements in parts of the Indus system; but that a quite different situation prevailed in the eastern Punjab and Haryana where, particularly in the second half of the millennium, there was an unprecedented expansion in the number of settlements. The situation in Sindh, we believe, arose from the deterioration of the environment brought about by changes in river courses and even the total disappearance of the Sarasvati, and exacerbated by a general decline in rainfall. We further saw how in the Late Post-urban Harappan period an increase in the number of settlements also began in the north-western parts of the Doab. The result was evidently a major reduction in population in the more arid regions. We cannot but wonder whether some part of the increase in settlements in the north-eastern province of the Indus system was not linked to population moving out of areas of increasing aridity and seeking new homes in better environments. Now we shall turn to the archaeological evidence from the Ganges plains, focussing in particular on the growth of settlements that can now be recognized as the precursor of the second urbanization.

At the outset we should try to make clear what we mean by the 'colonization' of the Ganges plains. We noticed in chapter 5 how scattered Mesolithic sites are found both in the Vindhya hills to the south, and also on the plains themselves. We further remarked on the appearance of Neolithic and later of Chalcolithic ways of life, including cattle-keeping and agriculture and the cultivation of rice, scattered widely over the southern margins and the central plains.

224   *Origins of a Civilization*

Clearly considerable areas of the Ganges plains were already settled, if sparsely. However, it is evident that from the Late Post-urban Harappan period onwards a population spread of a different order began in the northern parts of the Doab, and rapidly extended through the Upper and Middle Ganges plains. In the previous chapter we saw how studies of settlement patterns in East Punjab, Haryana and the northern parts of the Doab, suggest that this expansion was itself an extension of a similar, and perhaps slightly earlier, development to the south-west of this region. This leads us to infer that this series of interrelated developments led on to a movement of population south-eastwards into the Doab. This is what we refer to as colonization: but at the same time we must not forget that, as a result of the widespread adoption of rice cultivation by the incomers in the Upper Ganges plains, the increase of population could also be seen as an independent development. Probably, both factors were involved during this time.

Environment of the Ganges Plains. In chapter 2, we briefly reviewed the environment of the Ganges plains but we may now draw attention to some further features. The whole valley may be divided into three major sections; the Upper Gangetic plains, corresponding with the Doab of the Ganges and Jamuna rivers as far as their confluence (*sangam*), and comprising districts of modern Uttar Pradesh; the Middle Gangetic plains from Allahabad eastward, comprising eastern UP and Bihar; and the Ganges-Brahmaputra delta, comprising Bengal in the West and Bangladesh in the east. Throughout the course of the Ganges there are a number of major tributary streams, on the north from the Himalayas, and on the south from the Vindhyas and Mekhala ranges; but within the Doab the drainage is entirely local, with drainage streams such as the Rind flowing gently in a south-easterly direction, dictated by the underlying inclination of the plains. The northern plains are inherently liable to flooding by the major tributaries, and are consequently punctuated by former channels and meanders, many of which leave oxbow lakes. The rainfall is almost wholly monsoonal, and precipitation increases steadily as one travels eastwards. The vast alluvial plains have been, since their earliest settlement, the basis for highly productive agriculture. In the lower rainfall areas in the north-west predominantly wheat and barley are grown, and to the east the proportion of rice steadily increases. As we saw in the previous chapter, the agriculture of the Doab, as reported at Hulas, from the second millennium BC onwards, involved a utilization of cereal crops of all three classes wheat/barley, rice and millets. This has enabled farmers to maximize the yield in differing rainfall and climatic conditions, and to obtain both winter and summer crops from the same land.

The modern landscape as we move eastward is increasingly man-made. Anciently, much of the land was under forest, and initially there must have been a need for large-scale clearance and deforestation. How and in what circumstances this was accomplished has still to be worked out, but there is general agreement that burning was a major method of forest clearance, while the availability of iron axes must have played an important, if secondary, role. It would be a mistake, however, to think that the forest clearance was ever wholesale. It is probable that originally there would have been only limited clearance of the land required for cultivation around any settlement. Pollen and charcoal samples from excavated sites, such as Hastinapura and Atranjikhera, suggest that in the earlier stages of the settlements there was still extensive forestation in the vicinity (Lal, 1989: 38-39). This is supported by early textual references. For example, the Mahabharata refers to Hastinapura, the capital of the Kurus as situated in a forest, the *Kuru-Jangala*, and this is often mentioned in other texts, for example the Ramayana. It is probable that throughout the centuries there has been a direct correlation between the growth of population and the demands of increasing agricultural production, and the area of forest which was allowed to survive in any area. What we see today in the Ganges plains is very much the final stage, when continuing population growth and pressure has led to almost complete extinction of the forests.

Archaeological Sequence

Before we consider in more detail the development of settlements in the late second millennium BC, particularly with reference to the Doab, we shall briefly sketch in the outline of the wider culture sequence of the Ganges valley as a whole. In chapter 5 we saw how at various places, mainly in the Middle Ganges valley and on its southern margin, Neolithic sites appeared at a remarkably early date. We saw that the eastern Neolithic, of which they form a part, apparently also spread in course of time on to the Ganges plains themselves, for example at Chirand. Not all the excavated sites have been published and regrettably only a few radiocarbon dates are available, but it is clear that the earliest levels at such sites represent a Neolithic culture, with hand-made pottery, bone and stone

226   *Origins of a Civilization*

industries, but without metal. The subsistence included rice and other cereals, such as barley, and fish bones were a common occurrence. At Chirand this culture is dated to c. 2000-1700 BC, but its beginnings may well be earlier than these dates suggest. Around 1500 BC, items of copper begin to appear, along with Black-and-Red and painted pottery, and this phase has been called Chalcolithic. Somewhere after 1000 BC, perhaps around 800 BC, the first objects of iron are found.

The sequence in the Doab is slightly different. Here, the earliest settlements yield a predominantly red pottery, known in Indian archaeological writing as Ochre Coloured pottery (OCP), but which we prefer to call 'red ware of Harappan tradition'. This pottery is not clearly differentiated from the Post-urban red wares (of both Mature Harappan and even Early Harappan tradition) from sites in the Punjab and Haryana. Its chronology in the Doab is not as yet clearly established. The previously excavated site of Alamgirpur has often been regarded as a Harappan outpost in the Doab; but it may be questioned whether it can be called Harappan in any strict sense of the term. Rather, we believe, it is likely to be contemporary with the Early Post-urban period of the Punjab, that is to say from c. 2000 BC. We are not at present aware of any definite evidence of actual Harappan sites from east of the Jamuna. One of the most authoritative excavations to date is that at Atranjikhera in Etah district (Gaur, 1983). Here, the earliest occupation is assigned to the OCP period (I), for which a group of thermoluminescent dates were obtained extending from 2280-1170 BC. Our opinion is that this first period should be tentatively dated from c. 2000 to c. 1300 BC. It is succeeded by a second period (II) characterized by the presence of Black-and-Red ware, and generally datable from 1300-1000 BC. In this period, copper was found, but apparently no iron. This in turn is followed by period III in which Painted Grey Ware occurs, as well as a wide range of iron objects. There is still much uncertainty regarding the date at which the third period begins, both at Atranjikhera and elsewhere, but it seems reasonable to assign this event to a date of c. 1100 BC, and the period thus defined continues until the beginning of the subsequent period which is associated with the presence of Northern Block Polished ware, i.e. c. 550 BC.

The Spread of Iron Working. In view of the importance of human subsistence, and the technology of the development and manufacture of iron tools, it is a matter of some regret that the evidence for so

The Second Urbanization 227

momentous a change is as yet imprecisely dated in many parts of India and Pakistan. This imprecision is in part due to the tendency of archaeologists in India to use radiocarbon dates primarily as a means of dating broad periods of occurrence of certain common pottery types (Painted Grey Ware (PGW), Black-and-Red Ware (BRW), Northern Black Polished Ware (NBP), etc.), rather than for dating strata in which, for example, the first occurrence of iron objects is noticed, at a given site. In this situation it would probably be prudent to adopt a somewhat general approach to the matter, rather than attempt to suggest a certainty which is not warranted by the available data. In an earlier publication (Allchin and Allchin, 1982), we suggested a division of the early use and spread of iron in India into three stages, and in default of any major addition of new evidence we shall follow it here. This scheme was as follows:

> Period I. 1300-1000 BC. Iron occurs only rarely and then generally in small quantities. Early occurrences in western borderlands (Pirak), and in Karnataka (Hallur),
>
> Period II. 1000-800 BC. Iron more common and more widely reported. Occurrences in the Doab, Middle Ganges and Bengal.
>
> Period III. 800-500 BC. Iron now increasingly in common use in almost all areas.

In terms of this hypothetical framework one may postulate that while finds of early iron going back to dates between 1300 and 1000 BC are not impossible, it is more likely that in most cases they will date to the second or third stages. It is also interesting to note that there is no clear regional pattern in early finds of iron objects. The evidence does not point to any area being markedly earlier than others, nor for that matter markedly later. There appears to have been a broad spread of early iron working, and a steady increase in the prevalence of iron objects. We should do well to bear this in mind in considering the role of iron in the spread of settlements in the Ganges valley. In particular, it is the third period when iron becomes common, and it is probably only after c. 600 BC that its almost universal use in making agricultural and other tools becomes the norm.

The Iron Age and the Period of the Painted Grey Ware. The period we have now reached, and which may be designated both the Iron Age and the period of the Painted Grey Ware, thus appears to be one of

228   *Origins of a Civilization*

considerable importance in progress towards the second urbanization in the Doab. The fact that more than 700 settlements in the Upper Ganges plains are reported as producing the distinctive painted grey pottery (Lal, 1989: 43), is sufficient to indicate that there was a great increase in the number of settlements at this time. This is in marked contrast to the preceding Post-urban or Late Harappan period. J.P. Joshi's survey (Joshi et al, 1984) recorded 429 Late Harappan sites in Haryana and the Punjab, as against only 130 in the Doab. In the period of the Painted Grey Ware the figures are reversed, with less than 50 sites in Haryana and Punjab, as against more than 700 in the Doab.

The picture of the material culture and life-style is still far from complete, and as yet there does not appear to be any site excavated with a view to studying these aspects in an integrated way. The evidence recovered varies from site to site. At Bhagwanpura a many-roomed house with mud walls replaced the round huts of the previous period. Elsewhere, the picture is less clear: at Atranjikhera there appear to have been round wattle and daub huts throughout the period, but this may be due to the limited scale of the excavations at both sites. There is more evidence respecting agriculture and subsistence: rice is a regular occurrence, along with barley and wheat, and varieties of leguminous plants. Indeed, from this time onwards, rice is a ubiquitous component of the settlements of the Ganges valley, and must have served a major role in the growth of population. Cattle, buffalo, horse, sheep, goat and pig are all found, and were evidently domesticated and in most cases also used for meat. At Atranjikhera, the excavation revealed the apparent prodigality with which grain was treated, suggesting its abundance at this time. Iron tools are numerous, particularly in the middle and upper parts of the period, and include arrow and spear heads, chisels, axes, knives and other objects, Copper is less common and includes antimony rods and nail-parers, pins, bangles, fish-hooks, and dishes. A regular feature of the period is the presence of varieties of arrowheads and points made of bone, horn or ivory. There are a few small objects of glass, as well as beads of stone. Bangles are found in copper, glass, terracotta and faience. There are also regularly larger terracotta beads, presumably used to adorn cattle. Among the terracotta objects there are human and animal figurines, the former including females with 'violin'-shaped bodies, and the latter bulls and rams, and numbers of decorated discs. The pottery includes common

The Second Urbanization   229

ware as well as the fine Painted Grey Ware with its large number of painted patterns. This ware is technologically the precursor of the Northern Black Polished ware of the succeeding period. All in all we have every indication of a stable community with a thriving agriculture and a range of crafts producing their immediate requirements.

Settlement Patterns in the Doab

The impression we have is that during the centuries from c.1300 BC to c. 600 BC there was a continuous spread of settlement in the Doab. We would accept the expansion to have started in the north-west, and moved in a generally south-easterly direction. As we have seen, during the Post-urban Harappan period there appears to have been an eastwards spread of settlement in the Sarasvati and neighbouring valleys, and we infer that this tendency now continued into the Doab. This process is of paramount interest for several reasons. First, it is generally believed that a necessary prerequisite for the emergence of cities is the build-up of population, and the Ganges valley is an obvious place to examine this process in action. Next, we need to obtain a more accurate picture of the processes of growth and spread, in the hope that they may be able to lead us to a better understanding of what they involved in terms of the communities then living in the area. To us this appears to be of special interest in the light of the unusual demography of UP in later times. A third reason for interest is that a correct reconstruction of these processes is likely to prove of great value in understanding the spread of Brahminism and the Aryan ethos into new territories on the Ganges plains.

As a guide to the continuing growth of population during the period under review we may cite two important settlement surveys made in Kanpur and Allahabad districts respectively by Makkhan Lal (Lal, 1984) and Erdosy (1988). These pioneering projects aimed at providing, for the first time in the Ganges valley, a clearer picture of the increase in numbers and size of settlements through time, as they might be observed and recorded in the course of surface surveys in the two districts. The methodology followed was largely similar in both cases.

The Kanpur district forms a sector of the Doab between the Ganges and Jamuna. It is approximately halved by the course of the Rind. The sequence in Kanpur district is as follows:

230   *Origins of a Civilization*

1. The first period is characterized by finds of Black and Red Ware (for which we have suggested dates from c.1300-1000 BC). The survey recorded nine sites of this period. All sites are under five hectares in size.

2. In the following period, that of the Painted Grey Ware (c.1000-600 BC), there are forty-six sites., only one of which is on the banks of the Jamuna. Of these sites none is more than five hectares, and forty are less than two hectares.

3. In the third period, that of the NBP (c.600-300 BC), the number of sites is ninety-nine in all. Even in this period there are only three sites on the banks of the Jamuna. Of these sites, eighty-one are below two hectares, while seventeen are between three and six hectares, and one is between eight and nine hectares.

4. In the fourth period, which is called Early Historic, the total number of sites further increased to reach a hundred and forty-one. Of these sites ninety-one are below two hectares, twenty-six are between three and six hectares, seven are between six and eight hectares, and one is around ten to eleven hectares.

The Allahabad district survey produced fewer sites, but this may be due to quite extraneous reasons, and should not be necessarily seen as indicating that there are fewer sites awaiting discovery.

1. The first period in this survey is that of the Painted Grey Ware. There are sixteen sites (compared with the forty-six for that period in Kanpur). One at once notices an important difference with the Kanpur survey, in that while in Kanpur district there are no sites of more than six hectares prior to the Early Historic period, in Allahabad district from the start, Kausambi, with an estimated area at this period of ten hectares, stands out as already larger than the rest. This predominance continues and increases through the succeeding periods. Of the sixteen sites seven are on the banks of the Ganges, and only two (of which one is Kausambi) are on the Jamuna.

2. In the NBP period, defined as from 600-350 BC, there are twenty-one sites: in addition to Kausambi which now has an estimated area of over fifty hectares, there is one other site of more than ten hectares, one of six to ten hectares, and seventeen of less than six hectares.

3. In the Early Historic period, defined as from 350-100 BC, Kausambi is still the only site of more than fifty hectares; there is one site of ten to fifty hectares; two of six to ten hectares; and

The Second Urbanization   231

forty-one of less than six hectares. Thus, although the increase in the number of settlements is not as marked as in Kanpur district, the hierarchy of sites now reaches four clear levels, and culminates in one of the great cities of the ancient Ganges valley.

These two surveys command our attention, in that they provide a dramatic picture of how the number and size of settlements increased during the first millennium BC. The reader who wishes to follow the evidence more closely is recommended to consult the original reports for further details. We are not aware of any comparable surveys for the Middle Ganges plains or the Ganges delta region. This is a matter of regret, since similar surveys in different geographical contexts would afford an opportunity for making critical comparisons and arriving at a broader understanding of the settlement of the Ganges plains as a whole. Unfortunately, this means that the Lower Ganges plains must remain in this respect partially *terra incognita* until more work of this kind is done.

We are left without clear answers to a number of major questions, however. As we have seen there is evidence of Neolithic and Chalcolithic settlements in the Ganges valley, long before the time we are now discussing, and there is also evidence of the collection of wild rice, and at a later date, of the cultivation of domesticated rice. Such settlements presupposes small-scale forest clearance, but there is no indication of a density of settlements comparable to that which we encounter in the north-western corner of the Doab during Post-urban Harappan times, and subsequently throughout the Doab. What new stimuli were experienced in that area and during the subsequent spread of settlements through the Doab? The introduction of iron working does not appear to have had a major impact. Almost certainly the cultivation of rice was of greater importance. We have suggested that the combination of changes in river courses, reduction of rainfall and related developments may have provided an incentive for a substantial movement of people towards the east, in search of better water supplies for agriculture and for their beasts. Can this have been the driving force? Or is there also some other factor? One aspect which we have so far not mentioned is that during these centuries we are entering that period which is variously referred to as Proto-historic and as 'Late Vedic'. It appears to us that, even though the use of such literary and semi-historical evidence is somewhat problematic, and fraught with difficulties in its interpretation, it should be taken in account in the context of the present discussion.

Archaeology and Late Vedic Tradition

In the previous chapter we noticed that Manu offered four apparently expanding definitions of the land which provided the best standards of right conduct. The first and second of these were respectively, *Brahmavarta* and *Brahmarsidesa*. The time has come to introduce his third restatement of the area (Manu II.21). Here, he says that the region between the Himalayas and the Vindhya Hills, which is east of Vinasana (the point where the Sarasvati river disappeared into the sand, now in Patiala district), and west of Prayaga (Allahabad, the *Sangam* of the Ganges and Jamuna), is the *Madhya Desa* (Middle Land). The area thus defined is partly the same as the earlier two definitions, but it has been extended eastwards to embrace the whole of the Doab, and this as we have seen is the centre of the settlements which sprang up during the period of the Painted Grey Ware.

The *Brahmanas* and other Late Vedic texts clearly show that their focus has shifted away from the older *Brahmavarta* and is now centred upon the *Madhya Desa.* We find references to a number of tribal groups, including the Kurus and Panchalas, to their various rulers, and to actual events. We also get some hint of how these Indo-Aryan speaking groups came to occupy these territories. We learn the names of various of their settlements, among them are some which can be clearly identified, since their names have scarcely changed in the intervening centuries, and whose archaeology is well enough known to confirm their contemporaneity with the texts. Kausambi is one such example. There are also references to battles and tribal rivalries. Among these references one is of singular interest, since it gives a very suggestive clue to one aspect of the settlement of the Ganges plains. This is the well-known and often quoted passage from the *Satapatha Brahmana* (1.4.1.10-19). The anecdote is cited in explanation of the silence of a 'king' Mathava Videgha, when his Brahmana priest, Rishi Gotama Rahugana, uttered Vedic verses in the course of a sacrifice. The silence is explained by the following passage:

14. Mathava the Videgha was at that time on the (river) Sarasvati. He (Agni, the sacred fire) thence went burning along the earth to the east; and Gotama Rahugana and Mathava Videgha followed after him, as he was burning along. He burnt over (dried up) all these rivers. Now that (river) which is called the Sadanira (the Ever Water) flows from the northern mountain (i.e. Himalayas):

The Second Urbanization

that one he did not burn over. That one the Brahmanas did not cross over in former times, thinking 'it has not been burnt over by Agni Vaisvanara.'

15. Nowadays, however, there are many Brahmanas to the east of it. At that time (the land) was very uncultivated, very marshy, because it had not been tasted by Agni Vaisvanara.

16. Nowadays, however, it is very cultivated, for the Brahmanas have caused (Agni) to taste it through sacrifices. Even in late summer that (river) as it were rages along: so cold is it, not having been burnt over by Agni Vaisvanara.

17. Mathava, the Videgha, then said (to Agni), 'Where am I to abide?' 'To the east of this (river) be thy abode!' said he. Even now this river forms the boundary of the Kosalas and the Videhas; for these are the Mathavas (descendants of Mathava).

In the conclusion the king explains to the priest that he had remained silent, because he was carrying Agni in his mouth. When the priest recited a certain verse addressed to Agni he flashed out of the king's mouth.

The meaning of this extraordinary passage is quite clear. Here is an Aryan king, with his Brahmana priest, and with members of his tribal group, who as a result of a command from Agni carries the sacred fire eastward, leaving the Sarasvati valley, and proceeding down the Doab and beyond until he reaches the Sadanira river. There he receives a fresh command from Agni to take up his abode across this river; and there his descendants still lived when the text was composed. The identity of the Sadanira is not certain, but most probably it should be identified with the Gandak (as one of the few major tributary rivers actually issuing from the Himalayas in this part of the course of the Ganges, and therefore carrying melted snow). The meaning of such expressions as 'the king carried fire in his mouth', and 'Agni burned over' the rivers he crossed, is obscure, but they are clearly intended to suggest an eastward movement of peoples from the Sarasvati valley, establishing settlements, clearing forests, cultivating freshly cleared land, at the same time as drying out some of the swampy areas they would have encountered. One is even tempted to hazard a guess at the approximate date of the original Sarasvati episode and of the subsequent inclusion of the story in the text of the *Brahmana*. The latter one would expect to be around the seventh or eighth centuries BC, while the original episode is unlikely to have been less than a century earlier, and may well have been more. If Mathava accomplished Agni's command and

234 *Origins of a Civilization*

actually crossed the Sadanira, he must have travelled at least six or seven hundred miles from the Sarasvati on the journey!

On the evidence so far, we may make the following points. The archaeology suggests that there was a steady expansion of settlements in the Doab and an accompanying increase in population during the last quarter of the second millennium BC and on into the first millennium. Several contributory causes of this increase have been ·suggested in the foregoing pages. A combination of natural factors has been seen as providing an inducement for people to leave the Sarasvati area and move eastwards across the Jamuna and into the Upper Ganges plains in search of a better habitat. In this new environment they came in contact with a population who already cultivated wheat, barley and rice, and perhaps also millets. This offered a highly productive and adaptable agricultural regime to settlers prepared to undertake the initial clearance of forest land. Once this was accomplished it provided the basis for steady increase in population, to be followed no doubt by further land clearance from time to time. This may help to explain the onward expansion of population down the Ganges valley, in the end reaching as far as the delta.

It may be noted that the Painted Grey Ware tradition scarcely extends east of Allahabad and the Sangam, although occasionally (for example, at Tilaura Kot) a variety of Painted Grey Ware is found. Beyond that point, a somewhat different sequence prevailed. Black-and-Red ware, plain grey ware and a Black Slipped ware which appears to be a forerunner of NBP are the principal pottery wares during the period from c.1000-600 BC. Such changes of style and preference may have some deeper meaning in terms of ethnic character, local conservatism or innovation, but in our view they are likely to be more the result of human choice and whim than anything more profound.

Indian textual tradition offers another way of looking at, and possibly explaining, the expansion; namely that it involved the dispersal of Indo-Aryan speaking tribes, who had already spent some period of residence somewhere within the Indus system, perhaps the Punjab and Sarasvati valley. There, as we suggested in the previous chapter, they had come in contact with the local population, probably establishing rule over them, and contributing to the formation of a pluralistic society of acculturated 'Aryans'. It is these acculturated Aryans who, we believe, set forth in search of a more congenial climate and fruitful environment in which to establish for themselves new homes and perhaps new kingdoms. At the same time they would have

The Second Urbanization 235

carried with them 'Agni in their mouths', that is the social and political order which had evolved in their earlier settlements. The picture, which may be culled from passages in the Vedic and Late Vedic literature, has certainly been accepted by former generations of historians as an account of what has been called the 'Aryan expansion'. A lucid exposition of the textual sources is offered by Pusalkar (1951: 315-320), from which the following paraphrase is extracted:

> The colonization was not effected by conquest alone. It was also effected by small bands of adventurous Brahmanas and Ksatriyas, who went to new countries and after clearing the jungles and making tracts habitable, set up residences there. They colonized under the leadership of groups of Ksatriyas, and new settlements were named after their tribes.

So far archaeology can shed little light on what such a dispersal would have involved, nor how it might be recognized. We have long held the view that, during the early stages of contact between Indo-Aryan speaking groups and autochthons, most if not all culturally distinctive traces of the former would have disappeared. It is, however, perhaps an indication of Indo-Aryan involvement that horse bones are reported at such excavated sites as Bhagwanpura and Atranjikhera; and it may well be that the rock paintings of horse-drawn chariots at such Central Indian cave-sites as Morhana Pahar, Chatur Bhuja Nath Nulla, etc. carry the same indications. In our view, the demographic spread across the Ganges plains is likely to coincide with the spread of Indo-Aryan speech. We would like to know more of the archaeology of these sites. Further research and more sensitive and extensive excavations at key sites might be able to supply some of the answers.

The Rise of Cities and States

We have now reached a crucial point in our survey of the second, or Iron Age, urbanization of South Asia, and the scene is set for the final sections of this book. Henceforward, the way is more clearly defined than in the previous chapters. Our task, too, is made easier by the fact that the authors, along with three colleagues (D.K. Chakrabarti, R. A. E. Coningham and G. Erdosy), recently published a study of *The Archaeology of Early Historic South Asia* (1995), covering much of this ground in considerable detail. Readers who wish to

236   *Origins of a Civilization*

learn more of the rise of cities and states in the Ganges valley, and the way that, within a short space of time, cities and states appeared in almost every corner of the subcontinent, may refer to this work.

Culture Sequence and Chronology. It will be recalled that the preceding period in the Upper Ganges plains was associated with Painted Grey Ware; while in the Middle Ganges plains and the delta it was associated with Black-and-Red ware and Black Slipped ware. This period is seen as coming to an end around 550 BC, and is succeeded by that known from the presence of a fine Black Gloss ware, as the period of NBP (Northern Black Polished ware being the somewhat misleading name coined for it by Sir Mortimer Wheeler). It seems necessary to repeat what we have published elsewhere (Allchin & Allchin, 1982: 323-324), that both the Painted Grey Ware and the Black Slipped ware are fine wares, made from and exploiting the finely sorted alluvial clays of the Ganges plains; and both are in their technology and morphology, closely related to each other. Moreover, both are unmistakably the direct antecedents of the Northern Black Polished ware, which is made from similar clays, fired by similar routines, and has a closely related morphology. The one major advance shown by the NBP is that, after firing, vessels were coated with an alkali dressing, which when biscuit-fired in a reducing atmosphere and fluxed at the correct temperature, produced what is in effect a true glaze, very comparable to that of the Greek Black ware. Because there are technical differences between this surface treatment and the more frequently encountered frit glaze, lead glaze, etc., it seems to us more accurate to refer to the Northern Black Polished ware as Black Gloss (BG) ware (Hegde, 1978).

The close affinity of these three pottery wares is symbolic of the continuity linking other aspects of the cultural tradition through the Upper and Middle Ganges plains, from the earlier to the later period. But before we consider the ways in which change took place within the continuum, we must first indicate the chronological horizons of the NBP (BG) ware, since it is still necessary to use it as a type fossil for dating other categories of evidence. The NBP occurs over a span of several centuries, and it has long been recognized that it underwent some changes within this time-span. There is more or less general agreement that there are more than one chronological subdivisions of NBP. Roy (1983) has suggested two stages, Early and Late; while some others, including Erdosy (1988, 1995), have proposed three stages, Early, Middle and Late. The Early stage produces fine

The Second Urbanization 237

wares which overlap with PGW; the Middle represents the high period of the NBP ware; and the Late represents its decline into cruder varieties of surface gloss and colouring. Erdosy has made a careful analysis of the considerable number of radiocarbon dates relating to the NBP, and calibrated them accordingly. These give time-ranges for the three stages as follows: Early NBP, 550-400 BC; Middle NBP, 400-250 BC; and Late NBP, 250-100 BC. These provide us with the best available working time-scale for discussing the emergence of cities and states.

The Emergence of Cities

Although the evidence is still not very clear, and indeed in some respects is sadly inadequate, one can begin to see the appearance of cities as passing through several evolving stages. Viewed in terms of sequence, it seems that some at least of the settlements, which were later to become cities, had a history going back to the beginning of the second millennium BC, and the period of the Red ware of Harappan tradition which is referred to as OCP. These sites may well belong to the Early Post-urban Harappan period, or even the transition from Urban to Post-urban. This sequence is suggested at Atranjikhera and Ahicchatra. Other sites are not so clearly identified in this respect. We have regrettably very few city-sites whose settlement histories have been studied as organic processes, where we can map out the growth and change from period to period. Kausambi is an example of a site where we have at least some idea of the growth from a nuclear form during the period of the Painted Grey Ware, to its full city form, when the great ditch and rampart defenses were first constructed (which Erdosy associates with the Middle period of the NBP, i.e. c. 400 BC). The initial settlement seems to have been in the south-eastern corner of the later city, adjoining the banks of the Jamuna. This area occupied some ten hectares. Without more problem-oriented excavation we cannot determine either what was the stratigraphic history of this area and when it first was occupied; nor how it was related to the subsequent ditch and rampart fortifications which enclose the city, and which cover more than 200 hectares. The date of this major development is not firmly established, but it has been shown that it was most probably in the earlier part of the fifth century BC.

It is not our intention here to discuss in detail the age and character of each and every Ganges city-site. Moreover, much of this

Origins of a Civilization

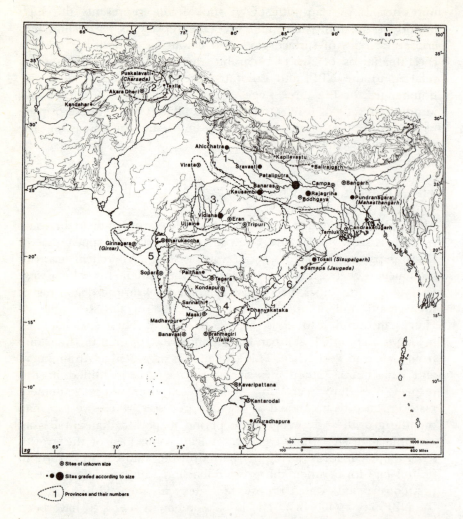

Map 7. *The distribution and relative size of principal cities of South Asia in the third century BC.*

data has been well-analyzed and published elsewhere (Roy, 1983). We can, however, draw certain general conclusions regarding the history of their growth.

Many of the settlements which later became cities appear to have been first established somewhere around 1000 BC. It also appears that they formed part of the primary settlement of the region. Looking at the distribution map of city-sites (Map 7) one is struck by

The Second Urbanization

how often they are separated from one another by considerable distances. Thus, if they are primary centres they are surrounded by ample space in which hierarchies of smaller sites could develop. This lends further support to our belief that at least some of the city-sites were from the outset the capitals of chiefdoms. Thereafter, in course of time, the central sites became capital cities and the chiefdoms became states.

At dates that are as yet unclear, but probably are all between 600 BC and 350 BC, significant changes took place. In most, if not all, of the city-sites the most obvious signal of the change was the construction of vast defensive moats and ramparts (*Plates 65 & 66*). This development appears to have already begun in the final stages of the period of Painted Grey Ware, although in none of the city-sites so far excavated is there clear evidence that it was early as this. Definite evidence comes from Rajghat, Banaras, where the earth rampart around the city was found to contain Black Slipped ware and Black-and-Red ware, and apparently antedated the NBP. This would indicate a date at least in the first half of the sixth century BC, if not earlier, but unfortunately there are no relevant radiocarbon dates to confirm this.

The overall city plans are of various shapes, some being more or less circular, as at Sankissa (*Fig. 28*), others crescentic, as at Sravasti, or triangulate, as at Ahicchatra (*Fig. 29*), some irregular rectangles, as at Kausambi, and some almost perfect squares, as at Sisupalgarh in Orissa (*Plate 67*) and Mahasthangarh in Bangladesh. The largest city area may be that enclosed by the city moat at Patna (Pataliputra), which we estimate to have been c. 340 hectares; while Rajagriha and Kausambi are over 200 hectares; and Ahicchatra, Sravasti and Mahasthangarh are between 100-200 hectares. On Map 7 we have attempted to indicate the relative size of the enclosed areas of a number of principal cities. This indicates that, by around the conclusion of the great period of city construction, the largest cities were concentrated in the Ganges valley, and on the two principal routes of trade and expansion, south-westwards towards Bharukaccha and the western coastal trade; and south-eastwards towards Orissa. Many of the less important sites have not yet been properly surveyed or published. The significance of this massive investment of labour in fortifying such sites is in our view fairly obvious. The fortifications served no doubt a variety of practical functions, such as keeping out robbers or wild beasts, but more importantly they served as symbols of royal or state power. This role is clearly seen in the *Arthashastra*, where the fortified city serves as protection for the king and for the treasury (*kosa*). Of course, the

240 Origins of a Civilization

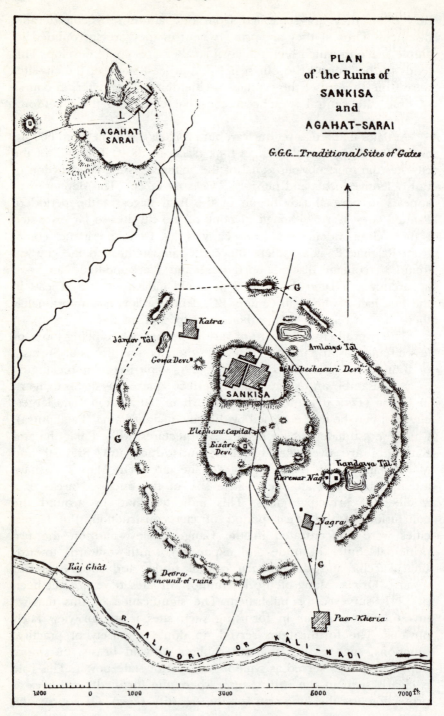

Fig. 28. Plan of Sankissa (Sankasya)

The Second Urbanization

fortified city further serves these roles in terms of interstate relations, including diplomacy and war.

The basic structure of the fortification is in most cases a broad moat (*parikha*) dug in the alluvial plain, the excavated earth of which was piled up to make the core of a rampart (*vapra*) (*Plate 68*). The rampart was probably finished with an outer coating of bricks, and had a city wall (*prakara*) constructed along its crest. This feature was also generally built of brick. An exception to this is found at Rajagriha where the walls are built over solid rock and there is no rampart or moat (*Plate 69*). The excavated examples suggest that the crowning walls were in need of frequent repair, and in some cases too the moat was enlarged, necessitating the addition of an extra layer to the *vapra*. But, we have the impression that once the basic layout of a city fortification was established it remained substantially the same from that time forward. Therefore, it is reasonable to use the area enclosed by a rampart as a basis for calculating the size of the city. Some attempts have been made to estimate the population of the cities and surrounding settlements; and others to consider the size of the work-force required to build the ramparts (Lal 1984: 989; Coningham, 1995). Coningham has estimated that to construct the rampart at Kausambi would have taken a work-force of over ten thousand, working for some five months, or correspondingly longer with a smaller work-force.

As yet archaeology has scarcely begun the study of the internal layout of any of these cities, and therefore it is not possible to make comparisons with the suggested layout offered by the *Arthashastra*. It is a great pity that the considerable resources available in India should not attempt to fill this gap.

One of the most striking things about the fortified cities is that many of them are already know to us from textual references as the capitals of the sixteen Mahajanapadas, 'Great territories or states', of early Buddhist sources. Ten of the sixteen Mahajanapadas are situated in the Ganges valley and their capital cities are well known from the same sources. Of these, no less than nine coincide with fortified city-sites independently identified by archaeology (Rajagriha, Campa, Vaisali, Kusinagara, Kasi, Sravasti, Kausambi, Ahicchatra, and Mathura) (*Map 8, p. 243*). Of these, Rajagriha, the capital of Magadha up to the early fourth century BC, is of particular importance. It assumed the role of capital already by the fifth century BC, if not earlier, and repairs to its walls are expressly mentioned in a Buddhist *sutta* of the time of the Buddha's death. It may, therefore, claim to be the first metropolis of the Ganges civilization, probably reaching this stage

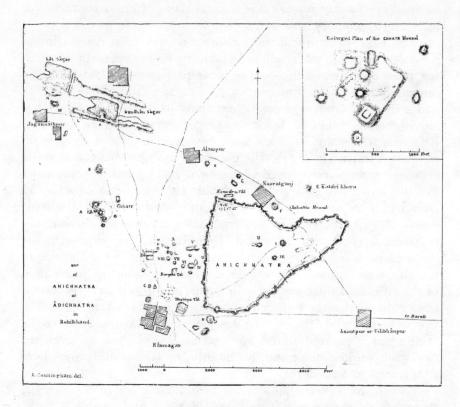

Fig. 29. Plan of Ahicchatra

during the rule of the Nandas, and almost at once losing it when the capital was moved to Pataliputra in the early fourth century BC.

Factors Favouring the Development of Urbanization. At this point in our narrative we think it might be useful to cast an eye back over the accompanying circumstances which appear to have favoured the development of urbanization. In an earlier publication (Allchin, 1990: 162-63) it was suggested that the general model for the development of urbanization required a sufficient and expanding population base, in a suitably hospitable environment, combined with the necessary technology and agricultural skills to produce adequate supplies of food. We also suggested that once this process was set in motion a number of secondary effects would also appear. These would be likely to include an expansion of the site hierarchy to include cities, an increase in social stratification and craft specialization, an increase in craft production of all kinds, evidence

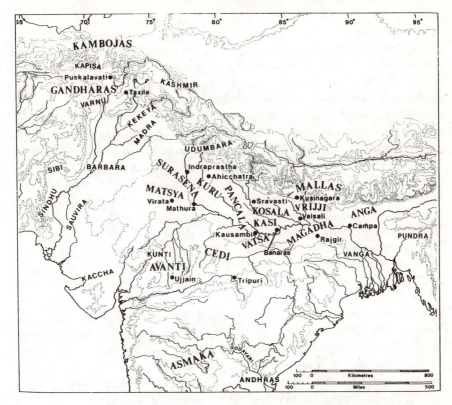

Map 8. *The approximate areas occupied by the Sixteen Great States (Mahajanapadas) and other major tribal Janapadas, 5th-6th centuries BC together with their probable capital cities*

of increased trading activities, and the emergence of a new political and economic structure (the state), with an appropriate ideology. To us it appears that this model well fits the conditions which we believe to have prevailed in the Gangetic plains during the second half of the second millennium BC and the first half of the first. Later, we shall consider how far the secondary effects were in evidence in the following centuries.

The Early City and the State

We wish now briefly to look into a particular aspect of the developmental process we have been investigating in the last two chapters. We realize that we are embarking on a hypothetical reconstruction of events, but we believe that it is a matter of sufficient importance to warrant our undertaking it.

There is general agreement that aspects of the urban society which flourished during the Harappan period were lost around 2000 BC. Around that date, cities declined and there was evidently a breakdown of the urban structure and much that went with it. This was probably accompanied by a re-emergence of a number of chiefdoms in the several provinces of the former Harappan domain. Our hypothesis, thereafter, rests on the assumption that in the Early Post-urban period, at least in some of these provinces, there was a seizure of power in some cases by Indo-Aryan speaking groups; and that in the ensuing centuries the rivalry of the older 'Harappan' ruling groups and the new 'Indo-Aryan' was at least in part resolved through a period of interaction which produced a new class of acculturated Aryans who, for whatever reasons, maintained that they were of direct Aryan descent. Some of these Aryan ruling groups would have won political power for themselves, perhaps by force of arms, and others may have done so by intermarriage, or other means. It is clear that at this time the population, whom such groups ruled, comprised a number of different ethnic elements.

As environmental factors led to the dessication of much of Sindh and the Sarasvati-Ghaggar valley, we expect that some Indo-Aryan speaking groups would have migrated towards the east into the Doab, taking members of the mixed population with them, and established for themselves chiefdoms in their new homelands. We would expect these chiefdoms to have been as complex as their predecessors, and that the Aryan chiefs might name such areas after their ancestral tribes. These tribal territories would therefore be known by such names as 'the *janapada* of the Kauravas, or of the Pancalas, etc.'

During the following centuries this socio-political situation must have continued to develop and, particularly with the emergence of the new cities, the old terms would acquire new meanings. The term *janapada* must have ceased to mean tribal territory and come to mean state territory; while the old tribal names tended to be shortened into geographical instead of ethnic terms which stood for the territory of the state. Thus the '*Janapada* of the Kauravas' became 'Kuru *Janapada*', and so on.

The Expansion of Urbanization in South Asia

Mechanisms for the Spread of City-formation

In this chapter we have hitherto focussed our attention on the Ganges valley, making virtually no reference to developments in other parts of South Asia. We have followed this course because we believe that, in terms of the rise of Indian civilization, the Ganges valley played a distinct and special role. By this we mean that the Ganges valley appears to have been the seat of the composition of a large part of the voluminous literature of the Late Vedic period, and of the subsequent period of the *Brahmanas* and *Upanishads*, not to mention its having been the homeland of Buddhism and Jainism; and the region which produced the two great epics, the Mahabharata and the Ramayana. Each one of these elements later became disseminated throughout South Asia, and it could be argued that each was a facet of the spread of Indian civilization as a whole. We do not, however, mean that the process of urbanization was confined to the Ganges plains. The newly emerging urban societies were in themselves responsible for the creation of all sorts of outward thrusts and stimulations which led to the spread of cities in all directions, and eventually to almost every part of South Asia. In the present section we wish to discuss first the mechanisms which contributed to the process of the spread of cities, and then to look briefly at the archaeological evidence for their continuation outside the Ganges region.

States and Tribes. One of the striking things about the period of the sixteen *Mahajanapadas* is the extent to which it is characterized by aggressiveness and expansionisim (Allchin, 1993: 332-4). Hardly had the states come into existence, than they began to fight among themselves, with a view no doubt to self-aggrandizement in terms of wealth, territory and prestige. Further, they started to look around for adjacent territories which they might annex. Such territories were largely in the form of uncleared forests, inhabited by a variety of tribal groups, some still living at hunting, fishing and gathering subsistence level, others as shepherds or pastoralists, and yet others practising agriculture of one form or another. Such tribal territories were obvious targets for expansive states and their rulers. This question was explored by Debiprasad Chattopadhyaya in his remarkable study *Lokayata* (Chattopadhyaya, 1959: 171-7), where he drew attention to the hostility felt in the time of the Buddha, by the

246 *Origins of a Civilization*

citizens of states, towards societies still organized in tribal sanghas, and to the persistence of the same ideas in Kautilya's *Arthashastra*, some centuries later. Wider aspects of state-tribe relationships have also been thoughtfully discussed by D.D. Kosambi in his *Introduction to the Study of Indian History* (1956, chapters 6-7).

All this leads us to think that the early states shared a mutual aggressiveness and expansiveness, and an acquisitive attitude towards neighbouring forests or tribal territories. In turn it leads us to expect that the expansion of urbanization would be likely to be closely involved with the expansive behaviour of states.

Colonization and Janapada Nivesa. A second mechanism of the spread of urbanism is what we have been calling colonization, and what the *Arthashastra* refers to as *janapada nivesa*. As we have already seen colonization is a difficult term because it can be used in different ways. We have used it for what we have called the Aryan colonization of the Ganges valley, but there are references in early Indian historical tradition for a similar process having been involved in the colonization of large tracts of western India, Central India (the modern Madhya Pradesh), the Deccan, and the coastal strips of the peninsula. We envisage it as involving sometimes whole military expeditions, perhaps with the support of an established ruler of another state, and sometimes no more than small parties of adventurers who targeted a likely area or settlement and by force, guile or whatever means, succeeded in getting the support of the local population in accepting their overlordship.

It seems that many parts of the regions south of the Ganges valley were colonized in this way, and we shall indicate below some examples which may represent this kind of situation. There seems to be every reason to believe that in some cases these entrepreneurs arrived in an area or chiefdom which was ripe for transformation to statehood, or incorporation into an existing state, and in either case they would be likely to advance the process of city-formation by enhancing the capital. The term *janapada nivesa* comes from the *Arthashastra*, a chapter in Book II being devoted to this topic, as one way in which a wise king should set up or take over territory. Although the treatment of the subject is different from the sort of free-booting activity which we have ascribed to many 'colonizers', there is also much which is common between them. To us it seems that this sort of colonization must incidentally have been a way of forwarding the process of social and economic change in far-flung regions of the South Asia.

The Second Urbanization

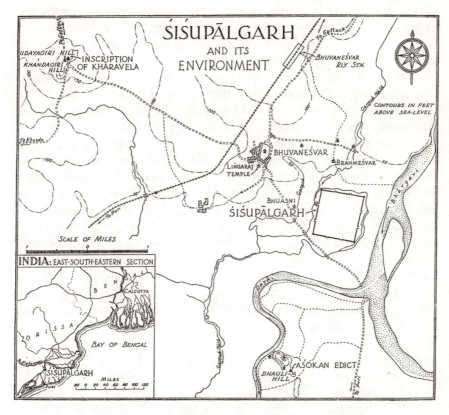

Fig. 30. Map showing the fortified city of Sisupalgarh in relation to neighbouring monuments

With the passage of time and the growing crystallization of states and their ideologies, such colonial expeditions were likely to become more political and larger-scale enterprises: one thinks of the reference in Kharavela's Hathigumpha inscription in Orissa, referring to an earlier occasion when the Nanda king constructed a water channel in the city now known as Sisupalgarh. This suggests that already in the fourth century BC state expeditions, emanating from Magadha in the Ganges valley, were being sent on missions of conquest to economically attractive regions; and the same inscription's account of Kharavela's own expeditions in various directions suggests that ideas of state interference and colonization were still very much alive in the first century BC.

248 *Origins of a Civilization*

Imperial Expansion. A special aspect of the foregoing mechanism is what we are calling imperial expansion. This refers in the first instance to the influence on other parts of South Asia of the emerging supremacy of the state of Magadha, first under the Nanda dynasty (whose chronology is still uncertain but probably spanned the first three-quarters of the fourth century BC), and more particularly under their successor, the Mauryan dynasty whose founder Chandragupta seized power after the retreat of Alexander the Great in c. 325 BC. It is hardly necessary to elaborate on our meaning. The distribution map of Ashokan inscriptions coincides with many sites which are linked to identified fortified settlements of that period: Sisupalgarh, Jaugada, Amaravati, Girnar, Kandahar and Taxila are examples. Some were evidently already cities before Mauryan contact was made, but others, we believe, were formerly large settlements which became elevated to urban status through Mauryan presence. Even more suggestive of this aspect are the remaining sites, some attached to Buddhist monastic settlements (Sanchi, Panguraria), and others on routes leading from the Ganges valley to the north-west and south. This Mauryan imperial contact may only have reinforced a trend that was already present. One is left with little doubt that it must have had an effect upon territories which it reached not unlike that of Roman imperialism on such far-flung places as Britain or Germany.

Trade. One of the features of the emergence of cities and states was that they provided a great impetus for the development of trade, both local and external. We believe it is self-evident that such long-distance trade, together with the search for precious raw materials and manufactures, provided an important stimulus to the spread of cities and accompanying institutions wherever merchants travelled or did business. Thus, colonization is not the only mechanism which served to spread the processes of state and city formation.

The Spread of Religion. A final mechanism which contributed to the emergence of cities and states is through religious missions. We have in mind the spread of Buddhism, both as it was taking place in the fourth and third centuries BC and more particularly as it was envisaged in the time of Ashoka when, according to the *Dipavamsa*, missions were sent to Gandhara, Mahisa (Karnataka), Aparantaka (the west coastal regions), Maharashtra, the Yavana region (presumably the Bactrian Greeks), the tribes of the Himalayan area, Suvarnabhumi (presumably Burma), and to Sri Lanka. Such missionary activities

The Second Urbanization

were not unique to Buddhism, there were also Jainas who travelled through the peninsula with similar aims, and doubtless others.

URBANIZATION BEYOND THE GANGES PLAINS

The North-West. The city of Kandahar is probably older than any other in South Asia; there is evidence of pre-Achaemenid and Achaemenid periods of city construction (McNicoll and Ball, 1996). Although it passed for a few decades under Mauryan control, it was never strictly speaking an Indian city, and played no direct part in the subsequent historical process we are discussing.

The North West Frontier region, ancient Gandhara, too has an interesting and largely independent history of early city formation. Its twin capital cities were Taxila and Puskalavati (Charsada). Taxila lies in an area settled since Early Harappan times, but the immediate precursor of the Early Historic city is a settlement belonging to a local culture of the second to first millennia BC, known as the Gandhara Grave Culture. A settlement of this period existed at Taxila, near the end of the Hathial ridge and surface collection indicates that it was already around 13 hectares in extent (Allchin, 1993). The distinctive pottery of this period is Burnished Red ware. Gandhara formed one of the satrapies of the Achaemenid empire from c.500-320 BC, but virtually nothing has been discovered which shows specific Achaemenid influence, except an Aramaic stone inscription of Priyadarsi, a small number of Achaemenid coins and the earliest indigenous silver coinage in the region, the silver bar coins.

Shortly before 400 BC a new city was laid out on a level area across the Tamra river, and is known as the Bhir mound. What is striking is that from the start it exhibited a strong influence from the Ganges area, visible for instance not only in the presence of a few shards of imported NBP, but also a fine black pottery, locally made, which imitated NBP and shared with it a range of more or less identical forms. This city occupied an area of c. 50 hectares. The date of its foundation is established by four radiocarbon dates from the earliest levels, as between 405 and 395 BC. The Ganges urban tradition is superimposed upon characteristically local elements.

It is probable that when we have more field results from Charsada we shall find that it had a broadly similar sequence of development for the early period. Certainly, Wheeler, in his excavation at the site

250   *Origins of a Civilization*

discovered an extended occupation belonging to the Red Burnished ware period, and further excavation and more solid dating are needed.

There is virtually no archaeological data relating to the rise of cities in Lower or Upper Sindh. The reasons for this are not clear, although environmental factors must have played their part. A number of possible sites are known, but none has so far produced evidence of city formation during the first millennium BC.

The Central Indian Belt. The belt of hills and forests, which extends from the Western Ghats in the west to the Ganges delta in the east, comprises an area of variations of terrain and offers an interesting context for further research on the emergence of cities. It includes several of the sixteen *Mahajanapadas* (*Avanti, Cedi* and *Asmaka*). From early times, the hill and forest belt was crossed by routes linking the Ganges valley with the coasts and with the Deccan plateau. The picture we gain from archaeology and history is that throughout it has been inhabited by a wide range of tribal peoples, such as the Bhils, the Gonds, Korkus, Santals, speaking languages of several different families, Indo-Aryan, Dravidian, and Munda. This region was the home of its own distinctive branch of Chalcolithic culture whose origins go back at least to the late third millennium BC. It is likely that a major substratum of the population of the region was formed at this time. Probably, from the mid-second millennium BC onwards, groups of Indo-Aryan speaking immigrants, of the kind we have referred to above, began to filter into the belt. They no doubt selected hospitable areas with agricultural potential for their settlements and established chiefdoms or kingdoms, clearing the forests around the central settlements, and over the centuries contributing to yet another complex, culturally plural social situation. Such kingdoms still appear like islands of settlement in the midst of oceans of forest. We suspect that archaeological research would be able to distinguish between them and the tribal population, who by and large occupied the more forested parts.

Evidence for this development could be obtained by research in and around such cities as Vidisha and Ujjain, both on the route running south-westwards from the Ganges valley to the west coast. Both seem to have had a development going back to times before the construction of the urban fortifications during the period of the NBP. Both show some divergence of material culture from that of the Ganges cities, and seem to have closer affinities with the Deccan and the western coastal region. The excavated sequence at Ujjain will serve as an example for the others. The earliest occupation here is typical of the peninsular Iron Age, with Black-and-Red burnished

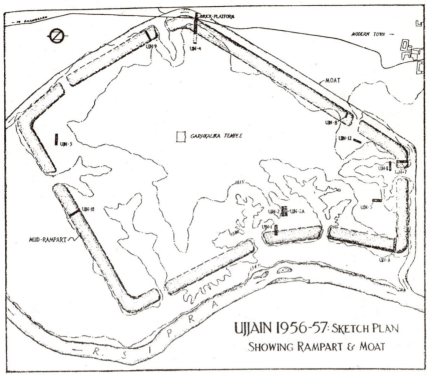

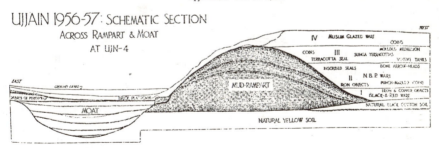

Fig. 31. *Ujjain, plan and section of ramparts*

pottery, and objects of iron and copper. The moat and rampart were constructed during this period (*Fig. 31*). It is followed by a second period which continues in much the same way, but the pottery is augmented by small quantities of imported NBP, and there are bone and ivory points, probably both styli and arrowheads (*Fig. 32, following page*). Two exciting finds are small ivory seals each inscribed in early Brahmi script, datable to the third to second century BC, and cast

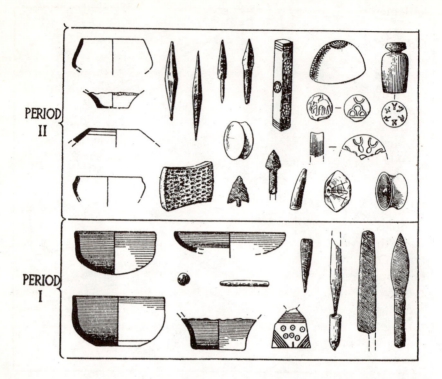

Fig. 32. Ujjain detail of culture sequence for periods II and III.

copper coins of types generally regarded as contemporary with the Mauryan period. Unhappily, the single radiocarbon sample from period I is quite implausible: we believe that this period dates from c.600-300 BC. Farther east, lie the cities of Eran and Tripuri, probably with roughly parallel histories. Farther south, in the neighbourhood of Nagpur are the fortified settlements of Pauni and Adam, surrounded by earth ramparts. Some of these sites appear to have started their development in the course of the second millennium BC, but others only developed during the period of the NBP, and they do not show the sort of closer Ganges links which one finds at Vidisha. Each city-site needs to be examined individually and its history evaluated before a clearer overall picture can be achieved. Our observation is that the extent of areas of forest clearance might

The Second Urbanization

usefully be considered and related to the history of the central settlements.

Cities in the Deccan. We are conscious that because the prime thrust of this book is directed towards the first and second urbanizations in South Asia, and thus towards the Indus and Ganges systems respectively, we may have neglected some other regions, for instance, the Deccan, including Maharashtra, Karnataka and Andhra Pradesh.

As we saw in chapter 5, these three states provide evidence of Mesolithic and Neolithic settlements probably going back to c. 3000 BC, if not earlier. The regions have a character of their own, which is expressed in their cultural development. This becomes very clear with the Chalcolithic period, extending from around 2000 BC down to the beginning of the Iron Age. As in Central India, we find complex societies which probably derive their roots, population-wise, from the co-existence of tribal and agricultural elements through time. One might expect that, left to its own resources, the internal development in the Chalcolithic period would in due course have led to city formation. During the first half of the second millennium there appears to have been a substantial settled population scattered through the three regions, but nothing as yet points to there being any settlements which were more than villages or at best small market towns.

In the second half of the second millennium, a widely noted change can be observed, around or after 1500 BC, associated with the culture known from its type site of Jorwe. It has been suggested that this change may have been somehow linked with the infiltration of Indo-Aryan speaking groups into the area, but no archaeological proof of this hypothesis exists. From early in the first millennium BC, iron becomes increasingly common in the settlements, in association with distinctive burnished Black-and-Red ware. A number of excavated sites indicate that this stage continued until c. the fourth century BC, when evidence of Ganges trade contacts begins to appear. It seems that it is only at this time that we should expect to find the beginnings of city and state formation.

In Maharashtra, Pratisthana is a likely candidate: there is a nuclear Jorwe period settlement, and its importance through to the early centuries AD is evident. An early Buddhist reference to the itinerary of the pupils of the sage Bavari, passing through Pratisthana en route for Sravasti, etc., in order to visit the Buddha, suggests that it was one of the earliest cities in the area. In Andhra and Karnataka the earliest evidence of fortified ramparts around settlements is

254   *Origins of a Civilization*

found at Amaravati, Sannathi and Banavasi, and although only the first of these has as yet been properly excavated or dated, it is interesting that all three have associations with Ashokan (or claimed Ashokan) inscriptions. The distribution of Ashokan edicts in Karnataka and Andhra points towards Mauryan imperial expansion being a prime factor in the development of cities in this area. Even major settlements like Maski and Brahmagiri and Koppal, contain areas of Early Historic structures whose dates are not clearly established but which *may* have a Mauryan beginning.

The West and East Coastal Strips. The discovery of cities or other sites, closely associated with ports or estuaries, on both the east and west coasts of the peninsula and the evidence that some of them actually pre-date the Mauryan period, while others are, sequence-wise, built on top of earlier settlements, points to the importance from early times of coastal trade, both within South Asia and with areas farther afield.

The west coast divides into two parts in terms of available data. The northern part includes Saurashtra where the city of Girnar, with its Ashokan inscriptions and tank, point to the likelihood of a major settlement lying under the later remains of Junagadh (Old Fort). This place was undoubtedly chosen because of its proximity to the mountain which gives the place its name (Girinagara), and provides a dominant landscape feature in Central Saurashtra; but it is more than fifty miles inland from the sea and the nearest port, Veraval. A major port settlement is undoubtedly awaiting excavation at Broach (ancient Bharukaccha) on the Narbada estuary. Here, excavation indicated a settlement going back to c. 800-600 BC, but such limited field research has been done that almost nothing can be said of the layout of the city during Early Historic times. Equally limited is our knowledge of the Ashokan inscription site of Sopara (Supparaka), north of Bombay, although excavation has revealed occupation compatible with an early date. From this point southwards, while early textual references and the *Periplus of the Erythrean Sea* (c. first century AD) lead us to expect a number of port sites, none has been as yet identified archaeologically as belonging to the Early Historic period. This is an interesting area for further research.

The east coast offers much firmer evidence for a whole series of ports or river-side sites along its entire length, from the Ganges delta to Kanyakumari. We remarked earlier that the Ganges offered an outlet to the outside world for the Ganges cities. The growth and vitality of the sites well matches this need. At the port site of Tamluk

The Second Urbanization

(ancient Tamralipti), in Midnapur district of West Bengal, excavation indicates that a settlement existed at least since the middle of the second millennium BC, and blossomed from the period of the NBP onwards. From the second century BC the presence of Rouletted ware and distinctive 'Hellenistic' black wares, reinforces the view that this area became an entrepot between the Hellenistic-Roman trade and the Ganges valley. Equally important for gaining a proper understanding of this area is the presence of major cities such as Chandraketugarh, 23 miles north-east of Calcutta. That so little has been published regarding the several excavations done at this site is extraordinary. One of the outstanding features of the region, from Mauryan times onwards, is the massive local manufacture of beautiful terracotta figurines: these also remind one of the excellent alluvial clays in the delta and lead one to wonder whether the Rouletted ware may not also have been manufactured by foreign (Yavana) merchants and craftsmen somewhere in this area.

Travelling southwards one encounters a whole series of ports and fortified Early Historic cities: in Orissa, Sisupalgarh near the later town of Bhubaneshwar, as we remarked above, was probably captured and developed by the Nandas in the fourth century BC. On a nearby hillock there is a set of Ashokan edicts (*Plate 67 & Fig. 30*). As we saw above, the Kharavela inscription, probably of the late first century BC, refers to the presence of the earlier intruder, the 'Nanda king' some three hundred years before (i.e. in the second half of the fourth century BC). Jaugada, likewise, lies some further 100 km to the south; so too does Dhanyakataka, Amaravati, on the Krishna river, later to become a Satavahana capital; and so on down to estuarine settlements such as Arikamedu, and the renowned city of Kaveripattanam on the mouth of the Kaveri.

Wherever excavations have established a stratified sequence they have shown more or less the same periods: an early period with typical Iron Age pottery and finds, followed by a period of exotic influence, with imports of Roman Arretine ware and amphorae, and distinctive Hellenistic-Roman influenced wares which were perhaps manufactured somewhere in the Indian peninsula, most notably the Rouletted ware (*Plate 70*). Finally, the island of Sri Lanka forms the southern-most major link in the series.

The coastal stations therefore form a vital element in the promotion of trade and in the southern spread of Gangetic influence throughout the peninsula. The coincidence of Buddhist sites with many of the cities points to the role of mission activities to which we referred above It is interesting to note that the earliest inscriptions

256 *Origins of a Civilization*

at these southern cities are almost always those of Ashoka and these are naturally all in Prakrit, in contrast to those found farther south, beyond the Mauryan frontiers.

The Southern Peninsula. There is as yet little evidence of early city formation from the interior of the peninsula, beyond the areas which were claimed by the Mauryans during their major expansion. This does not mean to say that there was not a substantial population in many parts of the peninsula from Iron Age times onwards, and that there were without doubt states at least by the time of Ashoka. Rather, it means that there is still much archaeological research required to elucidate such matters. It is also apparent that, under the influence of Hellenistic-Roman trade, routes into the interior must have been developed. One thinks particularly of the route which led from Kaveripattana, up the Kaveri valley, to Karur, and thence towards the Palghat gap, passing through Coimbatore and crossing over an area rich in semi-precious stones down to the west coast, to ports such as Muziris. On this route lies Karur, an ancient capital of the Cheras, where important early Tamil inscriptions have been discovered, and Kodumanal, also in the Chera kingdom, where excavations have revealed much evidence of bead-making and of Roman trade. As yet there is very little objective dating for all this activity, but we expect that when radiocarbon dates can be obtained they will provide a new perspective. It is interesting that the earliest Brahmi inscriptions from this area are in Tamil and indicate that a special Tamil Brahmi script was invented at an early date. How this relates to the earliest occurrence of the Brahmi script in Sri Lanka has still to be determined, archaeologically, but at present there is a dearth of objective dating for the early developments in the southern peninsula.

'As far as Tamraparni'. The beautiful island of Sri Lanka marks the southernmost part of the South Asian peninsula and offers a splendid opportunity of observing how and when urbanization arose and developed in this insular setting, and how these processes relate to those in peninsular South Asia and in the Ganges valley. Sri Lanka has a number of historical features which single it out from the rest of South Asia: here, Buddhism was declared the state religion around the middle of the third century BC and has by and large remained so to this day. In addition, because of its insularity Sri Lanka was spared the traumatic effects of the Muslim invasions which affected north India and some large parts of the peninsula, at the same time

The Second Urbanization 257

destroying much of the indigenous cultural heritage and contributing to the almost total eclipse of Buddhism there. One positive result for Sri Lanka is that, in contrast to India, much more of the ancient tradition was preserved within monastic libraries, and among these works are the several chronicles, particularly the *Mahavamsa* and the *Dipavamsa*. These texts give us much historical or quasi-historical data, among which are two episodes concerning the earliest period of Sri Lankan history. The first is the account of the expedition from North India of Vijaya and his companions and their landing and colonization of the island, probably in the fifth century BC. The second is the account of the mission sent by Ashoka to Sri Lanka in c. 246 BC. in the person of Mahinda, and of his relations with the king Devanam Piya Tisa.

The archaeological sequence of the first millennium BC in Sri Lanka appears to coincide to a remarkable extent with that found throughout the Indian peninsula. We saw in chapter 5 that there is much evidence of a well-dated Mesolithic culture in Sri Lanka. The archaeological sequence is known from a number of excavated sites, of which we shall mention two, Kantarrodai in the north of the island, and Anuradhapura in the centre. Both have produced reliable series of radiocarbon dates. Kantarrodai is a substantial site on the Jaffna peninsula, and is sometimes thought to have been the site of Tamraparni, where Vijaya first landed in Sri Lanka and where he 'laid out' the 'first city' in the island. It has produced a culture sequence, dated by radiocarbon, beginning with a characteristic South Asian early Iron Age (c. 500-130 BC); followed by a second and third period (from c. 100 BC).

The sequence at Anuradhapura begins with a spread of typical Sri Lankan Mesolithic artifacts on the natural rock surface in the centre of what was to become the fortified city. Radiocarbon dates suggest that this goes back to the fourth or fifth millennium, but it seems likely that the site was occupied from time to time thereafter. The more continuous occupation begins around 800-600 BC, with typical Black-and-Red ware pottery, some vessels bearing scratched symbols, and small quantities of iron tools and slag (Coningham and Allchin, 1995). The houses are circular in plan with timber posts and walls and (presumably) thatched roofs. In the following phase (dated between 450-340 BC), the main elements remain the same. However, in its final stage, a remarkable discovery has been made, a number of potshards with crude Brahmi inscriptions scratched on them (*Plate. 71, nos. 1 and 2*). Datable to c. 360-340 BC these are almost certainly the earliest dated Brahmi inscriptions from any part of South Asia.

258 *Origins of a Civilization*

Around 340 BC a remarkable change took place at Anuradhapura. Apparently, the city was largely replanned and rebuilt, and the houses too were now cardinally oriented. The structure was still of timber, with mud or wattle and daub infilling, and the single excavated building had several oblong rooms. The roof was still of thatch, but a few decades later the first evidence of the use of tiles has been found. Another new development of this time was the construction of the great moat and rampart which surrounds the city. The city now assumes its full size of c.100 hectares. It is significant that these events took place at a time when, according to the *Mahavamsa*, king Pandukabhaya was ruling, since the chronicle records that it was during his reign that Anuradhapura was refounded as the capital city, and laid out on well-planned lines. He is also recorded as having built or enlarged various irrigation tanks to supply the city, some of which can still be identified today. The excavations revealed evidence of greatly enhanced trade, with imports of lapis lazuli and other stones from India and Afghanistan. Another probable import is a fine grey ware, the source of which is still not clear, but which appears to have been related to the slightly later Hellenistic-influenced Rouletted ware. Several more inscribed shards were also discovered (*Plate 71, no. 3*), and at the end of the period (c. 275 BC) the first coins of copper appear.

The next period at Anuradhapura covers almost four centuries (from c. 275 BC – 150 AD). Its earlier phase coincides with the reign of Devanampiya Tisa, the junior contemporary of Ashoka Maurya, who received the Buddhist mission led by Mahinda. The main excavated buildings of this period show a complete change from the previous stage: materials used include burnt bricks and limestone blocks, and the roofing is of tiles. The ceramics now include quantities of 'Hellenistic' type grey ware and Rouletted ware, and imported glass appears. All the indications are that this was equivalent to the period of Hellenistic-Roman trade which played such a large part in the increasing wealth of sites from Taxila in the north to Arikamedu in the south. Appropriately, considerable numbers of local copper coins are found. Once again, there is close agreement on the excavation results with the details of the period described in the *Mahavamsa*.

Conclusion

We may now sum up a number of points that arise from this brief, somewhat impressionistic view of the rise and spread of cities throughout South Asia:

The Second Urbanization 259

a) A rapidly expanding settlement pattern developed in the Upper Ganges plain between c.1000 BC and 550 BC, and, more or less contemporarily, settlements began to increase in the Middle Ganges valley. This process continued thereafter for several centuries, raising the level of population to hitherto quite unprecedented levels.

b) The dates of the construction of the massive city defences in the Ganges valley are not as yet precisely defined. Therefore, we cannot know for sure which cities were earlier or which later; nor how far the appearance of fortifications was more or less simultaneous throughout. We believe, however, that the main work took place within two centuries, between 500 and 300 BC. On present showing, the stone walls of Rajagriha are probably older than any other major Ganges fortifications but they are not as yet objectively dated by archaeology.

c) In the Gandhara region the first cities emerged more or less simultaneously with those of the Ganges.

d) The principal cities of Central India and the Deccan probably arose in parallel with those of the Ganges, but some may be slightly later. This seems also to be the case for those of the eastern coastal strip and Sri Lanka. But it must be repeated that the whole time-scale is so compact that, without much more precise dating, it is really not possible to unravel their relative ages and sequence.

e) It is striking that the century from 400-300 BC, which must have seen city building reaching its climax, also witnessed two major developments: the first manufacture of indigenous Indian coinage, in the silver bar coins of the north-west and the equivalent coins of the middle Ganges valley; and the earliest use of an indigenous script, the Brahmi, at present first attested archaeologically in Sri Lanka.

f) It is also worthy of consideration that if we accept the shorter chronology for the life of the Buddha, such as that proposed by Bechert (1982, 1991), bringing the date of the *Mahaparinirvana* (the death of the Buddha) to c. 358-378 BC, it would follow that the Buddha was contemporary with the great period of city building. This is already indicated by the account of his visiting the new city of Pataliputra, then under construction, in his last years. We cannot here discuss the historical implications of such as a chronology, but it seems to us to raise problems in accommodating the Nanda dynasty in pre-Mauryan Magadhan history, and leads us to think that the date of the *Mahaparinirvana* should be somewhat earlier, and not later than 400 BC.

The Flowering of Early Historic Civilization

With the conclusion of chapter 11 we have reached our goal. The South Asia-wide expansion of cities and states which we have been reporting seems to herald the fourth and final definition of the expanding civilization referred to by Manu (II. 17-22) (see above pp. 218, 232). In this the author states that the region contained between 'the ocean in the east and the ocean in the west and the (Himalaya) mountains is known as Aryavarta. In our journey we have thought it important to juxtapose the evidence offered by archaeology with that which can be gleaned from early literature. The latter sources are obviously biased to the extent that they are written from a partial and largely Brahminical point of view. Helpful as they may be in pointing towards the way in which these centuries witnessed the spread of Indo-Aryan speakers, colonization and probable domination of local communities, they must not allow us to confuse such a view with the wider perspective offered by archaeology. The spread of Indo-Aryan speaking groups must have involved a continuation of the same culturally plural, poly-ethnic processes as those we have recognized as operating already during the final stages of the Indus civilization and throughout the Post-urban period. On the one hand we have the extension of the Brahminical web of literature, culture, ritual, and conscious planning as it appears in the *Arthashastra*: on the other the establishment of economic and social relations with the many communities and their differing life-styles throughout the whole subcontinent.

We stand at the threshold of the Mauryan age, when the youthful civilization whose emergence we have been following enters a fully literate stage. Henceforward, written records and approximately datable texts become part of the scene. Henceforward, we find a more or less continuous series of coins issued. Moreover, from now on, in addition to the massive defensive structures we have described, we begin to find a growing number of stone or rock-cut monuments of Buddhist, Jaina or Ajivaka dedication, and also the earliest Vaishnava and Saiva cult monuments. We find a rich variety of sculptures in stone and terracotta. In addition to all these things our knowledge and understanding of Mauryan society is enormously enhanced by the wealth of information that can be gleaned from the Ashokan edicts; the extraordinary source book, the *Arthashastra* (whatever we may believe regarding its author and age); and the fragmentary but illuminating account of India composed by Megasthenes, the Greek ambassador to the Mauryan court at Pataliputra.

The Second Urbanization 261

The sources add a new dimension to our understanding of many things. For example, we learn from early Buddhist texts that in the Buddha's time Bimbisara, the king of Magadha, resided in Rajagriha. A generation later we hear of his successor Ajatashatru constructing a newly-fortified city on the Ganges at Pataliputra (Patna), and of the Buddha on his last journey visiting the site and prophesying that the Patali village would become the foremost of cities. Shortly after, the Magadhan capital was transferred there from Rajagriha. It is not difficult to infer reasons for such a move, the new city on the Ganges bank must have included an extensive *putabhedana* (wharf) for the loading and unloading of ships bearing all kinds of merchandise. Thence they might go by river in both directions, and have contact with ships from distant places. Thus, Pataliputra was well-suited for its new role, not only as the capital of the state of Magadha, but also as the metropolis of the India-wide empire which within a few decades Chandragupta Maurya was to establish. Finally, we have Ashoka's own statement that he had issued an edict while residing at Pataliputra; and the clear descriptive accounts of the city given by Megasthenes. In this way historical sources henceforward provide invaluable support for archaeological data, and vice versa.

We are aware that the archaeological line of approach we have been following in this book is in some respects austere, and that it neglects many interesting aspects of life, but we believe that we are justified in doing this in the interests of our main aim in this part of the book—that is, to investigate the events around and after the end of the Indus civilization, and to try to discover what relationship they had to the subsequent development of urbanization in the Ganges system and beyond.

BIBLIOGRAPHY

Adams, R. McC. 1974. Anthropological Perspectives on Ancient Trade. *Current Anthropology* 15, 3: 239-258.

Allchin, B. 1963. The Indian Stone Age Sequence. *Journal of the Royal Anthropological Institute* 93, 2:210-234.

Allchin, B. 1966. *The Stone Tipped Arrow: Late Stone Age Hunters of the Tropical Old World.* Phoenix House, London.

Allchin, B. 1974. Siddhapur and Barkaccha, Two Stone Age Factory Sites in Uttar Pradesh. In: *Perspectives in Palaeoanthropology*, ed. A.K. Ghosh, 233-248. Firma K.L. Mukhopadhyaya, Calcutta.

Allchin, B. 1976. The Discovery of Palaeolithic Sites in the Plains of Sind and their Implications. *The Geographical Journal* 142 (3): 471-489.

Allchin, B. 1995. Early Human Cultures and Environments in the Northern Punjab, Pakistan: an overview of the Potwar Project of the British Archaeological Mission to Pakistan (1981-1991). In: *Quaternary Environments and Geoarchaeology of India, Essays in Honour of Professor S.H. Rajaguru*, eds. S. Wadia, R. Korisettar and V. S. Kale, eds. 150-168, Memoir 32, Geological Society of India, Bangalore.

Allchin, B. and R. Allchin, 1968. *The Birth of Indian Civilization.* Penguin Books, Harmondsworth, reprinted Penguin Books, India, 1993.

Allchin, B. and F.R. Allchin, 1993. Lewan—A Stone Tool Factory of the Fourth to Third Millennium BC. In: *Harappan Civilization*, ed. G.L. Possehl, 2nd Revised edition, Oxford and IBH Publishing, New Delhi.

Allchin, B. and R. Allchin. 1982. *The Rise of Civilization in India and Pakistan.* The University Press, Cambridge.

Allchin, B., A. Goudie and K. Hegde, 1978. *The Prehistory and Palaeogeography of the Great Indian Desert.* Academic Press, London and New York.

Allchin, F.R. 1960. *Piklihal Excavations.* Government of Andhra Pradesh, Hyderabad.

264　　　　　　　　　　*Origins of a Civilization*

Allchin, F.R. 1980. Antecedents of the Indus Civilization. *Proceedings of the British Academy* 66:135-160.

Allchin, F.R. 1989. City and State Formation in Early Historic South Asia. *South Asian Studies* 5:1-16.

Allchin, F.R. 1990. Patterns of City Formation in Early Historic South Asia. *South Asian Studies* 6:163-173.

Allchin, F.R. 1992. An Indus Ram: a Hitherto Unknown Sculpture from the Indus Civilization. *South Asian Studies* 8:53-54.

Allchin, F.R. 1993. The Urban Position of Taxila and its Place in Northwest India-Pakistan. In: *Urban Form and Meaning in South Asia*, eds. H. Spodeck and D.M. Srinivasan 60-81, National Art Gallery, Washington.

Allchin, F.R. 1995. *The Archaeology of Early Historic South Asia.* Cambridge University Press, Cambridge.

Ardeleanu, A., U. Franke and M. Jansen, 1983. An Approach Towards the Replacement of Artefacts into the Architectural Context of the Great Bath in Mohenjo-daro. In: *Forschungs projekt DFG Mohenjo-daro*, G. Urban and M. Jansen, eds. Aachen.

Atre, S. 1987. *The Archetypal Mother.* Ravish Publishers, Pune.

Bar-Yosef, O. 994. The Lower Palaeolithic of the Near East. *Journal of World Prehistory* 8 (3): 211-265.

Baskaran, M., A.R. Marthe, S.N. Rajaguru and B.L.K. Somayajulu. 1986. Geochronology of Palaeolithic Cultures in Hiran Valley, Saurashtra, India. *Journal of Archaeological Science* 413:505-551.

Bechert, H. 1982. The Date of the Buddha Reconsidered. *Indologia Taurinensia* 10:29-36.

Bechert, H. 1991. The date of the Historical Buddha. *Symposium zur Buddhismus forschung*, 2 vols. Vandenhoek and Ruprecht, Gottingen.

Bellwood, P. et al. 1992. New Dates for Prehistoric Asian Rice. *Asian Perspectives* 31, 2:161-168.

Bhan, K.K. and J.M. Kenoyer. 1980-81. Nageshwar, an Industrial Centre of the Chalcolithic Period. *Puratattva* 2:115-120.

Bhan, K.K., M. Vidale and J.M. Kenoyer. 1994. Harappan Technology: Theoretical and Methodological Issues. *Man and Environment* 19, 1 & 2:141-157.

Biagi, P., M. Mukhtiar Kazi and Fabio Negrino. 1996. An Acheulian

Workshop at Ziarat Pir Shaban on the Rohri Hills (Sindh, Pakistan). *South Asian Studies* 12:49-62.

Bisht, R.S. 1993 [1982]. Excavations at Banawali: 1974-77. In: *Harappan Civilization—A Recent Perspective*, ed. G.L. Possehl, 113-124, 2nd edition. Oxford and IBH Publishing, New Delhi.

Bisht, R.S. 1989. A New Model for the Harappan Town Planning as Revealed at Dholavira in Kachch. In: *History and Archaeology*, ed. B. Chatterjee, 397-408, Ramanand Vidya Bhavan, New Delhi.

Bisht, R.S. 1991. Dholavira: A New Horizon of the Indus Civilization. *Puratattva* 20:71-82.

Blumenschine, R.J. and U.C. Chattopadhyaya. 1983. Preliminary Report on the Terminal Pleistocene Fauna of the Middle Son Valley. In: *Palaeoenvironments and Prehistory in the Middle Son Valley*, eds. G.R. Sharma and J.D. Clark, 281-284, Dept of Ancient History, Culture and Archaeology, University of Allahabad.

Brooks, R.R. and V.S. Wakankar. 1976. *Stone Age Painting in India*. Yale University Press, New Haven and London.

Bryson, R.A. and A.M. Swain. 1981. Holocene Variations of Monsoon Rainfall in Rajasthan. *Quaternary Research* 16:135-145.

Casal, J.M. 1964. *Fouilles d'Amri*. 2 volumes, Publications de la Commission des Fouilles Archeologiques, Paris.

Chakrabarti, D.K. 1990. *The External Trade of the Indus Civilization*. Munshiram Manoharlal, New Delhi.

Chang, T.T. 1977. The Rice Cultures. In: *The Early History of Agriculture*, eds. G. Clark and J. Hutchinson, 143-155, The British Academy, London.

Chattopadhyaya, D.P. 1959. *Lokayata: a Study in Ancient Indian Materialism*. People's Publishing House, New Delhi.

Chattopadhyaya, D.P. 1986. *History of Science and Technology in Ancient India. The Beginnings*. Firma KLM, Calcutta.

Childe, V.G. 1952. *New Light on the Most Ancient East*. 3rd ed., Routledge and Kegan Paul, London.

Clark, J.D. and G.S. Khanna. 1989. The Site of Kunjhun II, Middle Son Valley, and its relevance for the Neolithic of Central India. In: *Old Problems and New Perspectives in the Archaeology of South Asia*, ed. J.M. Kenoyer, Department of Anthropology, University of Wisconsin, Madison.

Clark, J.D. and G.R. Sharma, eds. 1983. *Palaeoenvironments and Prehistory in the Middle Son Valley*. University of Allahabad, Allahabad.

266 *Origins of a Civilization*

Clark, J.D. and M.A.J. Williams. 1986. Palaeoenvironments and Prehistory in North Central India: a Preliminary Report. In: *Studies in the Archaeology of India and Pakistan,* J. Jacobson, ed. Oxford and IBH Publishing, New Delhi.

Coningham, R.A.E. and F.R. Allchin. 1995. The Rise of Cities in Sri Lanka, *The Archaeology of Early Historic South Asia.* F.R. Allchin. 152-183, University Press, Cambridge.

Coningham, R.A.E. 1995. Dark Age or Continuum. In: *The Archaeology of Early Historic South Asia.* F.R. Allchin, 54-72, University Press, Cambridge.

Costantini, L. 1984. The Beginning of Agriculture of the Kachi Plain: the Evidence of Mehrgarh. In: *South Asian Archaeology 1981,* ed. B. Allchin, 29-33, The University Press, Cambridge.

Cunningham, Sir A. 1875. *Archaeological Survey of India, Report 1872-73.* Superintendent of Government Printing, Calcutta.

Dales, G.F. 1962. Harappan Outposts on the Makran Coast. *Antiquity* 36:86-92.

Dales, G.F. 1965. A Suggested Chronology for Afghanistan, Baluchistan and the Indus valley. In: *Chronologies in Old World Archaeology,* ed. R.W. Ehrich, 257-284, University of Chicago Press, Chicago.

Dalmia, Y. 1988. *The Painted World of the Worlis.* Lalit Kala Akademy, New Delhi.

Davis, R.S. 1978. The Palaeolithic. In: *The Archaeology of Afghanistan,* ed. F.R. Allchin and N. Hammond, 37-70, Academic Press Inc., London.

Deraniyagala, S.U. 1992. *The Prehistory of Sri Lanka.* 2 vols, Department of Archaeological Survey, Government of Sri Lanka.

de Terra, H. and T.T. Paterson. 1939. *Studies in the Ice Age of India and Associated Human Cultures.* Carnegie Institute, Washington.

Dhavalikar, M.K. 1993. Harappans in Saurashtra: the Mercantile Model as Seen in Recent Excavations at Kuntasi. In: *Harappan Civilization: a Recent Perspective,* ed. G.L. Possehl, 335-363, 2nd edition, Oxford and IBH Publishing, New Delhi.

Dhavalikar, M.K. 1995. *Cultural Imperialism: Indus Civilization in Western India.* Books and Books, New Delhi.

Dhavalikar, M.K. and S. Atre. 1989. The Fire-cult and Virgin Sacrifice: Some Harappan Rituals. In: *Old Problems and New Perspectives in the Archaeology of South Asia,* ed. J.M. Kenoyer, 193-206, Department of Anthropology, Madison, Wisconsin.

Dikshit, K.N. 1984. Late Harappa in Northern India. In: *Frontiers of the Indus Civilization*, eds. B.B. Lal and S.P. Gupta, 254-269, Indian Archaeological Society, New Delhi.

Elwin, V. 1939. *The Baiga.* John Murray, London.

Erdosy, G. 1988. *Urbanisation in Early Historic India.* BAR International Series 430, Oxford.

Erdosy, G. 1995. The Prelude to Urbanization: Ethnicity and the Rise of Late Vedic Chiefdoms. In: *The Archaeology of Early Historic South Asia,* ed. F.R. Allchin, 75-88, Cambridge University Press, Cambridge.

Erdosy, G. 1995. City-states of North India and Pakistan at the Time of the Buddha. In: *The Archaeology of Early Historic South Asia,* ed. F.R. Allchin, 99-122, Cambridge University Press, Cambridge.

Fairservis, W.A. 1971. *The Roots of Ancient India.* Macmillan, New York and London.

Ferguson, D. 1993. The Impact of Late Cenozoic Environmental Change in East Asia on the Distribution of Terrestrial Plants and Animals. In: *Proceedings of the Third Conference on the Evolution of the East Asian Environment,* ed. Nina G. Jablonski, 145-196, Centre of Asian Studies, University of Hong Kong.

Flam, L. 1993. Fluvial Geomorphology of the Lower Indus Basin (Sindh, Pakistan) and the Indus Basin. In: *Himalaya to the Sea, Geology, Geomorphology and the Quaternary,* ed. J.F. Shroder, 265-287, Routledge, London and New York.

Foote, R.B. 1916. The Foote Collection of Indian Prehistoric and Proto Historic Antiquities. Madras Government Museum, Madras.

Frankfort, H-P. 1989. *Fouilles de Shortughai: Recherches sur l'Asie Centrale Protohistoriques.* 2 volumes, Diffusion de Boccard, Paris.

Furer-Haimendorf, C. von. 1943. *The Chenchus, Jungle Folk of the Deccan.* Macmillan, London.

Gabunia, L and A. Vekua. 1995. A Plio-Pleistocene Hominid from Dmanisi, East Georgia, Caucasus. *Nature* 375:509-512.

Gaur, R.C. 1983. *Excavations at Atranjikhera.* Centre of Advanced Study, Aligarh Muslim University. Motilal Banarsidass, New Delhi.

Gropp, G. 1992. A 'Great Bath' at Elam. In: *South Asian Archaeology 1989,* ed. C. Jarrige, 113-118, Prehistory Press, Madison, Wisconsin.

268 *Origins of a Civilization*

Halim, A. and M. Vidale. 1984. Kilns, Bangles and Coated Vessels: Ceramic Productions in Closed Containers at Mohenjo-daro. In: *Interim Reports vol 2,* eds. M. Jansen and G. Urban, 63-97, ISMEO, RWTH, Aachen.

Hegde, K.T.M. 1978. Analysis of Ancient Indian Deluxe Wares. *Archaeo Physika* 10:141-155.

Hegde, K.T.M. R.V. Karanth and S.P. Sychanthavong 1982. On the Composition and Technology of Harappan Microbeads. In: *Harappan Civilization, a Contemporary Perspective,* ed. G.L. Possehl, 239-244, Oxford and IBH Publishing, New Delhi.

Helms, S.W. 1982. Excavations at the City and Most Famous Fortress of Kandahar, the Foremost Place in all Asia, *Afghan Studies,* 3&4: 1-24

Hemmy, A.S. 1931. System of Weights at Mohenjo-daro. In: *Mohenjo-daro and the Indus Civilization,* ed. Sir John Marshall, 589-691, Probsthain, London.

Hemphill, B.E., J.R. Lukacs and K.A.R. Kennedy. 1991. Biological Adaptations and Affinites of Bronze Age Harappans. In: *Harappan Excavations 1986-1990,* ed. R.H. Meadow,137-182, Prehistory Press, Madison, Wisconsin.

Hunter, G.R. 1929 (1934). *The Script of Harappa and Mohenjo-daro and its Connection with Other Scripts.* Oxford University Doctoral Dissertation. Kegan Paul, Trench and Trubner, London.

Hutchinson, J. 1977. India: Local and Introduced Crops. In: *The Early History of Agriculture,* eds. G. Clark and J. Hutchinson, 129-138, The British Academy, London.

Indian Archaeology—a Review (IAR). 1983-84. Excavations at Banawali, 24-29.

Jacobson, J. 1986. The Harappan Civilization: An Early State. In: *Studies in the Archaeology of India and Pakistan,* ed. J. Jacobson, 137-174, American Institute of Indian Studies/Oxford and IBH Publishing, New Delhi.

Jain, J. 1984. *Painted Myths of Creation.* Lalit Kala Akademy, New Delhi.

Jansen, M. 1987a. *Vergessene Stadte am Indus.* Verlag Philipp von Zabern: Mainz am Rhein.

Jansen, M. 1993. *Mohenjo-daro: City of Wells and Drains.* Frontinus-Gesellschaft e.v., Bergisch Gladbach.

Jarrige, J.F. 1981. Economy and Society of the Early Chalcolithic/Bronze Age of Baluchistan. In: *South Asian Archaeology 1979,* ed. H. Hartel, 93-114, Reimer Verlag, Berlin.

Bibliography

Jarrige, J-F. 1984. Chronology of the Earlier Periods of the Greater Indus as seen from Mehrgarh, Pakistan. In: *South Asian Archaeology 1981*, ed. B. Allchin, 21-28, Cambridge University Press, Cambridge.

Jarrige, J-F. 1985. Continuity and Change in the North Kachi Plain at the beginning of the Second Millennium BC. In: *South Asian Archaeology 1983*, eds. J. Schotsmans and M. Taddei, 35-68, Istituto Universitario Orientale, Naples.

Jarrige, J-F. 1993. The Question of the Beginning of the Mature Harappan Civilization as seen from Nausharo Excavations. In: *South Asian Archaeology 1991*, eds. A. Gail and G. Mevissen, 149-164, Franz Steiner Verlag, Stuttgart.

Jarrige, J-F. 1994. The Final Phase of the Indus Occupation at Nausharo and its Connection with the Following Cultural Complex at Mehrgarh VII. In: *South Asian Archaeology 1993*, eds. A. Parpola and P. Koskikallio, 295-313, Suomalainen Tiedeaktemia, Helsinki.

Jarrige, C., Jarrige, J-F., Meadow, R.H., and Quivron, G. 1995. *Mehrgarh, Field Reports 1974-1985*. Karachi: Government of Sindh, Department of Culture.

Jarrige, J-F. and M. Lechevallier. 1979. Excavations at Mehrgarh, Baluchistan. In *South Asian Archaeology 1977*, ed. M. Taddei, 463-535, Istituto Universitario Orientale, Naples.

Joshi, J.P. 1991. Settlement Patterns in the Third, Second and First Millennia in India. In: *The Cultural Heritage of an Indian Village*. British Museum, London.

Joshi, J.P., Madhu Bala and Jassu Ram. 1984. The Indus Civilization: a Reconsideration on the Basis of Distribution Maps. In: *Frontiers of the Indus Civilization*, eds. B.B. Lal and S.P. Gupta, 511-530, Indian Archaeological Society, New Delhi.

Joshi, J.P. et al. 1993. *Excavation at Bhagwanpura 1975-76: and Other Explorations and Excavations 1975-81 in Haryana, Jammu and Kashmir and Punjab*. With contributions from Madhu Bala and others. Archaeological Survey of India, New Delhi.

Kenoyer, J.M. 1991. The Indus Valley Tradition of Pakistan and Western India. *Journal of World Prehistory* 5(4):331-385.

Kenoyer, J.M., M. Vidale and K.K. Bhan. 1994. Carnelian Bead Production in Khambat, India: An Ethnoarchaeological Study. In: *Living Traditions: Studies of the Ethnoarchaeology of South Asia*, ed. B. Allchin, 281-306, Oxford and IBH Publishing, New Delhi.

Khan, F.A. 1965. Excavations at Kot Diji. *Pakistan Archaeology* 2:11-85.

270 *Origins of a Civilization*

Khan, F., J.R. Knox and K.D. Thomas. 1991. *Explorations and Excavations in the Bannu District, North West Frontier Province, Pakistan 1985-1988.* British Museum Occasional Papers No 80.

Khatri, J.S. and M. Acharya. 1995. Kunal: a new Indus-Saraswati site. *Puratattva* 25:84-86.

Kosambi, D.D. 1952. Ancient Kosala and Magadha. *Journal of the Bombay Branch of the Royal Asiatic Society* 27: 180-213.

Kosambi, D.D. 1956. *An Introduction to the Study of Indian History.* Popular Prakashan, Bombay.

Koskenniemi, K. and A. Parpola. 1979. *Corpus of Texts in the Indus Script.* Department of Asian and African Studies, Helsinki.

Koskenniemi, K and A. Parpola. 1980. *Documentation and Duplicates of the Texts in the Indus Script.* Ibid, Helsinki.

Koskenniemi, K. and A. Parpola. 1982. *A Concordance to the Texts in the Indus Script.* Ibid, Helsinki.

Lahiri, N. 1992. *The Archaeology of Indian Trade Routes up to c. 200 BC.* Oxford University Press, Delhi.

Lal, Makkhan. 1984. *Settlement History and Rise of Civilization in the Ganga-Yamuna Doab.* B.R. Publishing House, Delhi.

Lal, Makkhan. 1989. Population Distribution and its Movement During the Second and First millennia BC in the Indo-Gangetic Divide and Upper Ganga Plain. *Puratattva* 18 (1987-88): 35-53.

Lambrick, H.T. 1964. *Sind: a General Introduction.* Sindhi Adabi Board, Hyderabad, Sind.

Lechevallier, M. 1984. The Flint Industry of Mehrgarh. In: *South Asian Archaeology 1981,* ed. B. Allchin, 41-51, Cambridge University Press, Cambridge.

Lechevallier, M. and G. Quivron. 1985. Results of the Recent Excavations at the Neolithic Site of Mehrgarh, Pakistan. In: *South Asian Archaeology 1983,* eds. J Schotsmans and M. Taddei, 69-90, Istituto Universitario Orientale, Naples.

McAlpin, D.W. 1981. *Proto-Elamo-Dravidian: the Evidence and its Implications.* American Philosophical Society, Philadelphia.

McNicoll, A. and W. Ball. 1996. *Excavations at Kandahar 1974 and 1975.* Society of South Asian Studies Monograph No. 1. BAR International Series 641, Oxford.

Bibliography

Mackay, E.J.H. 1937. Bead Making in Ancient Sind. *Journal of the American Oriental Society* 47:1-5.

Mahadevan, I. 1977. *The Indus script: Texts, Concordance and Tables. Memoirs of the Archaeological Survey of India 77*. Archaeological Survey of India, New Delhi.

Mainkar, B.V. 1984. Metrology in the Indus Civilization. In: *Frontiers of the Indus Civilization*, eds. B.B. Lal and S.P. Gupta, 141-152, Books and Books, New Delhi.

Mandal, D. 1983 A note on the Radiocarbon Dates from the Middle Son Valley. In: *Palaeoenvironments and Prehistory in the Middle Son Valley*, eds. J.D. Clark and G.R. Sharma, 285-289, University of Allahabad, Allahabad.

Marshall, Sir J. 1931. *Mohenjo-daro and the Indus Civilization*. 3 volumes, Probsthain, London.

Meadow, R.H. 1989. Continuity and Change in the Agriculture of the Greater Indus Valley: the Palaeoethnobotanical and Zooarchaeological Evidence. In: *Old Problems and New Perspectives in the Archaeology of South Asia*, ed. J.M. Kenoyer, 61-74, Department of Anthropology, University of Wisconsin, Madison.

Meadow, R.H. ed. 1991. *Harappa Excavations 1986-1990*. Prehistory Press, Madison, Wisconsin.

Meadow, R.H. 1993. Animal Domestication in the Middle East: a Revised View of the Eastern Margin. In: *Harappan Civilization*, ed. G.L. Possehl, 295-320, 2nd Revised edition, Oxford and IBH Publishing, New Delhi.

Meadow, R.H. and J.M. Kenoyer. 1995. *Harappa 1994 and 1995*. New inscribed objects from Harappa. Unpublished report.

Misra, V.N. 1968. Middle Stone Age in Rajasthan. In: *La Prehistoire, Problemes et Tendances*. 295-302, Éditions du Centre National de la Recherche Scientifique, Paris.

Misra, V.N. 1984. Climate, a Factor in the Rise and Fall of the Indus Civilization. In: *Frontiers of the Indus Civilization*, eds. B.B. Lal and S.P. Gupta, 461-489, Books and Books, New Delhi.

Misra, V.N. 1995. Geoarchaeology of the Thar Desert, Northwest India. In: *Quaternary Environments and Geoarchaeology of India*, eds. S. Wadia, R. Korisettar and V.S. Kale, Geological Society of India, Bangalore.

Mughal M.R. 1971. *The Early Harappan Period in the Greater Indus Valley: (c. 3000-2400 BC)*. PhD Dissertation, University of Pennsylvania, Philadelphia.

Mughal, M.R. 1990a. Further evidence on the Early Harappan Culture of the Greater Indus Valley. *South Asian Studies* 6:75-199.

272 *Origins of a Civilization*

Mughal, M.R. 1990b. The Protohistoric Settlement Patterns in Cholistan. In: *South Asian Archaeology 987*, volume 1, eds. M. Taddei and P. Callieri, 143-156, ISMEO, Rome.

Mughal, M.R. 1992a. The Geographical Extent of the Indus Civilization During the Early, Mature and Late Harappan Times. In: *South Asian Archaeology Studies*, ed. G.L. Possehl, 123-143, Oxford and IBH Publishing, New Delhi.

Mughal, M.R. 1992b. Jhukar and the Late Harappan Cultural Mosaic of the Greater Indus Valley. In: *South Asian Archaeology 1989*, ed. C. Jarrige, 213-221, Prehistoric Press, Madison, Wisconsin.

Murty, M.L.K. 1969. Blade and Burin Industries near Renigunta on the Southeast Coast of India. *Proceedings of the Prehistoric Society* 28:83-101.

Murty, M.L.K. 1994. Forest Peoples and Historical Traditions in the Eastern Ghats, South India. In: *Living Traditions: Studies in the Ethnoarchaeology of South India*, ed. B. Allchin, Oxford and IBH Publishing, New Delhi.

Oldham, R.D. 1926. The Cutch (Kacch) Earthquake of 16th July, 1819, with a revision of the Great Earthquake of 12th June 1897. *Memoir of the Geological Survey of India* 46 (2): 71-147.

Paddayya, K. and M.D. Pedraglia. 1995. Natural and Cultural Formation Processes of the Acheulian Sites of the Hunsgi Baichbal Valleys, Karnataka. In: *Quaternary Environments and Geochronology of India*, Statira Wadia, eds. Ravi Korisettar and Vishwas S. Kale, 333-352, Geological Society of India, Bangalore.

Parpola, A. 1987, 1991. *Corpus of Indus Seals and Inscriptions*. vol. 1. *Collections in India* (with J.P. Joshi); vol. 2. *Collections in Pakistan* (with S.G.M. Shah). Suomalainen Tiedeakatemia, Helsinki.

Parpola, A. 1994. *Deciphering the Indus Script*. The University Press, Cambridge.

Possehl, G.L. 1986. *Kulli: an Exploration of Ancient Civilization in Asia*. Carolina Academic Press, Durham, N. Carolina.

Possehl, G.L. 1990. Revolution in the Urban Revolution: the Emergence of the Indus Civilization. *Annual Review of Anthropology* 19:261-282.

Possehl, G.L. 1992. The Chronology of Prehistoric India: from the Earliest Times to the Iron Age. In: *Chronologies in Old World Archaeology*, ed. Robert Ehrich, 467-468, 3rd edition, Chicago University Press, Chicago.

Possehl, G.L. 1993b. The Date of Indus Urbanisation: a Proposed Chronology for the Pre-urban and Urban Harappan Times. In: *South Asian Archaeology 1991*, eds. A. Gail and G. Mevissen, 231-250, Franz Steiner Verlag, Stuttgart.

Possehl, G.L. 1994a. The Indus Civilization. *Man and Environment* vol. 19, No. 1-2: 103-113.

Possehl, G.L. 1994b. *Radiometric Dates for South Asian Archaeology*. University Museum, Philadelphia, Pennsylvania.

Possehl, G.L. 1996. *Indus Age: The Writing System*. Oxford and IBH Publishing, New Delhi.

Possehl, G.L. In press. Prehistoric Plant Exchanges between Africa and the Indian Subcontinent (paper presented at Cross-Cultural Plant Exchange, London, July 1996).

Possehl, G.L. and M.H. Raval. 1989. *Harappan Civilization and Rojdi*. Oxford and IBH Publishing, New Delhi.

Possehl, G.L. and P.C. Rissman. 1992. The Chronology of Prehistoric India: from Earliest Times to the Iron Age. In: *Chronologies in Old World Prehistory*, ed. R.W. Ehrich, vol 1: 465-490 and vol. 2: 447-74, 3rd edition. University of Chicago Press, Chicago and London.

Pusalker. 1951. Aryan settlements in India. In: *The Vedic Age. History and Culture of the Indian People*, Vol. 1, ed. R.C. Majumdar, 245-267, Bharatiya Vidya Bhavan, Bombay.

Rao, S.R. 1979, 1985. Lothal: a Harappan Port Town, 1955-1962. *Memoirs of the Archaeological Survey of India* 78:172, New Delhi.

Ratnagar, S. 1981. *Encounters, the Westerly Trade of the Harappa Civilization*. Oxford University Press, New Delhi.

Ratnagar, S. 1991. *Enquiries into the Political Organization of Harappan Society*. Ravish Publishers, Pune.

Ratnagar, S. 1994. Harappan Trade in its 'World' Context. *Man and Environment* 19:115-128.

Rendell, H.M. and R.D. Dennell. 1985. Dated Lower Palaeolithic Artefacts from Northern Pakistan. *Current Anthropology* 26:293.

Rendell, H.M., R.W. Dennell and M.A. Halim. 1989. *Pleistocene and Palaeolithic Investigations in the Soan Valley, Northern Pakistan*. BAR International Series, Oxford.

Roy, T.N. 1983. *The Ganges Civilization*. Ramanand Vidya Bhavan, New Delhi.

Sankalia, H.D. 1964. Middle Stone Age Culture in India and Pakistan. *Science 146*, 3642:365-375.

Saraswat, K.S. 1993. Plant Economy of Late Harappan at Hulas. *Puratattva* 23:1-12.

Schick, K.D. and N. Toth. 1993. *Making Silent Stones Speak.* Weidenfeld and Nicolson, London.

Sen, D.K. 1964 and 1965. Ancient Races of India and Pakistan. *Ancient India* 20 and 21:178-205.

Shaffer, J.G. 1982a. Harappan Commerce: An Alternative Perspective. In: *Anthropology in Pakistan: Recent Socio-cultural and Archaeological Perspectives,* ed. S. Pastner and L. Flam, 166-210, Cornell University, Ithaca, N.Y.

Shaffer, J.G. 1986. Cultural Development in the East Punjab. In: *Studies in the archaeology of India and Pakistan,* ed. J. Jacobson, 195-236, American Institute of Indian Studies, Oxford, and IBH Publishing, New Delhi.

Shaffer, J.G. 1992. The Indus Valley, Baluchistan, and Helmand Traditions: Neolithic through Bronze Age. In: *Chronologies in Old World Prehistory,* ed. R.W. Ehrich, 3rd edition, 2 volumes. Vol 1: 441-464, vol 2: 425-446, University of Chicago Press, Chicago and London.

Shaffer, J.G. 1993 (1982b). Harappan Culture: a Reconsideration. In: *Harappan Civilization: a Recent Perspective,* ed. G.L. Possehl, 41-50, 2nd edition, American Institute of Indian Studies, New Delhi.

Sharma, G.R., V.N. Misra, D. Mandal, B.B. Misra and J.N. Pal. 1980. *Beginnings of Agriculture, (Studies in History, Culture and Archaeology, vol. 4).* Department of Ancient History, Culture and Archaeology, Allahabad.

Shastri, S.V.S. and Sharma, S.D. 1974. In: *Evolutionary Studies in World Crops,* ed. J. Hutchinson, 55-61, The University Press, Cambridge.

Singh, G. 1971. The Indus Valley Culture (seen in the context of Post-Glacial Climate and Ecological Studies in North-west India). *Archaeology and Physical Anthropology in Oceania* 6 (2): 177-189.

Singh, G., R.D. Joshi, S.K. Chopra and A.B. Singh. 1974. Late Quaternary History of Vegetation and Climate in the Rajasthan Desert, India. *Philosophical Transactions of the Royal Society of London* 267:467-501.

Sonawane, V.H. and P. Ajithprasad. 1994. Harappa Culture and Gujarat. *Man and Environment* 19:129-139.

Sullivan, H.P. 1964. A Re-examination of the Religion of the Indus Civilization. *History of Religions* 4:115-125.

Swain, A.M., J.E. Kutzbach and S. Hastenrath. 1983. Estimates of Holocene Precipitation for Rajasthan, India, Based on Pollen and Lake-Level Data. *Quaternary Research* 10:1-17.

Thapar, B.K. 1995. *Recent Archaeological Discoveries in India,* UNESCO, Paris.

Thapar, R. 1984. *From Lineage to State.* Oxford University Press, Delhi.

Bibliography

Verma, B.C. 1991. Siwalik Stone Age Culture. *Current Science* 61(8):496.

Vidale, M. 1989. Specialised Producers and Urban Elites: On the Role of Craft Industries in Mature Harappan Urban Centres. In: *Old Problems and New Perspectives in the Archaeology of South Asia,* ed. J.M. Kenoyer, Wisconsin Archaeological Reports, Madison, Wisconsin.

Wanpo, H.R. Clochon, G. Yumin, R. Larick, F. Qiren, H. Schwarcz, C. Yonge. J. de Vos and W. Rink. 1995. Early Homo and Associated Artefacts from Asia. *Nature* 378:275-78.

Weber, S. 1991. *Plants and Harappan Subsistence.* American Institute of Indian Studies and Oxford and IBH Publishing, New Delhi.

Wheeler, R.E.M. 1947. Harappa 1946: the Defences and Cemetery R 37. *Ancient India* 3:59-130.

Wilhelmy, H. 1969. Das Urstromtal am Ostrand des Indusebene und dar Sarasvati-Problem. *Zeitschrift fur Geomorphologie Supplementband* 8:76-93.

INDEX

Achaemenids 249

Acheulean 50, 67, 53-4, 62, 67
    artefacts 45, 47, 61, 63
    hand-axes 45, 49
    late— 61

Aceramic Neolithic settlement 132, 136

Afghanistan 14, 258

Agate, 89
    miners of central Gujarat 123

Agni 233

Agni Vaisvanara 233

Agricultural Production, 125-35
    boost to— 135-45

Ahar, 123
    copper miners at Rajasthan 123

Ahicchatra 237, 241-2

Alamgirpur 226

Allahabad 224, 234

Allah Band 118

Amri 118, 137, 154, 210, 212

animal husbandry 94, 170

Arabian, Desert 16, 21

Aravalli hills 28

Archaeology, 1-11
    approaches 7-10
    culturally-oriented 9
    conservation of cultural heritage 10-11
    data 218
    ethno-archaeology, 58, 200

investigations, 3, 4, 9
interpretation, 200
'New', processual, post-processual 200
South Asian, 1

Archaeological Survey of India 8, 9, 208, 214

Archaeological Survey of Pakistan 38

arid, aridity, 16, 17, 21-2, 24, 53, 66-7, 109, 208, 223

Arthashastra 239-42, 246, 260

Aryans 222, 234-5

Aryan ethos, 229
    spread in new territories on Ganges plains 229

Aryan expansion 235

Asia Minor 112, 203

Asmaka 250

Ashoka 248, 254, 257, 258

Atranjikhera 225-6, 235, 237

Attock 15

Avanti 250

axes 129, 225

Bactria-Margiana archaeological complex 210-12

Badakshan, source of lapis lazuli, 168, 174

Bagor 105

Bajra 169

278 *Origins of a Civilization*

Balakot 124, 168, 174, 179
Baluchi hills 156, 185
Baluchistan 14, 21, 45, 67, 87, 122, 131, 136, 138, 161
Banaras 239
Banawali 143, 148, 159, 163, 216
bangles 149, 155, 173-6, 228
Bannu Basin 15, 105, 139, 142
Bannu District, 110
    Sheri Khan Tarakai 139
Bara 216
barley 103, 105, 134, 137, 147, 168, 205, 224, 226, 234
beads, 109, 149, 165, 167, 168, 171, 228
    carnelian, 167, 171, 173-4
    copper, 131, 149
Belan river 48, 96
Bhagwanpura 216-7, 228-235
Bhita 8
Bhils 250
Bhir mound 249
Birbal Sahani Institute, Lucknow 217
Bisht 164
bitumen 129
Black Slipped ware 236, 239
blade 41, 68, 72-75, 94, 139, 172, 179
Bodh Gaya 8
Bolan river 23, 110, 125-6
bone artefacts 41,
Bos indicus (zebu) 170, 198, 87, 132
Brahmagiri 254
Brahmanas, 232-3, 235, 245
    Satapatha Brahmana 232
Brahmanical tradition 218, 260
Brahmavarta 218, 232
Brahmarsidesa 218, 232

Brahui 185, 186
bricks 131, 136, 146, 155, 163, 165-6, 194
bronze 165, 186
    sculpture 196
    'dancing girls' 197
Bryson and Swain (1981) 207-8
Buddha, Buddhist 30, 242, 248, 253, 255, 259
Budha Pushkar 66, 77
buffalo, 112, 170, 195, 198-9
    bones of—, 170
bull deity
burials 3, 7, 93, 129-31
Burnished Red ware 249
Burzahom 152

Cambridge-Baroda Project 207
camel 66, 176
Campa 241
carts, 176, 186
    bullock 137, 150, 195, 206
cattle 112, 132, 138, 223
    domestication of—, 93, 94
cattle pens 94, 101-32, 104
caves 9, 99
Cedi 250
Central Asia 138, 189
Central India, 27-30, 47-9, 86-7, 98-9, 253, 259
    stone industries
Central Indian Belt of Hills and Forests 250-3
Chalcolithic 97, 105, 250, 253
Chambal river 15
Chanhu-daro 156-7, 168, 174, 202, 209-10
Chandragupta 261
Charsada (Pushkalavati) 249

Index 279

Chattopadhyay, D.P., 194, 245
Chatur Bhuja Nath Nulla 235
Chautang river 215, 219
Childe, Gordon 10, 115, 204
Chenchu 99
chickpea 169
chiefdoms 188, 239-44, 246
Chirand 217, 225-6
Cholistan 96, 140, 144-6, 158, 168,
212-13
Chopani-mando 93-4, 97
Chronology and dating 47-50
city sites, 188
climate 6, 16, 32
climatic change 16-19, 120, 207
growing understanding of,
cotton 147, 169, 171, 172, 217
coins 6, 252
convergence or collision, effects, 14-5
process of—, 14-5
copper 10, 31, 165, 160, 168, 178,
226
cores 58, 70, 172
Costantini 134-5
cultivation 135
Culture,
beginning of—, 39-42

'Dark Age' 207
Dasas 221
Dating, techniques, 3, 7, 33
carbon 14 (AMS) dating 33,
97
development of physical—, 33-4
Paleomagnetic method 37, 48
Radiocarbon dating 227-237
Thermoluminiscent dating 76,
226
Deccan 29, 259

cities in the, 253-4
deforestation 225
depopulation, 214
major causes of,
Derawar fort 212
Dera Ismael Khan 138
desert 16-19
Dhavalikar 167,176
Dholavira 160, 164-5, 185
Dipavamsa 248
doab, 116, 223, 224, 225, 231
settlement pattern in 229
domestication of animals, 93, 127,
129, 131-4, 170, 176-7
in the Ganges valley
dolorite 51
Dravidian language, 185, 250
Brahui 185
drainage systems 22, 49, 155
Drishadvati river 113, 118, 218
dunes 17, 47, 104

Eastern Ghats 99
Eastern India 99
Egypt 115, 187, 203
Elephant, 136, 195, 199
bones of,
Elamite 184-5
Eleusine Coracana (ragi)
End of the Indus Civilization 207-
218
changes in thinking on 207-
209
references to discussions on
post-urban period 214
fresh period of aridity
corresponding to end of Mature
Urban period 209-211
environment, 5-6, 13-32

280   *Origins of a Civilization*

over exploitation of—, 121-22
environmental change, 61
   during the Holocene
erosion of soil, 15
Excavations, 8, 143
   at Lothal 193-4
   Pakistan-American, at Harappa 148

factory sites 65, 77, 99, 109
Fatehpur Sikri 8
faunal remains 60, 148
faience 171, 197
field pea 169, 217
figurines, 195-7
   more than one role, 195-7
   terracotta, 195-6
fish, 66, 138, 186
   consumption of 112
flakes 43-45, 68, 70
flint 53, 129, 148, 172
Fort Abbas 219
fortification 141, 237, 239, 250
fossil 33, 34, 38

Gagghar (Ghaggar), 157-8, 188, 213
   see also, Hakra and Sarasvati
Ganges-Brahmaputra System 26-7, 224
Ganges river,
   valley, 2, 26-7, 97, 98, 112, 182
   agriculture and subsistence, 223, 224, 228, 242
   role of rice in growth of population, 224, 228-231
   culture sequence and chronology, 236-7
   emergence of cities, 237-42

evidence of Neolithic and Chalcolithic, 223, 225, 231
   settlements in, 223, 229-31
   Upper Ganges Plains 224
Ganga-Yamuna Doab 116
Gandhara 4, 248-9, 259
Ganeshwar, sites 105, 160
geography 5
Geological Survey of India 36
Geological Survey of Pakistan 37
geology 7,
glacial phases 17
goat 112, 132-3, 137, 170, 199, 205, 206
Gonds 98, 250
Godavari river 30
Gold 103, 186
Gomal 138
Gondwanaland 14
grapes 169
grafitti 138, 192-3
graves 8
Great Bath 165
Gumla 138, 158

Hakra 24, 117, 140, 144, 211
see also, Sarasvati and Ghaggar
hand axes 37, 42-7, 52, 69
   industries 53-4, 60
   pre-hand-axe tradition, 44
   tradition 44-7
Harappa, American excavations at, 192
Harappan civilization 113, 206
   —Early, 52, 117-118, 125, 137, 205
   Incipient Urbanism, 125, 140-52
   —Mature, 52, 137, 156, 205

—Post-Urban, or Late Harappan, 223-4, 228
preference for terminology, 137
seals, hallmark of civilization 171
terracotta cakes 168
Harappan Art, 197
seals, 167, 190, 197-9
simple figurines, 195-7
stone and bronze sculpure, 196-7
use of metamorphosed limestone or a talc schist, 196
Harappan language or languages 184
bilingual 184
Parpola 192
script, 138, 142, 150, 155, 184, 191-3
Harappan social complexity, 185-7
centralised state power 187-8
comparison with Mesopotamia 155, 188
'early' characteristics 187
external trade 151, 189
formation of small city-states 188
indigenous growth 191
populations of, 183, 186
element of heterogeneity 183-4
religion and tradition 199-203
need to apply systematic approach to, 149, 200
materials for study, 200-3
excavated sites 200-1
stone sculpture 201-2
seals, sealings and amulets 149, 202-3
concepts later found in

Rig Veda 202
special craft groups, 186
Hastinapur 225
Hathial 249
Hathigumpha inscription 247
Hemphill, Lukacs, and Kennedy 183
Hills, flat topped uppermost nodules 172
Himalayan uplift 48, 53, 62
Himalayas, 13, 14, 15, 28, 62, 211
Hindu Kush 13, 28
History and pre-history 2, 5, 6-7, 9, 11, 16
Holocene 17, 32, 88, 99, 104, 117
Hominids 33-9
honey 99, 112, 186
Horse, 177
remains (bones) 185, 235
Hulas 216, 224
Human remains, 7,
scientific study of,
Hunter 184
Hunsgi 51, 60, 63

Indian subcontinent, 12
cultural history of, 12-13, 32
Indo-Aryan speaking tribes/groups 221-2, 234, 244, 250, 253, 260
Indo-Iranian borderlands 206
Indra 219
Indus civilization, 153, 203-261
cities and sites, 161
end of, 207-18
major sites of Indus culture 11
Mature, 121, 153
Place of, 203-5
Indus response to Mesopotamian trade,
Mahadevan (1977), 190

282   *Origins of a Civilization*

Indus river, 70, 113-14
  greater Indus river system 141
Indus script,
  proto-Indoaryan 185
Indus sequence 204
  early urbanism of Early
  Harappan period, 205
  full urbanism of Mature
  Harappan period, 205
Indus system 22-5, 113-124, 153
  agriculture environment 115-16
  increase in rainfall 119
  Indus environment 116-22
  Lower Indus Valley 22, 114, 118-20, 122
  Northern Gujarat, Saurashtra and the Makran Coast, 123
  Punjab and Northern Rajasthan, 122-3
Indus Valley 2
Inscriptions 6,
Iron, 225, 228
  role in spread of settlements in Ganges valley, 227
  use and spread 226-7
  division in three stages 227
Iron Age, 102, 204, 227, 235, 250, 255
  and the period of Painted Grey Ware, 227-9
  presence of arrowheads and points made of bone, horn and ivory, 167, 171

Jacobson 187
Jainism 245
Jalilpur 47, 140, 144
Janapadas 244

aggressiveness and expansiveness among, 245
Janapada Nivesa 246
Jarrige, J-F. 125-6, 142, 154
jawar (*Sorghum bicolor*) 104, 169
Jhukar 209-10
Jorwe 253
Joshi, J.P. 159
jujube (Hindi, *ber*) 135, 169

Kacch 15, 22, 160, 214
Kachi plain 110, 126, 136, 156
Kalibangan 5, 10, 143, 147, 159, 161-2, 185, 201
  —ploughed field surface, 5, 148, 169
Kandahar 249
Karakoram 13, 15, 24, 28
Kasi 241
Kausambi 230, 232, 237, 239, 241
Kauravas 244
Kaveri 30, 255-6
Kenoyer 187-8
Khairadih 96, 217
Kharavela 247, 255
Khetri, copper mines 145, 160
kosa 241
Kosambi, D.D., 221, 246
Kot Diji 118, 140, 142, 154, 157, 212
Kshatriyas,
  colonization under, 235
Kunal 143
Kurram river 139
Kuru-Jangala 225
Kurus 225, 232
Kusinagara 241

Index

283

lapis lazuli 167-8, 174, 258

Las Bela 15, 45, 67, 110, 124, 156, 168

Lewan 105, 111, 139, 150

Levant 203

limestone 51, 68

linseed 169

Lothal 160, 166, 174, 180, 193

Luni 66-7

Madhya Desa, 232

Mahablipuram 11

Mahabharata 225, 245

Mahabodhi temple 8

Mahadaha 93

Mahagara 94-6

Mahajanapadas 241, 245

Mahasthangarh 239

Mahavamsa 257

Mandalas 219

Marshall, John, 8, 9, 180, 199-200

views on Harappan religion 200

Maski 254

Mathava Videgha 232-3

Mathura 11,

Mauryan 248, 260

Megasthenes 260

Mehrgarh 110-11, 125-39

gazelle, disappearance of 133

Periods 126

wheat, cultivation; *see* wheat

Mekhala ranges 224

Meluhha 177, 180

Mesopotamia 112, 114, 115, 161, 180, 188, 203

Mesolithic 43, 48, 88-94, 105, 139, 253

Microlithic 89, 94, 99, 105

Millets, 101, 103, 104, 169, 225, 234

African origin 104

Mohenjo-daro 8-11, 158

citadel, 161, 165-6, 201

great bath, 165-6

'Great granary' 166

Lower town 164

pillared hall 166

Morhana Pahar 253

Munda 250

mustard 169

Nallamalai Hills 99

Nandas 242, 247, 255

Narmada 213, 254

Nausharo 125, 142, 154

Nevasan, 57, 58, 60

Neolithic period, 11, 43, 94-112, 225

rice, major crop in, 206

sites of, 94, 100, 225

Southern Neolithic people of Karnataka 100-1, 124

North-West Frontier Province of Pakistan 5, 21, 121, 141, 142-3

North-West Frontier region 249

Northern Black Polished ware 227, 236, 237, 239, 249

as Black Gloss ware, 236

comparable to Greek Black ware 249

Paddayya, K. 51

Painted Grey ware,

Precursor of Northern Black ware 216, 217, 222, 226, 227, 228, 229, 230, 234

Pakistan 14

Palaeolithic 43

—Lower 43, 47, 53, 55

284 *Origins of a Civilization*

—Middle   43, 55-73
—Upper   43, 698, 70-81, 88
Pancalas   232, 244
Parjanya   203
Parpola   192, 203, 221
Patna (Pataliputra)   242, 259, 260-1
Patpara cycle, cycle of aggregation
   61-62
'Peking Man'   35
Peninsula India   55, 60, 62, 99
Petraglia, M.D.   51
Phulki river   167
piedmont zone   14, 15, 67, 124,
   126, 136-7, 153, 205
Piklihal   180
Pirak 125, 212
Pleistocene 17, 32, 35, 38, 49
   —four glacial periods during   17
Ploughs,   50, 169, 195
   without ploughshares   169
Possehl, 141, 151, 154, 155, 160
Post-Urban stage, 217
   Significant botanical finds   217,
   218
potter's wheel   136
pottery,   4, 102, 136, 160
   Black-and-Red and painted,
   226, 236, 239, 253, 257
   Black slipped ware   236, 239
   Burnished Red ware   139, 249
   Northern Black polished ware,
   226, 229, 234, 236-7, 250
   Ochre Coloured pottery, 226,
   237
   Painted Grey ware,   217, 222,
   226-87, 229, 234, 236
   Plain black ware   94
   rusticated ware   96, 140
Potwar   38-9,   44, 47, 67-9
prakara   241

parikha   241
Pre-History   2-3, 5, 6-7, 9, 11, 36-7,
   86
'priest king'   196, 202
provenance,
   point provenance   51, 109
   spot provenance   51, 78
Punt,   203
   mysterious land

Quarternary climatic change   62
Quetta valley   126, 136
   Kili Ghul Muhammad   136

radiocarbon dating   77, 125, 138-9,
   141, 154, 226, 237, 257
rice   96-8, 224, 234
ragi *(Eleusine coracana)*   104, 169
Rahman Dheri 138-9, 144, 158, 204
rainfall,   16, 17, 18, 19, 168, 207-8,
   211, 225, 231
Rajagriha   239, 259, 261
Ramayana   225, 245
Rann of Kacch   15, 67, 118-19
Ratnagar S. (1994) 156, 180-181, 187
'Red ware of the Harappan
   tradition', 226
   Red pottery,   226
Rig Veda   24, 202, 219, 222
   geography of 219
Rigvedic Aryans   221
   second wave of Indo-Aryan
   speakers   221
Rishi Gotama Rahugana   232
Riwat   37, 44, 76
rock art   11, 85-7, 98
Rohri hills   11, 53, 69-70, 117-8,
   157, 172

Index 285

Sabarmati river 166

Sadanira 233

Sakkhar, 178
    factory sites at, 173

Samhita 219

Sanghao cave 70

Sankalia, H.D. 60

Sankissa 239-40

Sanghol, 209, 216

Santals 250

Sarai Khola (Sarai Kala) 139, 143

Sarasvati, 118, 218, 232-3, 244
    see also, Hakra and Ghaggar

Sarasvati-Drishadvati Valleys, 214
    post-urban period in the, 214-18

Saraswat, K.S. 217

Sargon 189

Saurashtra 145, 160, 209, 214

Science and Technology, 193-5
    Chattopadhyay, D.P. 194
    stone weights 193
    Hemmy (1931) 193

Seals, 142, 143, 174, 197
    animals on, 174, 177
    showing mythological or socio-religious themes, 198
    stone seals, 143
    see also, writing

'Second' Urbanization, 2, 205
    Architectural sequence, 238, 239, 241
    beyond the Ganges plains, 225, 249, 250, 253, 256
    cereals crops, utilisation of, 224, 225, 226, 228
    charcoal samples, 225
    Chalcolithic ways of life, 223, 231
    colonization of the Ganges

    valley, 223
    culture, 225-6
    hand made pottery, bone and 226, 228
    stone industries without metal, 227
    Early city and the State 244
    Ganges plains, 236, 239
    Imperial expansion 241, 246, 248
    Mission activities 248
    Neolithic, 223
        early appearance 223
    trade 248

Sen, D.K., 183

Sessamum (*til*) 147, 169

Settlement patterns, 156-161
    in the Doab,

settlement surveys
    of Allahabad district by Erdosy, 229
    of Kanpur district by Makkhan Lal, 229
    methodology followed, 229-31
    no comparable surveys for the Middle Ganges plains
    or the Ganges delta 233

Shaffer, 137, 182, 209

Sheep 112, 206, 295

shell-working industry 167, 168

Shortughai 168, 180

Sichuan 14,

Sindh-Baluchistan border 9, 124

Sindh province 141-2

Sindhu river 219

Sisupalgarh 10, 239, 247-8, 255

Siwalik deposits 37, 67

Smelting and alloying
    bronze 171
    copper 167

286 *Origins of a Civilization*

Son river 49
Sopara 254
South Asia 1 ff.
  Climate 20
  Environments 21
  Expansion of Urbanization in, 245-61
  long history of cultural development, 13-
  physical features 13-19, 20
  surface sites 50-4
South Asian culture 1 ff.
South-East Asia 41, 97
South-West Asia 134
South India 30, 81-5, 100, 236, 256
South Indian Neolithic 100-4, 177
Sravasti 239, 253
Sri Lanka, 27-30, 47, 60-1, 81-5, 88-9, 248, 255-8
  Central and Peninsular India and—, 27-30
steatite 171, 180
Stone Age, 53, 60
  cultures, 50
  factory or work sites, 50, 53, 63, 69-70
  Lewan 139
stone artefacts 3, 9, 33, 37, 41-2, 93, 102, 105-9, 129, 149
  significance of 42-4
stone axe 96
stone tools 50, 58, 63, 172
stone weights 155
  part in mercantile practice 155,
store houses 136
Sudras 221
Sumeria 181, 186, 190
Sumerian 184
Surkotada, 160, 162, 185
  see also horse remains

Suktagen-dor 124, 156, 168
Sutlej 117, 143, 214
Swat 16, 140

Taj Mahal 8
Tamra River 249
Taxila 8, 10, 217, 248, 249
Tectonics 24, 118, 208
  Plate Tectonics 13, 211
Terracotta figurines, 102-3, 195-228, 255
  animal, 102
  female, 129, 136, 138, 195-6
  inanimate objects, 150, 195
  Harappan, distinct style 196
  headrest 103
  male, 142
Thar 21-22, 47, 52, 62, 64-6, 74, 77, 104-5, 207
thermoluminescent dating 61, 76, 226
Tiger, 65, 198-9
  horned, 199
Trade, 156, 248
  Effects on culture change, Harappan 149—
  Evidence of, 177, 178
  Indus trade with Mesopotamia 123, 155, 180-81
    —within Indus domain 176, 178
  within neighbouring regions or chiefdoms 179
  Powindahs, nomadic groups in trade 181
  Ratnagar, *Encounters* (1981) 180, (1994) 180-2
    pack animals 150, 177, 181
Tibetan Plateau 14

Index

287

Tripuri 252

Turkmenistan 138
  painted pottery sites
  such as, Altin Tepe and Kara
  Tepe 138

Upanishads 245

Ujjain 250

UNESCO 11, 173

Urbanization, emergence of first
  South Asian 2
  'second' urbanization 2, 206,
  208, 223-261

urban sites,
  factors for abandonment of
  211, 223

Vaisali 241

vapra 241

Veddas 99

Vedic,

late Vedic literature 218-22,
  231-2, 235, 245

Vidisha 250

Vinasana 232

Vindhyas, 27-8, 93, 96, 224

Water transport 178

West Asian languages, 184
  see also Sumerian and Elamite

Western Ghats 29

Wheat, 135, 137, 147, 168, 169,
  217, 224, 234,
  and barley, 103, 105, 137,
  147, 168, 205, 224, 226, 234
  Harappan economy based on,
  205

Wheeler, Sir Mortimer, 10, 131,
  136, 161, 249-50

Writing, 155, 191-
  Hunter 192
  Koskeniemi and Parpola 192
  Mahadevan 192
  Possehl (1996) 192